Understanding Criminal Careers

Understanding Criminal Careers

**Keith Soothill, Claire Fitzpatrick
and Brian Francis**

WILLAN
PUBLISHING

Published by

Willan Publishing
Culmcott House
Mill Street, Uffculme
Cullompton, Devon
EX15 3AT, UK
Tel: +44(0)1884 840337
Fax: +44(0)1884 840251
e-mail: info@willanpublishing.co.uk
website: www.willanpublishing.co.uk

Published simultaneously in the USA and Canada by

Willan Publishing
c/o ISBS, 920 NE 58th Ave, Suite 300
Portland, Oregon 97213-3786, USA
Tel: +001(0)503 287 3093
Fax: +001(0)503 280 8832
e-mail: info@isbs.com
website: www.isbs.com

First published 2009

ISBN   978-1-84392-502-6 paperback
       978-1-84392-503-3 hardback

British Library Cataloguing-in-Publication Data

A catalogue record for this book is available from the British Library.

Project managed by Deer Park Productions, Tavistock, Devon
Typeset by GCS, Leighton Buzzard, Bedfordshire
Printed and bound by T.J. International Ltd, Padstow, Cornwall

Contents

List of figures, boxes and tables

Figures

Boxes

Tables

Acknowledgements

This work was partially supported by the Economic and Social Research Council under its National Centre for Research Methods initiative (grant number RES-576-25-0019). The authors wish to thank colleagues for their support and advice in the writing and preparation of this book. Also we are grateful to Brian Willan and his team for their help throughout the publishing process.

Preface

This book is about criminal careers. It is a contentious and controversial area in some respects. We want to enter those dangerous waters but want also to give the reader what many would hopefully describe as a 'balanced' book. Our own position will emerge at times but on other occasions we will be much more in the background, for there are many issues relating to criminal careers in which the jury is still out.

We maintain that the study of criminal careers is fundamental to criminological study. The three foundation stones for understanding criminal careers are onset, persistence and desistance which feature prominently. But there is much more. One needs to focus on theoretical approaches and methodological issues which also – or, at least, should – resonate throughout criminology. However, there are also other issues, such as whether offenders specialise in offending behaviour and the concepts of dangerousness, prediction and risk, which are more specific to the study of criminal careers. Much has been written about criminal careers and not everything, of course, has been included in this book. However, we also think this is a useful time to take stock and consider not only the past but also the possible future in focusing on this area.

Authors rarely reveal their credentials for writing a specialised book. Perhaps one too readily assumes that the authors are specialists. In fact, criminological careers, rather like criminal careers, can be many and various. Over 30 years ago, one of us (KS) was offered the post of Research Officer to the Cambridge Development Study. Later in this book we describe the Cambridge Development

Study as the major longitudinal criminological study in the United Kingdom. Sadly, in contrast to the United States, there has been little competition – although more recently the Edinburgh Study of Youth Transitions and Crime has begun to fill this gap. KS turned the offer of the post down and later it was very successfully taken up by David Farrington, who has become one of the foremost authorities on criminal careers in the world. The Cambridge study goes on and the four hundred or so boys who started in the study are now in their mid-50s. So why turn down such an attractive offer? This kind of academic 'turning point' is almost as complex to explain as the 'turning points' that some try to describe in the lives of criminals. There are both personal and structural reasons.

The Cambridge Development Study focused on 411 boys from a working-class area of south-east London recruited in 1961 and 1962 when aged 8–9. The absence of females, minority ethnics and virtually none from a middle-class background seemed to limit the message such a study could bring to what seemed a rapidly changing world. The project seemed heavily dominated by psychological approaches – and psychology was changing rapidly so it was thought that the tests used would soon be outdated. Furthermore, the numbers in the study were comparatively few so the likelihood of being able to comment on serious crime, such as murder, rape, arson and other serious violence offences, seemed negligible.

All this remains true and yet the Cambridge Development Study has still become very famous, known throughout the world whenever criminal careers are discussed. The commitment and dedication of Donald West, who started the study, and the subsequent stewardship of David Farrington remain very impressive.

However, academic careers are not built on rational grounds alone, any more than criminal careers are – despite the beliefs of some rational choice theorists. Some had told KS of the difficulties of working at Cambridge at that time and the *éminence grise* of the Institute of Criminology, Professor Leon Radzinowicz, was daunting. More seriously, Tony Gibson – the previous occupant of the post of research officer - did not seem to gain much recognition for his pioneering efforts on that project. And so we move on from one turning point to another.

Twelve years ago, on a rainy autumn morning, the three of us sat in an undergraduate criminal careers course in a small teaching room at Lancaster University. One of us (KS) was convening the course, while the other two were sitting in as student (CF) and academic colleague (BF). For CF, this course was a key turning point that sparked her interest in the topic area. Since this rainy Lancaster morning, we have all continued to follow our own particular research interests within the arena of criminal careers, both individually and in collaboration with one another. CF is now convenor of the criminal careers course at Lancaster, while KS and BF continue to work at a national and international level in this area.

While our interests span both quantitative and qualitative research, we all share the view that such distinctions may not be helpful in seeking an understanding of human activity. Quantitative and qualitative approaches may provide a very different lens through which to view the trajectory of individual offending and, indeed, may also provide quite different ways of thinking about the issues, yet both approaches are needed to develop a full understanding of the development of criminal careers. This book is undoubtedly a result of our combined experience and reflects the particular interests of three very different researchers. We hope that it will help those who are either starting, or are already on, their own journey of studying criminal careers.

Keith Soothill, Claire Fitzpatrick, Brian Francis

Chapter 1

Introduction

There is a renewed interest in studying crime across the lifespan. However, the interest has been fragmented and the aim of this book is to build bridges between theoretical criminology, the study of criminal careers and policy-relevant research. Certainly there has been a burgeoning, or perhaps we should say resurgent, interest in criminal careers research. As we shall see when we consider the major longitudinal studies, there are phases when there are enthusiasms for this type of research and then it seems to go out of fashion. Much of the recent resurgence – that is, over the past decade or so – has been related to the opportunities that advances in computer and statistical work can deliver. There is scope for doing statistical manipulations which previously would have taken many person-years to complete but are now undertaken in minutes. However, there has also been a renewed interest in qualitative work whereby interviewing offenders produces new insights. The discovery of the original worksheets of the major longitudinal study by the Gluecks in the vaults of Harvard University and the subsequent re-interviewing of many in this cohort around the age of 70 produced a captivating book by Sampson and Laub in 2003. In this respect, something of the origins of criminal career research and the recent resurgence of interest were brought together.

In short, there are some masterpieces to share but, curiously, there has never been a text that usefully summarises this burgeoning field. This is what we aim to achieve in the chapters that follow. It is tempting to launch into displaying the wares in the warehouse of criminal career research. However, firstly, we need to define this area of study.

What is 'criminal careers' all about?

According to David Farrington, who is a leading authority on the criminal careers approach, a criminal career is 'the longitudinal sequence of offences committed by an individual offender' (1997: 361). In other words, it is the sequence of offences committed by an offender over time. The *time* focus is particularly important here, as a career suggests a trajectory or a pathway, or a development over a period of time in an individual's life.

Importantly, Farrington (1997: 364) distinguishes between the two dictionary definitions of the term 'career' which underpin two different concepts – firstly, a course or progress through life, and, secondly, a way of making a living. Farrington stresses that in understanding criminal careers the term is being used in the first sense. Hence, a 'criminal career' describes the sequence of offences during some part of an individual's lifetime, with no necessary suggestion that offenders use their criminal activity as an important means of earning a living.

Farrington further notes that the criminal careers approach has a particular focus on the factors and experiences in childhood that can impact on later adult development.

> (F)or example, hyperactivity at age 2 may lead to cruelty to animals at 6, shoplifting at 10, burglary at 15, robbery at 20 and eventually spouse assault, child abuse and neglect, alcohol abuse, and employment and accommodation problems later on in life. (Farrington 1997: 361)

As one can see from the above quote, Farrington is concerned with certain sorts of behaviour that act as stepping-stones to other types of behaviour. According to him, a career of childhood antisocial behaviour typically leads on to a criminal career and other problems in later life. While this may be true, there are difficulties here when we consider the criminal justice implications and try to predict who is likely to become criminal. For example, on the basis of Farrington's argument, should we intervene in the lives of all hyperactive two-year-olds? Of course this is unrealistic. There are probably quite a lot of hyperactive two-year-olds out there, not all of whom will eventually go on to commit crime. If we presume that all two-year-olds who are hyperactive will go on to offend, we are likely to end up over-predicting and labelling many individuals who will in reality live relatively crime-free lives. This relates to the problem of 'false positives' in assessing the risk of individuals, an issue that we return to later in Chapter 7.

Another crucial point to make at this stage is that the criminal careers approach is not regarded as one specific theory, but as a paradigm that can embrace various theoretical approaches that are concerned with the sequence of individual offending. As Farrington notes, it is 'a framework within which theories can be proposed and tested' (1992: 521) (see also Blumstein *et al.* 1986a, 1986b; Blumstein and Cohen 1987). Within the criminal careers framework there are a number of theoretical ideas, not just one. Some of these ideas, and the debates and controversies that surround them, are explored in Chapter 2, but for now we move on to outline some key definitions.

Definitional issues

Ensuring that everyone sees the notion of a 'criminal career' as no more than a metaphor is important. Blumstein *et al.* (1986a), for example, usefully distinguish between 'criminal careers' and 'career criminals' with the former being the metaphor and the latter being the few high-rate or long-duration offenders who really do make a career out of crime. While researchers recognise that it is possible to study the criminal careers of larger aggregates, such as families, gangs or whole communities, the main focus has tended to be on the offending of individuals over time. (As we argue at various points in the book, this individual focus has narrowed the vision in some respects in that there is far less of an emphasis on social forces and the impact of the wider society than should be the case.)

At a minimum, a criminal career has a beginning (normally called 'onset'), an end (mostly called 'desistance') and a criminal career in between (normally identified as 'duration'). However, what actually constitutes a beginning and what really constitutes an end is contentious and will be a focus in Chapters 4 and 5 on 'onset' and 'desistance' respectively. So, for instance, does 'onset' mean the first time that a mother notices her child taking money or an object without permission? Perhaps, if you asked the child it might even be before that, that is when he or she was taking money or objects without even the mother noticing. In some studies, 'onset' often has more of an official imprimatur; in other words, it is when some form of officialdom gets involved. The police may arrest a child, a young man or even an old man for the first time. Perhaps a social worker – and not a policeman – may get involved and note that the child has a habit of taking things without permission. In brief, defining 'onset' is not necessarily straightforward.

There are similar problems in defining 'desistance'. How do we know when someone has stopped committing crime? If we rely on someone's account that they have given up, the next day he or she may take something without permission or be stopped for dangerous driving. Is it like smoking or having cancer when one can begin to say after a certain period of time that a person is no more likely to start smoking or have a further outbreak of cancer than the next person? Perhaps it is just safer to wait until a person dies before deciding that a person really has given up crime. Yet while death really does bring an end to things, there is still really no knowing whether the years before a person's death were, indeed, completely crime-free. For example, the paedophile who has no longer been caught committing offences against young children may have got more circumspect in his activities and simply not been caught.

There are many other terms used in thinking about criminal careers. However, like the term 'career', most of the terms also have everyday uses and so it is important to know the precise use of a term for the purposes of studying criminal careers. Box 1.1 lists the more usual ones.

The definitions in Box 1.1 are useful in highlighting some of the key terms used within criminal careers research. However, one term not mentioned in the box that has a crucial impact on research in this area is the concept of 'crime' itself. How we define crime, and what kinds of behaviours we include within the category, has clear implications for the kind of research and analysis that is possible. For example, if such offences as 'speeding' are included, then obviously more people come within the ambit of this type of research than if they are not included.

Furthermore, we need to embrace the distinction between serious and less serious crime. While this distinction has always been recognised, the offences regarded as serious in one era or in one place may not be so regarded in another era or in another place. In most countries there have been some massive shifts. In England and Wales the so-called 'Bloody Code' in the eighteenth century whereby over 200 offences had the possibility of the death sentence seems barbaric in contemporary terms. In the nineteenth century the focus for seriousness was largely on offences involving property rather than offences involving the person. Indeed, in the late nineteenth century more than a half of the cases involving non-consensual sexual crime which actually reached court – which itself was most unusual

Box 1.1   Definitions of some important concepts

Criminal career	the longitudinal sequence of offences committed by an individual offender.
Recidivism	a term for reoffending.
Onset	the beginning of a criminal career.
Desistance	the end of a criminal career.
Duration	career length between onset and desistance.
Prevalence	proportion of the population who are committing offences.
Participation	another name for prevalence.
Frequency	rate of committing offences for active offenders.
Seriousness	a measure of the importance of the offence as determined by the criminal justice system or by the general public.
Severity	a measure of the punitiveness of a criminal sentence or sanction.
Escalation	a measure of how far an offender's criminal career increases in seriousness.
Specialisation	how far offenders focus on certain types of offending.
Diversification	the opposite of specialisation; how far offending covers all types of offences.
Switching	the ending of one 'form' of offending and the beginning of another.

Sources: Adapted from Farrington (1997) and Loeber and Le Blanc (1990).

– resulted in acquittals (Soothill 2008). While current convictions for rape, for instance, are not impressive, there is now at least a greater recognition among the populace that rape is a very serious offence which can be committed against both women and men (whether they are sexually experienced or not). As this discussion highlights, the behaviours that are regarded as 'crime' and the perceived seriousness of these particular behaviours clearly vary across time and space. This is very important for us to bear in mind as we begin to assess the contribution of criminal careers research.

Who are the criminals?

Another important issue for consideration concerns whether criminal activity is a marginal activity in society or, indeed, in people's lives.

The latter question is comparatively easy to answer. Even the lives of the most hardened criminals involve much more than simply crime. The successful criminal may have many other roles, including family, leisure activities and so on. Even close neighbours may not know the source of their lifestyle. Not surprisingly, not much is really known about such people for their criminal activity is often hidden from public view, only coming to light if they make a mistake or their crimes are found out.

In contrast to the successful criminal is the totally unsuccessful criminal. Often they are found residing in prison, usually for quite petty crimes. As petty offences theoretically equal shorter sentences, the reality for many unsuccessful criminals is that they have a life in prison by instalments – the 'revolving door' phenomenon[1]. Prison, sadly, becomes their home so that they may, indeed, throw stones at police station windows in the hope of being captured and returned to prison for Christmas. In other words, there are few aspects of their lives which are not in some way tainted by their possession of a criminal label.

There are also those who have never been involved in criminal activity either knowingly or unknowingly. However, it is questionable whether such a category actually exists. In other words, has anyone never committed a crime? Of course, it relates to what one calls 'crime' – if speeding is included, then many more are captured in the portals of crime than if it is not included. Meanwhile, putting aside the concern of whether anyone has led a totally crime-free life – even Jesus seemed to be involved in some considerable malicious damage as he cleared the money changers from the temple – for the rest of us there is a balance or a relationship between criminal activities which come to public notice (i.e. they become visible within the public domain) and crime which remains invisible.

Curiously, those whose crime lives have complete visibility have some strange bedfellows. It includes those who cannot seem to do very much crime without getting caught as well as those whose only crime (allegedly at least!) is a passionate murder committed when the balance of the mind may have been disturbed. However, most of the criminal activity of people who are engaged in crime is invisible (what is conventionally known as the 'dark figure'). Criminal activity may emerge from the darkness and come into public notice with police enquiries and the like but there is nothing 'official' yet. An arrest, for instance, makes alleged criminal activity 'official' – that is being formally dealt with by officials.

It is conventional wisdom that social control agents (such as the police) aim to make 'invisible' criminal activity 'visible' and punishable. This, however, is only a partial truth. At worst, a corrupt police force will take payments – or 'protection money' – so that villains can, thus, avoid being brought to justice. This can be at the individual level – that is, a policeman simply takes a bribe – or at a more systemic level – that is police routinely taking payment to prevent those involved in a certain type of activity, usually prostitution or drug dealing, being brought to justice.

However, social control agents can also act quite legitimately in keeping criminal activity more or less invisible. So, for instance, the development of a formal system of 'warnings' and 'cautions' arises from two concerns – to regularise a more informal system of control on the one hand, and to avoid the alleged dangers of the stigma of a court appearance in the development of a deviant identity on the other. In other words, while the 'visibility line' has been breached in these circumstances, the records that are maintained are much more circumscribed than would be the case if the rigmarole of court proceedings was invoked.

The point of all this discussion is simply to stress that much work on criminal careers essentially engages in visible crime, that is crime known to public authorities. Greenberg (2006) has recently noted that criminal career research has tended to concentrate on the most common crimes of interpersonal violence, theft, vandalism, illegal drug use and so on. It has had far less to say about crimes that are less commonplace. Related to this, there has been little research done on white-collar crime, like insurance fraud, price-fixing, tax evasion and money laundering. Furthermore, Greenberg notes that the criminal career approach has not had much to say about arms trafficking, war crimes and genocide. Yet, as he argues, some of these offences can only be carried out by those who are highly educated and who hold office in legitimate organisations and governments. For these offenders, onset is expected to be late, and involvement in crime is likely to occur at older ages. Also, predictors of common criminality (like school difficulties and low socio-economic status) may not predict involvement for these sorts of offences (Greenberg 2006: 93).

In brief, criminal careers research, like criminology more generally, tends to focus on the most common, most visible crimes, with little attention being directed at the crimes of the powerful. Furthermore, with respect to the most visible crimes, there are additional limitations in that quantitative research in particular mainly focuses on crimes which have been through the court process and which come out of the criminal justice 'sausage machine' as convictions. In other words, rarely is even the information on 'final warnings' and 'cautions' included in the analysis.

However, there is a concession which seems to put a bucket down the well of invisible crime, and this comes in the form of self-report data whereby researchers may ask respondents about crimes they have committed which have not come to the attention of the public authorities. Known as 'self-reported' crime, this information can be very important. While such 'self-reports' may not always produce quite the insights hoped for, there is no doubt that they provide a valuable tool in efforts to overcome the mystery of the 'dark figure' of crime.

Why bother studying criminal careers?

Having established some of the key concerns of the criminal careers approach, as well as highlighting some of the limitations of research in this area, we move on now to consider the 'so what?' question. In other words, what is the point in studying criminal careers and why is so much time and research attention devoted to this area of study?

Criminal careers research provides us with crucial information about patterns of offending behaviour over time, such as data relating to onset, offending frequency, career duration and desistance. This information has the potential to feed directly into decisions about criminal justice policy and practice. The academic debates and controversies within the field relate directly to 'real-world' issues and have serious implications for how far we might intervene in the lives of real people, particularly those we label as 'criminal'. For example, Piquero *et al.* (2007) argue that the criminal careers paradigm suggests three general orientations for crime control strategies: prevention, career modification and incapacitation. In their view, '(k)nowledge concerning the patterning of criminal careers is intimately related to these policy issues' (2007: 16). They go on to elaborate on each of the three strategies.

- *Prevention strategies* – are intended to reduce the number of non-offenders who become offenders. This involves general deterrence.

- *Career modification strategies* – seek to reduce the frequency and seriousness of the crimes committed by those who are already known offenders. This involves individual deterrence and rehabilitation.
- *Incapacitation strategies* – focus on the crimes reduced as a result of removing offenders from society during their criminal careers (for example by imprisonment) (Piquero *et al.* 2007).

Undoubtedly criminal careers research has important implications for how we deal with offenders. However, like criminological research more generally, it also raises a number of questions about how research findings may be used by policy-makers and practitioners. With respect to the emphasis on 'prevention strategies' above, it is worth noting that there is currently increasing concern among some commentators in the UK about the government's focus on earlier and earlier intervention into the lives of very young children who are simply perceived to be *at risk* of offending (Goldson 2007). This 'pre-emptive' approach being proposed by New Labour (described by one commentator as 'Spotting tomorrow's criminals in today's pushchairs': Lettice 2007) seems to presume a level of certainty, in our knowledge about risk factors and the most 'risky' individuals, that may not necessarily exist. Indeed, in many respects, the current policy discourse surrounding notions of 'risk' overplays the predictive power of risk assessment methods. By labelling certain individuals as 'risky', it also arguably individualises the problem of crime, redirecting attention away from structural inequality and societal conditions. All this is not to suggest that the idea of general deterrence is necessarily a bad thing, but just that as we come across research evidence we need to consider how it might be used (or misinterpreted) to justify specific policies or interventions.

Questions about how early we should intervene in the lives of non-offenders (prevention), how far we are able to redirect criminal pathways (modification) and how long we can justify locking people up for (incapacitation) inevitably raise moral as well as policy and practice dilemmas. At a conference in London in January 2008, Shawn Bushway highlighted an important finding from recent research based on official police contact data from the US – that ten years of non-offending is a reasonable (and conservative) signal about the prospects of rehabilitation (Kurlychek *et al.* 2007). In other words, if an offender has not had contact with the police after ten years we can reasonably assume that they are unlikely to be convicted in the future or, rather, that they have about the same chance of being convicted as a non-offender of the same age and gender. Notwithstanding our earlier comments about the limitations of conviction data, there is a need to seriously consider the implications of this finding for how we deal with offenders. So, for example, should such individuals be treated like 'non-offenders' after ten years?

The point of all this discussion is simply to highlight that while in understanding criminal careers it is necessary to engage in academic and scholarly debate, it is also important not to forget about the real world and the real people within it whose lives may be profoundly affected by research in this area. Indeed, certain commentators adopt a methodological approach that focuses specifically on the narratives of offenders, and attempts to capture something of the reality of their lives. Tony Parker, whom Sir Stephen Tumin, the former Chief Inspector of Prisons, once called 'the Mayhew of our times',[2] for example, has been widely regarded as the best interviewer of criminals since the Second World War (Soothill 2001), and is someone who kept alive the flame of talking to offenders for over three decades from 1962 to his last book on offenders in 1995. The following quotations from Parker's work highlight some of the offenders we need to embrace as well as some of the critical points in their lives.

The plea of Charlie Smith to the judge –

> I – the recidivist, the repeating offender, the habitual criminal, call me what you will, my Lord – I am left to get on with living, while I am outside, as best as I can. So long as I do not trouble you, you ignore me – until I lay hands on your property. Then you hit me hard. You fall back, regularly and with increasing severity, on the ineffectual, irrelevant concept of deterrence … 'Three years didn't change you, we'll try seven.' 'Seven makes no impression? Let's try ten.' (Soothill 1999: 29)

Donald, whose offences had all been the same sort of thing –

> I don't think I was born to be a criminal at all; when I was a little kid I always used to be very lucky at finding things – sixpences that people dropped in the street, fountain-pens, packets of foreign stamps, bars of toffee, all sorts. I thought it was a kind of magic thing, you know the silly ideas you get when you're a kid; I thought I'd been picked-out to have special good fortune. Now I think the exact opposite, that I must have been one of those chosen to have sorrow and loneliness all through my life. (Soothill 1999: 55)

The painful saga of Wilfred Johnson, who had prison sentences of six months, two years, 21 months, eight years and five years for indecent assaults on young boys:

> ... And that was when my first trouble came on. There were always lots of kids about in the boat-yards, asking could they help you, would you take them out in your boat for a ride. One Saturday afternoon there were two of them, two little boys, I said all right they could come out with me because they'd helped me push my boat down into the water from the shed. A very hot day it was. They went over the side for a swim. They'd no costumes on. When they got back in the boat they were running about skylarking and laughing. And I did you know, I must admit I did go so far as to forget myself, I laid hands on them. Nothing serious, please don't think that, I didn't attack them or anything of that kind. Only playing about, touching them, that was as far as it went. They didn't object, they didn't complain, it was a harmless bit of fun you might say. It never crossed my mind they hadn't liked it, they seemed willing enough.
>
> That was why it was such a surprise to me the next weekend. I was down there again tuning up the old engine, and these two plain-clothes policemen came into the shed .... (Soothill 1999: 125–6)

While Parker's work is inspirational and thought-provoking, harsher critics might argue that his work is not rigorous and question how he got his respondents and whether his methods are valid. Yet the importance of exploring the lives of offenders in depth is increasingly emphasised as important in the academic field. Indeed, in a recent special edition of the journal *Theoretical Criminology*, a number of respected scholars spend the entire issue analysing the narrative of just one individual. As editors of the special issue, Maruna and Matravers (2007: 437) observe that 'deep exploration into the life narrative(s) of a single individual can generate at least as much insight into offending as getting to know a little bit about 200 or 2000 human beings in a large-scale survey'. As we noted at the beginning of this chapter, statistical advances have been partially responsible for renewing interest in criminal careers, and much of this is related to the ability to undertake complex analysis of large-scale data sets. Certainly there is much to learn when the number (N) of individuals studied is high and N equals anything from 100 upwards, but what Maruna and Matravers (2007) helpfully remind us is that there is also the potential to learn much when N equals 1! A concern with improving our qualitative understanding of the lives of offenders, as well as emphasising the power of recent statistical evidence on criminal careers, runs throughout this book.

Conclusions

This chapter has introduced some of the key concepts that relate to the study of criminal careers. Many of these concepts are contentious and seem sometimes to be contradictory, but the basic building blocks of onset, persistence and desistance are common to many approaches within the criminal career paradigm. In the subsequent chapters we hope to be appreciative of the fine efforts that many have contributed in developing an understanding of these issues. However, we think that much of the work has also had its limitations by failing to emphasise various features which should, we feel, be central to a consideration of criminal careers research.

Firstly, the notion of the criminal career of an *individual* offender has in some ways narrowed the vision. It has tended to limit the study of criminal careers to psychological approaches where the focus is on the individual. We contend that the individual is only part of the story. The individual is embedded in a society that may have relevance in understanding the type of crime that is committed. In our view, the psychological approach is a necessary but not sufficient condition for understanding criminal careers. While developmental psychology has made an imperialist bid in terms of explanatory power, such a bid is doomed if it cannot account for the crucial factors of social context and social reaction.

Furthermore, we believe that our conceptions of criminal careers should be dynamic, not static, that is lifestyles may not be the same in each generation. Forms of crime do change and, thus, the same kinds of persons are not necessarily 'recruited' into these new forms of crime. Computer crime, for example, needs a skill that is not available to the unskilled. Finally, we argue that there should be more focus on serious rather than on less serious activity. During the last ten years of New Labour government in the United Kingdom, there has been an expanding policy focus. On the one hand, there has been an awakening of a concern about terrorist activity whereby everyone's civil liberties are increasingly under challenge to combat the threat while, on the other hand, there has been considerable focus on nuisance activity which has come under the umbrella term of 'antisocial behaviour' and which has been increasingly criminalised. The criminologist interested in criminal careers, however, must focus on the full range of criminal offences which include those with a high tariff in terms of sentencing, both in theory and in practice. Do persons who start off with comparatively trivial activity necessarily 'graduate' to these more serious offences? There are many important questions and the answers are often complex.

Our mission, however, is one of correcting the balance. While the quest for some 'iron laws' of criminal careers without any thought about social change has produced some answers, while the psychological approach has developed some useful insights and while the focus on less serious offences is (as we discuss in the next chapter) understandable, there is much more to do. As we shall now see, theories and methods can produce either liberation or entrapment. In brief, we need to recognise when we are trapped as well as the potential for liberation.

Notes

1 The 'revolving door' phenomenon is a term that was probably first used in relation to chronic inebriates (Pittman and Gordon 1958) to describe the repetitious legal punishment of persons accused of public intoxication (Lovald and Stub 1968). However, its use has been extended to mentally disordered patients (Haywood et al. 1995) and other groups.
2 Henry Mayhew was a social researcher, journalist and advocate of social reform. He published an extensive series of newspaper articles in the *Morning Chronicle*, later compiled into the book series, *London Labour and the London Poor* (1851) which provided an influential survey of the poor of London. As Shore (2000) notes, 'Mayhew's skills as an interviewer of nineteenth-century street types were unparalleled, and are of value both in terms of social history and in revealing the ways in which the model of the juvenile criminal was constructed.'

Chapter 2

The Great Debate: competing theoretical approaches and methodological issues

In order to understand a subject area, one needs to grasp what is the 'Great Debate'. Usually, of course, there is more than one major debate which captures a subject area and one can often identify a series of debates or issues. So, for example, in philosophy one can point to the major historical debate about free will versus determinism which spilled over in the nineteenth century into the arenas of science and religion. The relationship between the mind and matter is another pivotal issue which engages philosophers and scientists. The nature of reality is yet another. Such philosophical debates are rarely, if ever, resolved. Certainly particular debates excite more interest at one time rather than another. During more quiescent times, there usually remains an underlying and unstated tension. The major proponents of each position have perhaps exhausted their gunfire and have little new to say. Positions may be slightly modified over time but, in broad terms, very little changes, for often these arguments expose the great mystery of the human condition. Are there debates of this significance in studying criminal careers? We maintain that there certainly are and each generation studying the phenomenon of criminal careers needs to be aware of them.

Many commentators see the issues in terms of competing theoretical explanations on the one hand, and competing methodological approaches on the other. However, we wish to stress that we see both these types of debates as part of the same coin and they need to be addressed together rather than having a chapter on 'theory' and a chapter on 'methods'. While this may make more difficult reading, it underlines the point that theory and method should not be separated. First, one needs to understand why.

Discussions about method are empty unless one understands the question being posed. In other words, methods are like scaffolding. One can talk about different kinds of scaffolding and the different shapes that one can create, but it is not worth while to do that until one understands the type of building that one is trying to construct and then particular types and shapes of scaffolding usefully come into play. Essentially, our view of the world and what it is that we are trying to find out is likely to influence the methodological approach that we find most useful. This becomes clearer as we delve into some of the key controversies and debates relating to the study of criminal careers.

Competing theoretical explanations

To some, the issue of theory is not a happy thought. Yet it should be. While many approach the arena of 'theory' with a sense of trepidation, it is important to recognise that theories are pivotal to understanding a phenomenon. They help us to make sense of the world, and their aim is to explain rather than confuse (Soothill *et al.* 2002). However, as Osgood and Rowe (1994: 518) have stressed, 'research on criminal careers has been largely divorced from theoretical criminology'. Undoubtedly, this divorce needs some sort of reconciliation.

Certainly on the theory side there are many candidates for this marriage between theory and methods, and many theories that are used both explicitly and implicitly in the study of criminal careers. However, we wish to try to avoid confusion at the outset. It is perhaps easiest at this point to identify two competing theoretical explanations that have been important in this area over the last two decades. Underpinning this focus on two types of explanation is a concern about the proper approach to studying crime across the lifespan (Osgood and Rowe 1994). On the one side are the proponents of what has been described as the criminal career model and, on the other, are the proponents of the propensity model. It is the supporters of these two rival positions who represent the key competitors within the 'Great Debate'.

The criminal careers approach

Firstly, it is important to reiterate a key point made in Chapter 1, which is that the 'criminal careers approach' is not a specific theory but an overarching framework, or a paradigm as this is sometimes called. Appreciating the approach as a framework means that the framework can encompass a range of theoretical ideas which are sometimes competing. These various theoretical ideas share certain features – they focus on individual change and on processes such as onset (see Chapter 4) and persistence and desistance (see Chapter 5). As Farrington (1997) notes:

> The Criminal Career approach focuses on within-individual changes over time and on the predictors of longitudinal processes such as onset and desistance, recognizing that the same person can be an active offender at one age and a non-offender at another. It also aims to explain the development of offending over all ages. (Farrington 1997: 365)

The criminal careers approach was formally developed in the USA during the 1980s, when a panel of experts was convened at the request of the National Institute of Justice to consider research on criminal careers. The panel was chaired by Alfred Blumstein, and he and his colleagues went on to publish many of their findings in a two volume collection called *Criminal Careers and 'Career Criminals'* (1986a, 1986b). Certainly these volumes provide a useful introduction to many of the ideas underpinning the criminal careers framework.

In 1983 when the panel of experts was convened, the US prison population had experienced a rapid growth, more than doubling in eleven years to 437,000 (Blumstein *et al.* 1986a: ix). The crime rate was also a major public concern at this time. Consequently, there was a strong policy interest in seeking alternatives to rapidly escalating prison costs and what was regarded as relatively ineffective crime control. So in many ways, the panel on criminal careers was convened in response to the policy concerns of the day and the feeling that crime control needed to be far more effective. Hence, there was a clear relationship between the development of the criminal careers framework and the apparent needs of United States criminal justice policy.

One approach considered was to direct attention at 'career criminals', those high-rate or long-duration offenders who contribute most to total crime rates. Research at the Rand Corporation had highlighted the massive variation in individual rates of criminal activity. So, for instance, in US surveys of prisoners, it was shown that the worst 10 per cent of offenders reported committing more than 50 robberies a year, but half the prisoners reported committing fewer than five robberies a year (cf. Blumstein *et al.* 1986a: ix). While this finding may not be true for all prisoners, it was felt that there was a need to explain this extreme variation and be able to distinguish high-rate from low-rate offenders – hence the focus on what are known as 'career criminals'.

A further point noted by the panel was that any attempt to identify the career criminals in a population inevitably requires examination of the criminal careers of *all* offenders, and issues such as onset, career duration and desistance. In other words, to find the characteristics that distinguish the most serious offenders, such as high frequencies of offending and longest careers in crime, data was also needed on the less serious offenders in order to act as a comparison. So this dual focus is why Blumstein *et al.*'s subsequent publication was titled *Criminal Careers and 'Career Criminals'* to reflect the interest in both low-rate and high-rate offenders.

In terms of the rationale for conducting research on criminal careers, Blumstein *et al.* note that the panel was interested in assessing the feasibility of predicting the future course of criminal careers (1986a: x). Would it be possible to gain the knowledge to say who was going to be a criminal in the future? (It is interesting to note that this concern with prediction very much remains a preoccupation of politicians today.)

There was also an interest in developing insights into individual offending as well as in improving criminal justice decision-making. The panel commented that they hoped to be able to estimate the impact of policy changes on crime rates and prison populations. In fact, these are aspirations which still remain largely unfulfilled although the Home Office (representing England and Wales) has developed statistical models which attempt to throw some light on such questions.

So this is the background to the official beginnings of the criminal career paradigm. The work of the panel usefully identifies some of the furniture, such as onset, duration and desistance, which will fill the House of Criminal Careers. With its focus on the development of behaviour across the life course, the criminal career model raises the possibility that factors that may influence early involvement in crime may be unimportant in later stages of a career. An obvious example is that involuntary unemployment might impel someone to steal. If you find such a person a job then he might well abandon stealing. However, there may be some who find these illegal sources of income sufficiently lucrative and attractive not to abandon them, even if opportunities for lawful income later arise. Hence, in such a case the inability to earn income lawfully at one point can be said to influence the onset of a criminal career but be irrelevant to its persistence when other motivating or social forces may come into play.

The criminal careers approach clearly highlights the apparent importance of life events or life contingencies. In that respect, the surrounding environment reflecting life chances and life opportunities seems to be crucial. In other words, what happens to an individual is the pivot around which a criminal career might or might not develop. With respect to the methodological implications of all this, longitudinal research, which involves studying the same individuals over a period of time, is regarded as crucial in understanding how criminal careers may develop.

Interestingly, the development of a research programme on criminal careers did not occur quietly nor was it something that was accepted universally by criminologists. Far from it. There was a great deal of debate and controversy over the criminal careers paradigm and its value for controlling crime.

The Great Debate, as it became known, was played out quite publicly and very vocally on the pages of the American journal *Criminology* during the 1980s and early 1990s. And the debate was essentially between two parties – criminal careers advocates such as Alfred Blumstein and David Farrington on one hand, and criminal propensity enthusiasts such as Travis Hirschi and Michael Gottfredson on the other (e.g. see Blumstein *et al.* 1988a, 1988b; Gottfredson and Hirschi 1987, 1988). So what provoked this very public controversy? The challenge came from Gottfredson and Hirschi and so it is important to try to understand their standpoint which involves a particular approach to explaining criminal behaviour.

The criminal propensity approach

Criminal propensity refers to an inclination or trait or tendency to commit crime. However, according to Gottfredson and Hirschi (1990), criminal propensity is not biologically determined through genetic inheritance but is acquired in early childhood by good or bad parental skills. From around age 8, these individual level-traits within a person remain relatively stable throughout life. The emphasis on stability here is very important as it implies that once you have propensity you will always have that propensity, as it stays with you over your lifetime. Thus supporters of the propensity model believe that experiences in later life, such as finding employment, are irrelevant to understanding criminal behaviour (Gottfredson and Hirschi 1990).

This approach has quite considerable methodological implications. In the first place its supporters see no value in longitudinal research. Longitudinal research involves observing behaviour over long periods of time and occupies our attention throughout this book. Hence, such a challenge is important to investigate. Gottfredson and Hirschi's (1990) claim that individual criminality is stable over time means that intervening events are of little or no importance.

A crucial part of Gottfredson and Hirschi's thesis is the distinction between criminal propensity and crime committed. They make the claim that crime declines uniformly over age for all adult offenders, regardless of offence, region of the world or historical epoch. For that reason, it is argued that it is meaningless to speak of different stages in a criminal career such as onset and desistance. As Gottfredson and Hirschi see it, criminals do not desist; the likelihood that they will commit crime simply diminishes over time. Thus the authors maintain that there is no reason to study the impact of such factors as unemployment on the development of criminal careers. Why? Because in their view such impacts are non-existent or too weak to be of any substantial interest (Greenberg 1991).

How do Gottfredson and Hirschi reconcile the contradiction between criminality being stable over age and crime declining with age? They do this by saying that whether a crime is actually committed is determined by other factors – such as opportunity, availability of goods or targets, activity of the person, etc. – as well as criminality of the individual. It is these 'other factors' which change as one ages, not criminality.

While Gottfredson and Hirschi have a particular theory which does not propose a genetic cause, those who espouse this type of individual-level approach will also include those who point to genetics or DNA or something within the psychology of an offender that causes them to be criminal. In short, Lombroso's (1876) early work on the born criminal emphasising the physical traits of offenders such as big ears and big noses would fall under the general approach of criminal propensity. The implication of this kind of approach is that the problem or the flaw is located within the individual. In other words, it is analysis at an individual level, with little focus on the impact of the social structure or society. While Gottfredson and Hirschi (1990) distance themselves from biological positivism, their propensity theory suggests that criminals have been flawed since childhood, having the tendency or inclination to commit crime from an early age. In fact, the age–crime curve is used to support their claims.

The age–crime curve

The age–crime curve describes the pattern of known crime or convictions within the population across the life course and generally shows a very similar pattern across a range of crimes and populations. When crime rates are plotted against age on a graph, one sees a rapid increase in crime during the teenage years, culminating in a peak at around 18 or 19 depending on the study. There is then a rapid decrease in crime for many of the population, and the crime rate then gradually declines but at a steady rate during the 30s, 40s and so on. Figure 2.1 shows a typical example of an age–crime curve. It is important at this juncture to emphasise the distinction between the prevalence of offending within a population and individual frequency

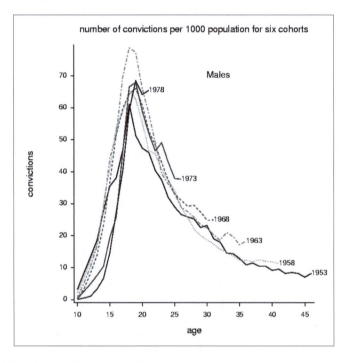

Figure 2.1 A typical example of an age crime curve - number of convictions per 1000 population for six birth cohorts

of committing offences. Prevalence provides a measure of how many individuals in the population participate in crime in any given period. The age–crime curve in Figure 2.1 is based on this kind of aggregate measurement (that combines data from many individuals) and thus reflects the prevalence of offending within a population. Whether an *individual's* offending frequency would follow a similar curve is a different issue entirely and has been less well studied, although we do know that individual offending frequencies tend to vary considerably (Piquero *et al.* 2007).

The age–crime curve means more to some theorists than others. For example, theorists such as Hirschi and Gottfredson focus on it because they believe it supports their age–crime invariance thesis. According to this, they argue that the age distribution of crime is invariant across a broad range of social and cultural conditions. In fact, they go further and maintain that 'the identification of the causes of crime at one age may suffice to identify them at other ages as well' (Hirschi and Gottfredson 1983: 554). Hence they are arguing that the causes of crime at, say 10 or 12 years will also be the causes of crime at 30 or 40 years, and the age distribution will follow a similar pattern regardless of wider social changes. Thus, for Hirschi and Gottfredson, social, cultural or policy changes are irrelevant because the age distribution of crime will remain the same regardless of them.

Interestingly, this approach challenges any generational differences in the criminal careers of offenders. For example, it implies that the patterns of offending for those born in 1953 will be the same for those born in 2003, providing the distribution of propensity is the same. Yet there are many ways in which social and cultural conditions have changed during these periods. For example, the role of women has changed in society; in some respects they have more equality than they once did and perhaps more opportunities for committing crime. The prevalence of drug-use and binge drinking amongst young people has also shifted.

The Gottfredson and Hirschi critiques

There are a number of other critical claims that have been made by Gottfredson and Hirschi about criminal career research and work on 'career criminals'. The following are taken from their 1986 essay 'The true value of lambda would appear to be zero'.

- They question the originality and value of studying 'career criminals', noting that this is not a new idea and has been recurrently studied by researchers (1986: 214–15).
- They point out that we often only identify someone as a 'career criminal' when they are older and their lengthy criminal record becomes apparent (1986: 217). (The implication here is that this is unhelpful in terms of thinking about intervention, and particularly the policy of selective incapacitation, because by the time we identify someone as a high-rate offender they are likely to be older and past their peak age of offending anyway, having effectively already done their 'worst'.)
- Gottfredson and Hirschi further argue that even the offending path of high-rate offenders follows the age–crime curve and declines over time. For all of the reasons mentioned above, they believe that ongoing efforts to try and chart 'career criminals' longitudinally are not justifiable and have limited thinking about crime (1986: 231).

Gottfredson and Hirschi's approach has serious methodological implications. They argue that because the one cause of crime which lies within the individual is time-stable, longitudinal studies of crime that follow up cohorts over long periods of time are redundant. Not only are they expensive and time-consuming, but also pointless as they maintain that we can identify the causes of crime at an early age. Therefore, there is no need to follow up people for, say, 30 or 40 years because this type of study will not tell us any more than we already know. For Gottfredson and Hirschi, cross-sectional data that examines offenders at any one point in the life course is more than adequate for testing our theoretical ideas. Cross-sectional research does not seek to follow the same individuals over time, but rather captures individuals at a particular moment in their life. According to Gottfredson and Hirschi (1987):

> In the 'cross-sectional' view of crime, differences across people and their life circumstances are sufficiently stable over time that day-to-day variability is uninteresting or likely to be nothing more than measurement error. In this view, apparently large changes in circumstance are themselves perfectly predictable from the explanation of crime itself. Lack of perseverance in school or in a job or in an interpersonal relationship are simply

different manifestations of the personal factors assumed to cause crime in the first place. Taking up with delinquent friends is another example of an event without causal significance. Since such 'events' are predictable consequences of the causes of crime, there is little or no point in monitoring them. (1987: 609)

By delving into the Gottfredson and Hirschi critiques of criminal career research, it becomes clear that theoretical concerns are very closely interlinked with methodological ones. Furthermore, the particular views that we hold in relation to human nature and offending behaviour will inevitably impact upon the particular methodological approaches that we find most helpful. If we believe (as Gottfredson and Hirschi do) that criminality is something static that remains relatively stable throughout life, cross-sectional research that measures individuals at one moment in time is likely to fit the bill. If, by contrast, we believe (as criminal career researchers do) that human behaviour and criminality are dynamic, and may develop and change across the life course, then longitudinal work that follows the same individuals over time seems far more appropriate. Whichever approach is embraced helps both to shape the formulation of the research questions, the methods used and the interpretation of the empirical evidence. To add further confusion, evidence that seems to point to one conclusion can take on a very different significance when viewed from a different perspective (Greenberg 1991).

Essentially, what we have classed in this chapter as the 'Great Debate' is a debate about the fundamental issue of how we view human nature. The debate continued throughout the late 1980s in a series of heated exchanges between the key competitors (for example see Blumstein *et al.* 1988a, 1988b; Gottfredson and Hirschi 1987, 1988). Interestingly, DeLisi (2005: 95) argues that 'what was not included in the exchange between propensity theorists and advocates of the criminal career paradigm is noteworthy for its absence'. In his view, 'the central challenge, levied by propensity theory, and the reason why it is often challenged, is that career criminals are simply bad. Career criminals are bad people who recurrently do bad things to other people' (2005: 95). While this observation arguably oversimplifies the propensity position, DeLisi's comment is interesting in that it does allude to an underlying tension in understanding criminal careers which concerns the relationship between heredity and environment. We return to this important theme in our conclusions in Chapter 9.

A General Theory of Crime

While many of Gottfredson and Hirschi's ideas about crime and criminality appeared in the pages of the journal *Criminology* in the 1980s (e.g. Gottfredson and Hirschi 1986, 1987, 1988), they finally culminated in a book, *A General Theory of Crime*, published in 1990. In this book, the authors bridge insights from the classical and positivist traditions and define crime as 'acts of force or fraud undertaken in self-interest'. They also suggest that the majority of crimes are trivial, mundane affairs that result in little loss and little gain.

In fact, *A General Theory of Crime* presents a version of control theory that is explicitly based on the idea of self-control. In stating that their theory is 'general', Gottfredson and Hirschi are making the very bold claim that it can explain all crime at all times. In other words, it can explain everything about criminality. One of the central ideas is that the essential nature of criminality is low self-control, and that this is *the* common factor in a host of problematic behaviours including accidents as well as crime and delinquency. They argue that low self-control can lead to crime when it is combined with appropriate opportunities and attractive targets (cf. Cohen and Felson 1979). So by acknowledging the importance of opportunity, Gottfredson and Hirschi also highlight the relevance of situational factors. However, despite mentioning the variable of opportunity, in reality it is the issue of low self-control that they focus most of their attention on (cf. Taylor 2001). They argue that the origins of self-control in an individual come from our early family experiences and the way we were brought up, so they link self-control to early socialisation.

In defining self-control, Hirschi and Gottfredson identify a number of factors that they believe characterise the concept of low self-control. In their view:

> People who lack self-control will tend to be impulsive, insensitive, physical (as opposed to mental), risk-taking, short-sighted, and non-verbal, and they will tend therefore to engage in criminal and analogous acts. (Gottfredson and Hirschi 1990: 90–1).

For Gottfredson and Hirschi (1990), low self-control is the individual-level cause of crime at all ages. They maintain that it is set by about the age of 8 years as a result of child-rearing experiences. Therefore, our propensity to commit crime will be established by the time we are eight years old. Furthermore, if we are offenders, low-self control will explain our criminality at every age.

Clearly this is a very bold claim, yet how do we begin to assess it? We now move on to evaluate Gottfredson and Hirschi's position, considering, in particular, some of the strengths and weaknesses.

Evaluating propensity theory

As proposed by Gottfredson and Hirschi, criminal propensity theory underpinned by its self-control themes has some immediate and understandable appeal. In focusing upon self-control it has a popular resonance, for criminals do often seem to lack self-control in apparently doing things without much thought. However, its appeal goes beyond a rather simplistic understanding of crime. It has also attracted a considerable amount of political interest and popularity. Soothill (2005) notes that in many ways the political interest is easy to understand. The theory emerged in its full form during the early 1990s when conservative values, particularly in support of the nuclear family, were paramount. Furthermore, promoting policies that emphasise the quality of family life and child-rearing practices is far easier and certainly less challenging than trying to promote polices that seek to change the social structure and the whole fabric of society. The implications of self-control theory are manageable for policy-makers and do not pose a particular challenge. Nevertheless, the theory is not simply a political gimmick and has some academic strengths to consider.

Certainly one of the strengths is that it does promote an interdisciplinary approach. It seeks to avoid offering a purely sociological explanation of criminality, but it weighs up the evidence from sociology, psychology, economics and biology. However, in the final analysis, the theory is also attractive because of its simplicity and boldness. Following the principle of Ockham's Razor – the notion that, when there are two competing theories and other things are equal, one takes the simpler – the theory reigns supreme!

However, as Soothill (2005) argues, general theories are often difficult to confront and pose particular challenges. Usually there is enough support from empirical evidence to encourage supporters of a particular general theory, but there is not enough evidence to convince concerned critics. This is the case with Gottfredson and Hirschi's general theory. Its major conclusion that low self-control is related to criminal involvement is difficult to dispute. But saying that there is a relationship or an association between low self-control and criminal behaviour is very different from saying that low self-control is the general causative link for all offenders. As critics have pointed out, that is a very questionable claim indeed. Indeed, is it believable?

Despite their claim that white-collar crime can be explained by their theory (see Chapter 9 in *A General Theory of Crime*), evidence on white-collar crime clearly undermines the self-control theory. For example, many individuals involved in white-collar crime have demonstrated that they can cope with delayed gratification and delayed rewards – which is the opposite of low self-control – by achieving an advanced education. Similarly, many organised criminals and terrorists have to make detailed plans and think through strategies very clearly before they act – recent research by Simpson and Piquero (2002) supports this view. Again this does not fit with low self-control and its emphasis on impulsiveness and risk-taking. Certainly the attackers of the World Trade Center on 11 September 2001 must have had to plan their strategy in incredible detail over quite a long period of time to ensure that they could carry out their plans. So, in many ways, self-control is a very limited and limiting concept in explaining criminal behaviour.

While simplicity is a virtue, with this theory it has the cost that important aspects of the approach, such as the role of opportunity, are not fully developed. Although they emphasise that low self-control needs to combine with appropriate opportunities to lead to crime, in reality they do not say much more than this about the variable of opportunity.

Their confidence about the completeness of their approach is also a shortcoming. Gottfredson and Hirschi have been reluctant to engage with competing theoretical explanations since publishing their influential work in the 1990s. In many ways they believe they have said all they have to say or that needs to be said, but this failure to engage with ongoing debates means that the influence of their approach is likely to reduce over time.

There is no doubt of its importance as a theoretical approach. In the decade following its publication, Gottfredson and Hirschi's book was certainly one of the most quoted criminological works, rather polarising criminological opinion. Sadly, polarisation usually fails to encourage rational debate. Enthusiasts fail to recognise weaknesses and critics fail to appreciate strengths. In such a climate certain puzzles are neglected. For example, it is difficult to disentangle the relationship between self-control and the social control components that were emphasised in Hirschi's earlier work (cf. Taylor 2001). In this sense, it is arguable that what we have termed as the 'Great Debate' has in some ways simplified the discourse around understanding criminal careers. Certainly the 'Great Debate' did not capture everything and may have missed some key issues. Later theoretical developments within criminology suggest that, with hindsight, the effort expended on defending one position against another may have been put to better use elsewhere. In trying to understand criminal careers theoretically, it is useful at this stage to consider an alternative approach which stands in many ways in direct opposition to some of the basic tenets of Gottfredson and Hirschi's position.

Developmental criminology and the life-course approach

As usual, nomenclature can be a puzzle. Similar theories seem to have different names. However, here we are more concerned with identifying an alternative approach to that of Gottfredson and Hirschi rather than trying to clarify the differences between the variants. For our purposes both developmental criminology and the life-course approach fall under the general heading of criminal careers, that is they both fit within the criminal careers paradigm.

In contrast to Gottfredson and Hirschi, those working within the criminal careers paradigm believe that antisocial behaviour and criminality are not simply the result of an individual trait or tendency. They are something which has to *develop* over time within an individual. So rather than focusing on a time-stable individual trait, developmental theorists are interested in tracing the *development* of behaviour within individuals. Their focus is very much multi-disciplinary and links are made between criminology and psychology, particularly studies of child development in the early years. Many, if not most, child psychologists, for example, are very interested in developmental approaches.

What advocates of this approach tend to do is focus on early predictors of later offending, Hence they are interested in how early childhood experiences and family experiences can impact on later behaviour. In fact, the focus on early family life seems to have echoes of the Gottfredson and Hirschi approach, but there is a difference. The essential distinguishing feature is that developmental criminologists are interested in the possibilities for charting development and change within an individual. In other words, they recognise that change is possible and that individual behaviour is not necessarily time-stable throughout life. Within developmental criminology, the life-course approach is one perspective that has proved particularly popular with those working within the framework of criminal careers.

The life-course approach is spelt out in detail by Robert Sampson and John Laub in their 1993 book, *Crime in the Making*. While they acknowledge the stability that propensity theorists refer to and recognise the existence of the age distribution of crime, an additional feature of their approach is the recognition of change in antisocial and deviant behaviour throughout life. On this aspect they have more to say.

Sampson and Laub (1993) argue that attachments formed in later life, such as joining the labour force and getting married, can divert criminal pathways and redirect life trajectories (this is explicitly refuted by Gottfredson and Hirschi). This key point has important implications for the way that we deal with offenders. For example, it means that we can be optimistic about the prospects of reforming and rehabilitating offenders. Life-course theorists imply that rehabilitation and change is possible, and that there is a variety of pathways we may take through life. In other words, just because individuals have offended at an early age, say at 12 years, this does not mean we should give up on them for the rest of their lives. Instead, we should seek to provide opportunities for change, whether that means getting them back into education, helping them to improve relationships with family or eventually helping them to get a job.

Given the emphasis on change and the possibility of criminal life courses being diverted, Sampson and Laub (1995) argue that longitudinal data is very valuable in exploring criminal careers. This is because studying people over time can highlight the different stages in the life course where change may occur. They also challenge Gottfredson and Hirschi's rejection of the collection of longitudinal data on the basis that it is costly and tells very little. In contrast, Sampson and Laub (1995) argue that the crux of Gottfredson and Hirschi's theory lies with the time-stable criminal propensity of individuals, but any demonstration of this requires longitudinal data. In other words, you need to study people over the life course in order to prove their criminal propensity is time-stable. If this crucial point is accepted, then the relevance of longitudinal data for whichever approach one espouses is clear (although presumably Gottfredson and Hirschi's response to this would be that once the stability of criminal propensity has been established, longitudinal data will no longer be required).

Sampson and Laub (1995) also challenge the Gottfredson and Hirschi approach on the latter's own territory. In brief, if Gottfredson and Hirschi's claim that self-control must be taught in early child-rearing and must be set by the age of eight years is true, then Sampson and Laub argue that self-control does, in fact, change over the life course, that is up to the age of eight years. Therefore it is only actually a time-stable construct from middle childhood onwards. (A related question of interest concerns why self-control becomes stable at eight and not before.)

It is arguments like these – on both theoretical and methodological grounds – that characterise the Great Debate between criminal careers and criminal propensity theorists. There are commentators in both camps whose viewpoints make the positions seem far apart and impossible to reconcile. Indeed, if one believes in complete stability over time, then it is impossible to appreciate the possibility of change. In contrast, if one accepts the possibility of change, then the pessimism of complete continuity in behaviour cannot be accepted.

Evaluating developmental criminology

Developmental criminology draws on a range of theoretical ideas from a spread of disciplines such as psychology and child development in order to inform its contribution. Furthermore, it takes a two-pronged approach to explaining criminal behaviour, emphasising continuity but also change and variability over the life course. It also focuses on various stages of the life course and is interested in looking for individuals' motivations and rationale for offending. This emphasis on motivation stands in direct contrast to propensity theorists, such as Gottfredson and Hirschi, who believe that motivation is irrelevant when someone has a criminal propensity or low self-control.

Perhaps most importantly in terms of what this means for the real lives of offenders and policy makers and criminal justice workers is that developmental and life-course approaches suggest we have reason to be reasonably optimistic about the prospects of getting individuals out of crime and encouraging them to go straight. In other words, the message is that all is not lost when someone offends at an early age. In contrast, while propensity theorists do not fully spell it out, the implication of their approach is that the opposite is the case.

In terms of the challenges and limitations, the theoretical basis of the work of developmental criminologists has been questioned by some. The favoured focus of integrating lots of different theoretical ideas and approaches means that it is not always clear whether the developmental theorist is offering anything new or original, or whether they are simply choosing a 'pick 'n' mix' of the best ideas from other theorists but without considering the tensions and contradictions in trying to amalgamate disparate theories (Soothill 2005).

Other criticisms include the fact that developmental criminologists in general, like many researchers, tend to work with data on known offenders. The problem with this, of course, is that their work inevitably focuses on lower class males committing rather mundane offences which often involve public order offences. This type of criminology can be interpreted as simply maintaining the control of the poorest in society rather than including the broader spectrum of crime. Certainly developmental psychologists and criminologists have had far less to say about the criminal careers of white-collar criminals and organised crime which may reveal very different life course trajectories.

A further point of concern is that developmental and criminal careers work does encourage an individualistic focus. The criminal records and convictions of individual offenders are often the main source of measurement. However, this leaves little room to consider the impact co-offenders have on one another, the impact of peer pressure on young people and the mechanisms underpinning offending in groups or organisations. Furthermore, the broader structural and cultural features underpinning a particular society are rarely given any prominence. Hence changes within a society over time or differences between societies are rarely part of the currency with which developmental criminologists deal.

Having briefly assessed some of the strengths and weaknesses of developmental and life-course approaches, we now consider a final theoretical approach provided by Terrie Moffitt (1993). While Moffitt's work certainly comes under the umbrella of the criminal careers paradigm and developmental criminology, it differs from the general theory of Sampson and Laub (1993) in that it seeks to offer a typological approach to understanding criminal careers.

Moffitt's developmental taxonomy

In short, Moffitt's developmental taxonomy is one approach which many criminologists interested in this area are currently willing to embrace in some form. However, theories – like behaviour! – can change and Moffitt's work continues to evolve. Here we first focus on her early work which seeks to distinguish between different types of offender. In Chapter 3 we go on to consider some later developments and modifications advocated by Moffitt and her colleagues.

Writing in 1993, Terrie Moffitt proposed that there are two distinct categories of antisocial behaviour and offending – these are life-course persistent offenders on the one hand and adolescence-limited offenders on the other. The first type refers to offenders who have an early onset and continue offending throughout their life. The second type, adolescence-limited, refers to those whose involvement in offending increases rapidly in early adolescence and then, after a peak of activity at about 18 years, rapidly declines. For this second group, offending only really takes place during adolescence (Moffitt 1993).

Smith (2007) notes that the two groups of offenders are hard to distinguish from each other in adolescence as their offending rates and patterns are similar. Yet the causes of offending are entirely different in the two groups as are their patterns of past and future offending.

According to Moffitt's theory, the substantial continuity of offending over the life course is entirely due to life-course persistent offenders – they explain all the continuity. This is obviously an important concession to the Gottfredson and Hirschi approach which insists on continuity. However, for Moffitt, this is only half the story. The substantial change in rates of offending is, she argues, entirely due to adolescent-limited offenders. So group 1 explains all the stability and group 2 explains all the change in crime patterns. When the two groups are combined together and superimposed on a graph, the result is the age–crime curve (see Figure 2.1). So, for Moffitt, these two offender types explain the pattern of the age–crime curve, and yet the two categories contain some very different and distinct types of offenders.

Certainly Moffitt's approach has encouraged various empirical studies (e.g. Nagin et al. 1995) and in many respects the results are supportive (see review in Moffitt 2006). Nevertheless, Moffitt's approach is not without its critics. Indeed, Sampson and Laub (2003) argue against the existence of a life-course persistent criminal 'type', as in their view all offenders desist but simply at different points over the life course. Interestingly, Moffitt has more recently added the category of 'low-level chronics' to her existing typology (Moffitt et al. 2002), although Blokland (2005) raises the issue that typologies may lose their theoretical power and become diluted as more categories are added. Later work by Moffitt has also added a crucial gender dimension to understanding criminal careers (Moffitt *et al.* 2001) highlighting that the 'Great Debate' was limited in its tendency to draw almost exclusively on data with males. This important gender dimension is discussed in the following chapter. For now, we conclude our theoretical discussion by summarising the approaches discussed in Table 2.1.

There are various ways of trying to summarise the various theoretical approaches that we have discussed in this chapter. Others have also tried (e.g. Blokland 2005 and Piquero *et al.* 2007). The latter is perhaps the more straightforward, cross-tabulating the notion of whether theories embrace change or not (i.e. static or dynamic) on the one hand, and whether they are general or developmental theories on the other.

The top left-hand cell in Table 2.1 refers to static/general theories of which Gottfredson and Hirschi's approach is a prime example. As Piquero *et al.* (2007: 35) stress, the static general theories 'assume that there is a general cause and one pathway to crime for all offenders and that once this causal process has occurred change is highly unlikely'. In contrast, they point to Sampson and Laub as espousing a dynamic general theory which 'maintains the assumption of general causality but allows for the possibility that life circumstances can materially alter an individual's criminal trajectory above and beyond persistent individual differences' (*ibid.*).

What is perhaps not stressed enough is that these two types of theory herald rather different methodological approaches. If one does not recognise that change owing to life circumstances is possible, then the potential value of longitudinal research seriously diminishes. So Gottfredson and Hirschi see little value in longitudinal research compared with those who point to the possibility of general

Table 2.1 Theories and types of explanation

	General	Developmental
Static	Gottfredson and Hirschi's theory	Moffitt's life-course persistent offenders
Dynamic	Sampson and Laub's theory	Moffitt's adolescence-limited offenders

Adapted from Table 2.1 in Piquero *et al.* (2007: 36).

or developmental change. Hence, for Gottfredson and Hirschi the less costly and quicker results which emanate from cross-sectional research are good advertisements for the theoretical approach that they tend to embrace. The sadness is that these very different stances have tended to increasingly become ideological positions rather than the outcome of careful and systematic research.

Moving on from general theories to developmental theories, these are more complex 'in that they assume that causality is not general and that different causal processes explain different offender types' (*ibid.*). Moffitt's life-course persisters and adolescence-limited offenders are portrayed as the former being less likely to respond to changes in life circumstances, while the latter do, indeed, respond to changing life's circumstances and give up committing crime.

The diagram looks neat but should only be read as a guide towards recognising that theories are different and have different implications. In fact, one suspects that, as Piquero and his colleagues themselves acknowledge in a footnote, the pathways of most offenders are a mixture of static and dynamic processes. Continuums rather than the dichotomies implied in Table 2.1 are probably a better way of understanding criminal careers.

Piquero *et al.* note that empirical research has attempted to adjudicate between these theoretical models and suggest that 'thus far the evidence tends to favour a middle-ground position' (2007: 36). Blokland (2005: 157) is perhaps less cautious arguing that general static theories oversimplify at best, while suggesting that his own work provides support for the *dynamic* assumptions made by general dynamic theories. However, he can also see the dangers in the assumption of one *general* cause underlying all change in criminal behaviour. In fact, there seems little doubt that various *criminological* careers will continue to flourish expounding a wide variety of criminological theories in the area of criminal careers!

Policy implications

So what are the implications of some of the opposing theoretical positions discussed in this chapter for how we deal with offenders in the real world? Clearly the policy implications may vary according to which side of the 'Great Debate' one is considering.

Prospects of rehabilitation and reform vs stability of criminal propensity

On the one hand, the criminal career paradigm emphasises the importance of turning points throughout life and highlights that events such as finding employment and getting married can alter the course of offending trajectories. Thus rehabilitation programmes aimed at finding jobs for offenders and encouraging them to change their behaviour are believed to offer the potential for reform and change. Yet a far less optimistic view is taken by criminal propensity theorists such as Gottfredson and Hirschi (1990). Their belief in the relative stability of criminal propensity throughout life renders meaningless attempts at rehabilitation and reform and suggests that attachments formed in later life are irrelevant. Indeed, taken to its logical conclusion, Gottfredson and Hirschi's (1990) work implies that a wide range of currently popular measures such as drug and alcohol rehabilitation programmes, mentoring programmes and initiatives aimed at getting offenders back into education or employment are unlikely to impact upon involvement in crime.

Selective incapacitation

Interestingly, while Gottfredson and Hirschi (1990) are frequently misrepresented as right-wing theorists (e.g. by Young 1999b), in actual fact their general theory of crime specifically argues against the right-wing policy of incarceration (cf. Taylor 2001). By contrast, researchers within the criminal career tradition such as Piquero *et al.* (2007: 23) argue that their work on individual crime rates and career lengths is particularly useful for policies and decisions relating to incarceration, specifically with respect to sentence length and time served in prison. So selective incarceration is a particular policy implication arising from work on criminal careers although, as Piquero *et al.* point out, their work may 'provide powerful arguments against lengthy incapacitation policies' (2007: 23).

Pre-school family interventions

Finally, it is important to highlight a potential area of 'policy convergence' between theorists on both sides of the Great Debate and that is the area of early intervention within the family. Researchers working within both the criminal careers and criminal propensity tradition recognise the importance of early experiences within the family and good child-rearing practices. Criminal career research, such as that on early family risk factors (Farrington 2007), seems to have an obvious connection with pre-school intervention policies, but there is actually no reason why Gottfredson and Hirschi's general theory (1990) could not be used to justify quite progressive policy programmes (such as intensive health visiting) (cf. Taylor 2001).

The increasing emphasis on early intervention as a policy priority is evident in the UK government's Youth Crime Action Plan, which was published in July 2008. The plan describes a range of interventions available, ranging from universal services such as Sure Start to projects that provide 'non-negotiable support for the families of children engaged in anti-social behaviour' (Home Office 2008: 29). While universal services like Sure Start have the potential to provide valuable family support, it is questionable how supportive targeted 'non-negotiable support' will be perceived as. Indeed, the current enthusiasm for early, targeted intervention into the lives of specific families deemed to be 'high-risk' may be overstating the case about how far we can truly predict the criminals of the future, and indeed such policies may risk stigmatising already vulnerable populations. As Sampson and Laub (2003) observe, 'there are important differences in adult criminal trajectories that *cannot* be predicted from childhood, contra the National Summits of the policy world, and apparently much yearning among criminologists' (2003: 588, emphasis added).

Conclusions

Returning to our theoretical and methodological discussion, Moffitt's current work arguably represents one of the most popular and compelling approaches within criminology, although it is certainly not accepted uncritically (see Sampson and Laub 2003; Laub and Sampson 2003). In some respects, the challenges to Moffitt's work concerning the value of her typology signal a new era and a new 'debate' within the criminal career paradigm itself.

Like any paradigm, the criminal careers approach provides a framework for presenting research and analysis as well as a potential target for challenge. Hence, the scientific battle for understanding is never over. However, Moffitt's work – together with that of others such as David Farrington, Robert Sampson and John Laub – all use the language which frames the following chapters, such as onset, persistence and desistance.

We have identified the 'Great Debate' in this chapter as a heated theoretical and methodological dispute between supporters of the criminal careers and criminal propensity approaches. Furthermore, we have argued that the particular theoretical approach that one favours is likely to dictate the particular methodological approach that one finds most useful for examining criminal behaviour. However, our own view is that whichever side of the 'Great Debate' one is on, the necessity for longitudinal studies remains paramount. Even propensity theorists require empirical data from longitudinal research to support their claims about stability in criminal behaviour (cf. Sampson and Laub 1995). Meanwhile, both those who believe there is merit in distinguishing specific offender types (Moffitt *et al.* 2001) and those who argue against typological explanations (Laub and Sampson 2003) use longitudinal data to support their claims. So now we move on to consider whether longitudinal studies are, indeed, the 'Great Solution' and to describe some of the main attempts to provide that solution.

Chapter 3

The Great Solution? Exploring the major longitudinal studies

In the last chapter we stressed that, among many criminal careers researchers, longitudinal studies are regarded as the gold standard in providing us with important information on issues such as onset, persistence and desistance within an individual. However, before focusing on these topics in some detail, criminologists studying criminal careers need to know about longitudinal studies in their own right. Are they indeed the 'Great Solution' to understanding criminal careers? There are two strategies in talking about longitudinal studies. Firstly, one can try to cover in detail all the longitudinal studies. This would be both tedious and repetitive in that many of their findings do replicate from one study to the next. However, in Box 3.1 we have listed some of the major longitudinal studies in criminology, beginning with the pioneering efforts of Sheldon and Eleanor Glueck and moving to some of the more contemporary developments. There will be others that are not mentioned – partly because new studies are emerging each year but also because in some studies the interest in crime and criminal behaviour is only tangential to the main issues of the project.

Rather than trying to discuss all the longitudinal studies in existence in this chapter, we have selected a few studies which are particularly relevant and/or illustrative of longitudinal studies in general. The three studies which are our focus are the Gluecks' study, the Cambridge Study of Delinquent Development and, finally, the Dunedin Health and Development Study. However, before outlining the specifics of these particular studies, it is important to emphasise a number of methodological points with respect to the value of longitudinal research in general.

Box 3.1   Ten major longitudinal studies

1. **The Glueck's Unravelling Juvenile Delinquency study** – Boston, USA (see Laub and Sampson 2003)
   500 delinquent and 500 non-delinquent males from Massachusetts.

2. **The Cambridge-Somerville Youth Study** – Massachusetts, USA (see Powers and Witmer 1951).
   506 boys from Cambridge and Somerville, Massachusetts

3. **Delinquency in a Birth Cohort** – Philadelphia, USA (see Wolfgang *et al* 1972).
   (a) 1945 cohort: 9,945 boys born in Philadelphia in 1945 and who lived in Philadelphia through age 17.
   (b) 1958 cohort: 27,160 boys and girls born in Philadelphia in 1958 and who lived in Philadelphia through age 17.

4. **The National Survey of Health and Development** – England, Scotland and Wales (see Douglas *et al.* 1966)
   5,362 persons selected from all those born in the first week of March 1946 in Great Britain.

5. **The Cambridge Study in Delinquent Development** – Cambridge, England (see Piquero *et al.* 2007).
   411 London males selected at ages 8–9 from registers of six state primary schools.

6. **The Dunedin Multi-disciplinary Health and Human Development Study** – Dunedin, New Zealand (see Moffitt *et al.* 2001).
   1,037 youths from an unselected birth cohort from Dunedin, New Zealand, born in 1972–73.

7. **The Pittsburgh Youth Study** – Pittsburgh, USA (see Loeber *et al.* 2003).
   1,517 boys in Pittsburgh public schools, ages 7, 10, 13.

8. **The Edinburgh Study of Youth Transitions and Crime** – Edinburgh, Scotland (see McAra and McVie 2007).
   4,300 young people in the city of Edinburgh recruited when they were aged around 12.

9. **The Dutch National Crime Study** – The Netherlands (see Blokland 2005).
   5,176 persons who represented 4% of all criminal justice cases in the Netherlands in 1977.

10. **The Peterborough Youth Study** – Peterborough, England (see Wikstrom and Butterworth 2007).
    700 young people living in Peterborough recruited in 2002 when they were 11 years old.

Longitudinal designs

There are several different ways in which longitudinal research can be carried out. Blumstein *et al.* (1986a) note that one approach is the prospective design that is forward-looking. This involves identifying a cohort at birth and then following that cohort prospectively over the course of (or over a period of) their lifetime. One obvious disadvantage here is the very long time required to develop research results. The research will take decades to complete, and is likely to be expensive and resource-intensive. A related difficulty is that by the time the final results become available, the historical environment in which the cohort is observed may no longer be relevant (Blumstein *et al.* 1986a).

A different approach to longitudinal design that Blumstein *et al.* (1986a) describe is the retrospective longitudinal design. This approach aims to avoid the long delay associated with the prospective study by defining a cohort and reconstructing its prior criminal involvement. So the retrospective study casts its gaze backwards and examines what has occurred in the past. An example of the retrospective approach was described by Wolfgang and his colleagues in 1972. Wolfgang *et al.* (1972) first defined their cohort which was all boys born in 1945 and living in Philadelphia between the ages of 10 and 18. They then retrospectively collected their records of contact with the police and used this information to make comments on individual criminal careers.

Not only can a longitudinal study be prospective or retrospective, it can also be single cohort or multi-cohort. Wolfgang *et al.'s* cohort of all boys born in 1945 was in the first instance a single-cohort study. However, if the researchers had decided to compare this data with boys born in 1947 and 1949, for example, it would have become a multi-cohort approach. An additional feature of the longitudinal design is that data may be collected on more than one occasion and at more than one time period. When this is done, the design becomes multi-wave. Importantly, a multi-wave, multi-cohort design has the potential to make crucial distinctions between age, period and cohort effects in understanding patterns of criminality (cf. Francis and Soothill 2005).

In common with cross-sectional research, longitudinal work has the potential to draw on a wide range of data sources. One of the main sources of information used on offending over the life course are official statistics. They are often based on conviction data and court appearances, but they can also be related to numbers of arrests and the number of times that an individual comes into contact with the police. Yet, as most students of criminology are aware, official statistics are very limited and only represent a fraction of all criminal incidents. Only a minority of all offences will ever be reported to the police and recorded by them, and an even smaller number lead on to someone being arrested or charged (*see* Soothill *et al.* 2002).

A second key data source is the self-report study which involves individuals reporting their own involvement in crime to researchers. Since the early 1960s, self-report data have been used to provide a more complete account of offending, and Smith (2007) notes that the balance of research evidence suggests that it is the best method available for collecting data on criminal offending over the life course. Yet self-reports clearly have limitations too, and there is always the possibility that respondents may lie or exaggerate when asked to report their experiences as an offender or a victim. Thus it is often argued that the most reliable research studies are those that combine official records with self-reports. Research can be made even more reliable if data are included that are based on the reports of others. For example, if we combine official records and self-report data with reports from teachers, parents and peers we are most likely to gain a complete picture of someone's offending behaviour (Smith 2007).

The pros and cons of longitudinal research

Without wanting to repeat the comments made in the previous chapter, the following quote by Blumstein *et al.* (1986a) reiterates the reasons why criminal careers researchers tend to regard the longitudinal method as superior to cross-sectional research:

> Many issues about criminal careers cannot be adequately addressed in cross-sectional research: the influence of various life events ... the effects of interventions on career developments; and distinguishing between developmental sequences and heterogeneity across individuals in explaining apparent career evolution. Answering these and related questions requires a prospective longitudinal study of individuals of different ages. (Blumstein *et al.* 1986a: 199)

Indeed, cross-sectional research designs that seek to collect information from individuals of different ages on one occasion (for example, a one-off survey of women in prison) very much provide us with a 'snapshot' picture or a slice of reality from one moment in time. Cross-sectional surveys can, of course, be repeated at different time periods if required (as in the case of the British Crime Survey), but not necessarily with the same individuals. Thus, as Blumstein *et al.* explain in the quote above, it is only longitudinal research that enables us to consider developmental sequences within individuals, and the influence of various life events on individual trajectories.

A number of more general advantages of longitudinal data have been identified by Rutter (1988):

- precision in timing and measurement (with respect to measuring specific variables, such as involvement in antisocial behaviour);
- heterogeneity of outcome (capturing a range of different individual outcomes in adulthood);
- subdivision by age of onset (for example, dividing age groups into strips, such as 5–10, 10–15 and so on, in order to identify the onset of a range of different childhood disorders and behaviours);
- intra-individual change (identifying changes within individuals and not just between individuals);
- causal chain analysis (helping us to understand the correct order and sequence of behavioural events, such as when there is a link between involvement in crime and drug use).

While the advantages of longitudinal research for measuring continuity and change within individuals seem clear, it is also important to highlight the limitations of this type of research. We have already noted that large-scale longitudinal work is often expensive, time-consuming, resource-intensive and slow to provide policy-makers with key findings. A number of other limitations have been highlighted with respect to work on criminal careers in particular.

Blokland (2005) identifies several limitations of existing studies on the age–crime relationship.

- While longitudinal data has become more widely available, the majority of studies only cover a limited period of the entire lifespan.
- The primary focus of longitudinal research has tended to be on the period in which participation in crime is the highest, namely during adolescence. As a result of the bias towards youth, not much is known about offending in later life.
- Most longitudinal studies only consider the criminal behaviour of boys. This leaves the behavioural development of girls a neglected

area and calls into question the applicability of developmental theories to females.

- Many studies are not able to control for what is known as 'false desistance' or the forced reduction of criminal behaviour due to incarceration, deteriorating health or death. This can result in underestimations of the persistence in crime for offenders experiencing such circumstances (Blokland 2005: 11).

Interestingly, Blokland's final point is emphasised in a different way by Francis *et al.* (2008) in their discussion of the England and Wales Offender Index, which is an extensive Home Office research data set. While the Offender Index has numerous advantages for examining crime patterns over time, Francis *et al.* (2008) note that it does not contain information on death, or immigration or emigration. Thus an individual might have left the country (perhaps to Scotland), but this would be viewed as a period of not offending in the data set. The authors identify a further problem with all long-term longitudinal data sets, which is that, as new offences are passed into law or some offences become viewed as more or less serious, definitions of standard list offences may well change over time (Francis *et al.* 2008: 7).

It is of course important for any student of criminal careers to be aware of the methodological concerns outlined above. Yet, in spite of these limitations, longitudinal studies have undoubtedly revealed much about the nature of criminal behaviour over time. We move on now to address some of the substantive findings that have arisen from three major longitudinal pieces of research across the globe. Our journey will take us from the USA to the UK and on to New Zealand. Each study started with a bold ambition which was at least partially fulfilled. So what were their origins and outcomes?

The Gluecks' study

One of the most influential studies in the history of criminological research was conducted by Sheldon and Eleanor Glueck of the Harvard Law School in the USA. The Gluecks' data came from a three-wave prospective study of juvenile and adult criminal behaviour that originated with their book *Unravelling Juvenile Delinquency* (1950) (see also Glueck and Glueck's 1968 *Delinquents and Nondelinquents in Perspective*). The research design involved a sample of 500 male delinquents aged 10–17 and 500 male nondelinquents aged 10–17 matched case by case on age, race/ethnicity, IQ and low-income residence in Boston. The delinquent group had been remanded to reform school in Massachusetts during their adolescence. Extensive data were collected on the 1,000 boys at three points in time – at ages 14, 25 and 32.

The Gluecks were pioneers in the sense of presenting evidence for the first time which is now part of the established canon of criminal careers research. While the findings have been repeated so often in other studies that they are no longer surprising, it is important to grasp the implications of these 'laws' of criminal careers research. These are described by Piquero *et al.* (2003: 366) whose work is a rich source summarising key theoretical, empirical and policy developments in criminal careers over the previous two decades.

1 They found a strong relationship between age and crime. In particular, they found that, as the sample of offenders aged, their individual crime rates declined.

2 They observed that an early age of onset was related to a lengthy and persistent criminal career.

3 They found strong evidence of the stability postulate: that is, that the best predictor of future antisocial behaviour was past antisocial behaviour. They observed that many of the juvenile delinquents went on to engage in criminal activity as adults.

4 Their analysis uncovered strong family influences. They found that those families with lax discipline combined with erratic/threatening punishment, poor supervision and weak emotional ties between parent and child generated the highest probability of persistent delinquency.

The Gluecks collected a wealth of information on their sample of men between 1939 and 1948. Between 1949 and 1963 they followed up the same individuals at the age of 25, then again at age 32. Interestingly, while their data could easily have become forgotten in historical archives, it was, in fact, rediscovered in the basement of Harvard University library by contemporary researchers Robert Sampson and John Laub. This enabled Sampson and Laub (1993) to re-analyse the Gluecks' vast data set which led them to formulate their own life-course approach to explaining criminal behaviour (as outlined in Chapter 2).

In re-analysing the Glueck data, Sampson and Laub (1993) found patterns of both stability and change in criminal behaviour over the life course. In particular, they found that, even after controlling for stable individual differences in offending propensity, life events (such as marriage) and in particular the attachment to informal social control agents fostered cessation from criminal activity (Laub *et al.* 1998).

Most recently, Laub and Sampson (2003) have followed up the Glueck men to the age of 70 by tracking down the official criminal records of the original delinquent group and interviewing a sample of 52 surviving men. The resulting publication *Shared Beginnings, Divergent Lives* has won a number of prestigious awards and arguably represents the longest longitudinal study of criminal careers in the world (Laub and Sampson 2003). The benefits of this very long-term follow-up study arguably overshadow some of the limitations of the Gluecks' original work, with its fairly narrow focus on lower-class males. Interestingly, such a limited focus is a difficulty that spans international borders and is evident as we move on from Boston, USA to South London, England.

The Cambridge Study in Delinquent Development

The Cambridge study is one of the most famous and influential longitudinal studies of delinquency in England. Owing to its wide range of publications it is also well known throughout the world. It is a prospective longitudinal survey of 411 males and seeks to explore the development of offending and antisocial behaviour. The 411 members of the sample were all first contacted in 1961 and 1962 when they were living in a working-class inner-city area of South London. The sample was chosen by taking all the boys who were then aged 8–9 and on the registers of six state primary schools within a one-mile radius of the research office that had been established. The most common year of birth for these males was 1953. In nearly all cases, the family breadwinner at the time (usually the father) had a working-class occupation (skilled, semi-skilled or unskilled manual worker). Most of the males were white and of British origin (Farrington *et al.* 2006a).

The study was originally directed by Donald J. West. However, since his retirement, it has been directed by David Farrington. Farrington has worked on the Cambridge study since 1970 and directed it since 1982. The study has received a great deal of its support and funding from the Home Office. The early major results of the study can be found in some key books (e.g. West 1969, 1982; West and Farrington 1973, 1977). More recent publications, usually authored by David Farrington, have often been published as journal articles and some findings have been published as Home Office Reports (e.g. Farrington *et al.* 2006a, 2006b). The latest follow-up (see Farrington *et al.* 2006b) takes the sample up to 50 years of age and so, while they are not yet as old as the Gluecks' sample, they are not far behind!

The original aim of the Cambridge study was to describe the development of delinquent and criminal behaviour in inner-city males. It also wanted to investigate how far delinquency could be predicted in advance and why it did or did not continue into adult crime. As a result, it had a focus on onset, desistance and prediction from the very outset. In particular, one of its major contributions has been in identifying a range of risk and protective factors for offending behaviour. Indeed, Farrington (2007) has noted that the following six categories of variables predicted offending independently of one another:

- impulsivity;
- intelligence or attainment;
- poor parenting;
- criminal family;
- socio-economic deprivation;
- child anti-social behaviour.

Thus he observes that despite the interrelations between the above variables, it could be concluded that all contribute independently to the development of delinquency (Farrington 2007). One of the obvious policy implications of the Cambridge study, with its emphasis on identifying predictive risk factors, has been the promotion of risk-focused prevention programmes. We elaborate on issues of prediction and risk in Chapter 7.

For now, it is enough to note that the Cambridge study has a fairly unique combination of factors. Not only does it consider a very wide range of variables, it is also based on a considerable amount of empirical data. Nine personal interviews have been undertaken with the male participants, from the age of 8 to 48 years (Farrington *et al.* 2006a, 2006b). Farrington also notes that with a sample size of around 400 males, he is able to do many types of statistical analyses as well as focusing in depth on individual case histories. Thus the wealth of research data that this study has created is phenomenal.

Furthermore, Farrington notes that there has also been a very low attrition rate, with 93 per cent of the males who were still alive providing data and information at the age of 48. This has been a quite remarkable achievement to keep in touch and maintain contact with the research participants for such a long time. Some modest incentives have been offered to the sample of males but, however achieved, the low attrition rate is very impressive for a study of this kind. In addition, information has been collected from a very wide range of sources – not just from the males being studied but also from their parents, their teachers, peers and official records.

Challenges of the Cambridge study

So the Cambridge study has a lot to commend it, but what about the challenges? Farrington himself notes that the individuals in the study were all born in the 1950s and so were growing up in the 1960s and 1970s when conditions were very different from today. One question raised by critics is whether or not the risk factors for offending identified by the Cambridge study would still apply to young people growing up today. Farrington suggests that they probably would. Writing in 1999 with Rolf Loeber (Farrington and Loeber 1999), he compared the results of the Cambridge study with the Pittsburgh Youth Study which explores young people growing up in the 1990s. They demonstrated that most results were replicated.

Other major limitations of the Cambridge study concern the predominant focus on white, British males. This raises a number of crucial questions. For example, what about issues of race, what about non-British people and what about females? Can the results be generalised to understand the development of these populations? Similarly, the Cambridge study (like the Gluecks' work before it) focuses on those born in working-class areas, but what about crimes of the powerful and white-collar crime? In many ways the Cambridge study captures a fundamental concern with criminal careers research generally in that it does not address crimes of the powerful. However, recently, Piquero and Benson (2004) have reviewed what is known about the intersection of white-collar crime and criminal careers, citing the contribution of David Weisburd (1991, 2001) in particular. Perhaps, though, one also needs to be reminded of the work of Frank Pearce (1976), not cited by Piquero and Benson, to move from the middle classes to the really powerful. Pearce's analysis of the relationship between corporations and crime, explicitly laying the foundations for a Marxist criminology rooted in an analysis of the mode of production in society and the social relations between classes, provides a rather different approach which is very far removed from Farrington's type of criminology.

A further criticism of Farrington's work is that much of it has been atheoretical (or outside of theory), focusing particularly on empirical variables and risk factors rather than theoretical constructs. Farrington (2005) has recently responded to such concerns by proposing an Integrated Cognitive Antisocial Potential (ICAP) Theory. Yet why does the criticism of being atheoretical matter? This brings us round to the important question of why we ever bother with theory in the first place.

Theories, as Chapter 2 has earlier tried to make clear, are attempts to help us make sense of the world around us. They can provide us with an important framework for thinking through the implications of research data. Theories can provide coherence to research findings and empirical data. Perhaps most importantly, they are often used to justify criminal justice policy and interventions into people's lives. Thus the criticism of being atheoretical centres partly around concerns that it is not good enough just to produce statistics and data, but we have a responsibility to try and establish theoretical positions in which to justify how we deal with those who offend. The danger of producing data without theory is that we leave our work open to interpretation by those who may have their own political agenda. Interestingly, as we move away from South London to South Island, New Zealand to consider our next longitudinal study, we will see that it clearly integrates empirical data with a specific theoretical position.

The Dunedin Health and Development Study

The Dunedin Health and Development Study is a longitudinal follow-up study of 1,000 males and females from ages 3 to 21. The study sample is based on a complete cohort of births between April 1972 and March 1973 in Dunedin, which is a provincial capital city on New Zealand's South Island. With regard to racial distribution, the study members are of predominantly white European ancestry, which matches the ethnic distribution of New Zealand's South Island. When the study members were born, less than 2 per cent of mothers identified their babies as Maori or Pacific Islander. About half of the study members still live in or near Dunedin. The rest have primarily emigrated as young adults to other cities in New Zealand

and Australia, and a minority are now living in Britain, the USA and Asia.

Further details about the study were published in a book by Terrie Moffitt and colleagues in 2001 called *Sex Differences in Antisocial Behaviour*. Moffitt *et al.* argue that the Dunedin study is unique because it focuses on health, development and behaviour in the first two decades of life. In other words, it traces the development of very young children and does not just start looking at individuals during the teenage years which is a feature of many other studies. Furthermore, Moffitt *et al.* believe the study is unique because it focuses particularly on gender differences in understanding development and risk of antisocial behaviour. The Dunedin study is also multi-disciplinary so it is not just concerned with delinquency like the Cambridge study, but considers antisocial behaviour within the wider framework of an individual's health and development.

Two types of antisocial behaviour

Moffitt *et al.* argue that the findings in their book, when taken together, show that young people develop antisocial behaviour for two main reasons. According to them, the first form of antisocial behaviour may be understood as a disorder having neuro-developmental origins. They argue that this form, along with autism, hyperactivity and dyslexia, has a strong male preponderance. Furthermore, it is linked with early childhood onset, subsequent persistence throughout life and low prevalence in the population. In other words, it starts early, goes on for a long time but is not particularly common. The Dunedin study shows that extreme gender differences are linked with this form of antisocial behaviour, and it is argued that molecular and quantitative genetic research could further our understanding of this particular type.

On the other hand, the Dunedin study shows that the bulk of antisocial behaviour, especially by females, is best understood as a social phenomenon originating in the context of social relationships. This second type generally starts in adolescence and has a high prevalence. It is the more common type, and gender differences associated with this type are fairly negligible. Moffitt *et al.* argue that the antisocial activities of males and females are especially alike when alcohol and drugs are involved, near the time of female puberty and when females and males are involved in intimate relationships. It is argued that this second antisocial form requires more basic research on the processes of social influence.

So we have these two types of antisocial behaviour that have been identified within the Dunedin study. One is associated with males and neuro-developmental disorders. It is not that common but it persists. The other is associated with males and females and is believed to explain the great majority of female offenders. This second type is linked to social processes specifically during adolescence.

In fact, these two antisocial types relate directly to Moffitt's earlier work (1993) on life-course persistent and adolescent-limited offending. Type 1 in the Dunedin study is the life-course persistent type. Type 2 is the adolescent-limited. Basically, what Moffitt *et al.* are doing in the Dunedin study is extending and elaborating on these theoretical ideas. A gender dimension is introduced which is something that has too rarely been addressed in criminology generally and longitudinal work specifically.

Key findings on sex differences

In terms of the key findings, Moffitt *et al.* found that males fare worse than females on a number of levels with regard to health and development. Firstly, they fare worse on conduct disorder. More males than females were found to have conduct disorders at *every* age, and girls were less likely than boys to present behaviour extreme enough to warrant a diagnosed disorder. Conduct disorders were identified by various symptoms that individuals had, including setting fires, cruelty to people and animals, forcing sex and physical fights.

Moffitt *et al.* also found that males exhibited more serious and violent behaviour, such as physical aggression, at every age. Even the most active serious female offenders offended at a rate that was much lower than the active males. Thirdly, males were found to fare worse in terms of exposure to risk factors and were found to have more hyperactivity and more peer problems. Moffitt *et al.* argue that this supports the hypothesis that males are more likely to be antisocial than females because they are exposed to greater levels of individual and social risk for antisocial behaviour.

Finally, males were shown to fare worse than females in relation to developmental pathways. The female life-course persistent antisocial individual is extremely rare. Moffitt *et al.* found that when males and females are held to the same criteria, fewer than 1 in 100 females in a cohort are on the life-course persistent path. The male : female ratio is 10 : 1. So for every 1 female life-course persistent offender there will be 10 males. These figures are similar to the results in a study in England and Wales that tried to estimate the numbers and percentages of persons who had been persistent offenders at some point in their lives. Soothill *et al.* (2003: 389) calculate that 4.7 per cent and 0.4 per cent of the relevant male and female population respectively could be so categorised, again demonstrating the massive discrepancy between males and females. It is argued that these outcomes follow on naturally from the finding above that males are exposed to greater levels of risk factors. Given this, it is not really surprising that they fare worse in terms of developmental pathways.

On the basis of the results of the Dunedin Health and Development Study, the situation looks rather bleak for males. There was only one area where females actually fared worse than males and that was with respect to adult depression. It was found that for females, major depression frequently follows conduct problems. Furthermore, the depression of females with an antisocial history grows more severe as they enter adulthood.

Key findings on sex similarities

As well as highlighting sex differences, Moffitt *et al.* also found that the sexes resembled each other in various ways. It was found that males and females were most alike in their behaviour during middle adolescence, at around age 15. During this period, the prevalence and incidence of conduct disorder among females rises to produce the narrowest gap between the sexes seen at any time in the life course.

There are particular similarities in relation to types of antisocial behaviour. Firstly, males and females were found to be similar in their drug- and alcohol-related offences. And at every age, similar numbers of males and females began to engage in drug- and alcohol-related offences. Interestingly, the second type of antisocial behaviour where similarities are found is partner abuse, and the study found that the physically violent behaviour of males against their partner is matched or even exceeded by females.

The authors argue that the sex similarity on partner violence appears to be robust and it cannot be explained by the hypothesis that women's aggression is self-defence. There are also similarities between the sexes in terms of age at onset, and the study found that antisocial males and females onset within six months of each other.

There is also stability of individual differences in antisocial behaviour across the first two decades of life. Both sexes were shown to have at least moderate stability. Other similarities concern the risk factors which explain antisocial behaviour. Moffitt *et al.* argue that the same risk factors predict antisocial behaviour for males and females, and they did not detect any sex-specific risk factors for antisocial behaviour. Risk factors, such as family adversity, low intelligence, difficult temperament and hyperactivity, affected both sexes, although they appeared to have a stronger effect on males than females. This is another interesting finding and relates to evidence from Hayslett-McCall and Bernard (2002), who argue that males are particularly vulnerable to early disruption at home and negative experiences in the early years. What the evidence is unable to tell us is why this is so, and this represents a real gap in our understanding of gender differences.

Having highlighted some of the key findings from the Dunedin study, we move on now to consider some of the implications.

Implications of the Dunedin study

The Dunedin study confirms that females are less antisocial than males. Like many studies before it, it found that fewer females than males exhibit antisocial behaviour. For females this behaviour is generally less frequent and less serious. Such findings are well documented in criminology (see Heidensohn and Gelsthorpe 2007). However, Moffitt *et al.* do note that the sex differences were less universal than they had originally assumed. And so there were three very robust exceptions to the sex differences. These were that females' antisocial behaviour resembles males in three ways – when alcohol and drugs are involved, near the time of female puberty and in intimate relationships with men. Moffitt *et al.* note that these findings persuade them to move away from more research on the differences between the sexes. For them, it would be far more profitable for future research to examine in greater detail the circumstances that promote similarity between males and females.

Moffitt *et al.*'s work is useful because it moves us beyond purely sociological understandings of gender differences in offending which emphasise factors such as 'double deviance', where female offenders may be condemned for both breaking the law as well as for transgressing common female stereotypes. In contrast, Moffitt *et al.* build on psychological ideas, and much of their thinking is influenced by psychology and psychiatry.

However, the emphasis is very much on the individual in explaining antisocial behaviour, particularly with regard to the life-course persistent type of offender whose behaviour is presented as having neuro-developmental origins. While this could be viewed as encouraging an individual-blaming approach, it is noteworthy that

Moffitt's most recent work with colleagues over the last decade has also acknowledged the importance of environmental risk factors. There has been a focus on the interactions between genes and environmental risk factors in relation to psychopathology in particular (Caspi and Moffitt 2006; Moffitt *et al.* 2006). With the increasing rise of interest in genetics, this is an area which is crucial to clarify in criminology.

What is the importance of genetic and environmental factors in the development of crime? With discoveries about genetics that will certainly continue to impact upon medicine, providing scope for understanding in more detail numerous medical conditions, the temptation is to see genetics as an important ingredient in the development of crime. Mainstream criminologists tend to be dismissive of the potential impact of genetics as, quite correctly, they recognise crime as a social construction rather than a biological condition. Indeed, they see the dangers of a return to the excesses of Lombrosian claims about criminal behaviour. The beauty of the recent work by Moffitt and her colleagues is that they espouse a much more measured approach basing their claims on carefully accumulated evidence. Nevertheless, at times the evidence remains difficult to interpret and to understand.

In focusing upon measured gene–environment interaction (often referred to as $G \times E$), Moffitt *et al.* are concerned with the behavioural effects due to a variation in the DNA sequence and a specified measured environment. While they stress that the interaction of nature and nurture has a long history (Haldane 1946), it is noted that more recently $G \times E$ has played 'a central role in developmental psychology's resilience theories about children who have good mental health despite adversity' (Moffitt *et al.* 2006: 6).

Increasingly social scientists are recognising the importance of gene–environment interplay or interaction. In other words, in most fields where genetics may play a part, a strong deterministic claim that genetics directly causes behaviour is too simplistic. While there are extreme examples where this may be the case, crime has the intervening variable of the social environment which needs to be considered. It is rare, indeed, for the genetic effect to be so overwhelming that the environment has no effect. It is this gene–environment interplay or interaction that is crucial to try to understand. Indeed, this area is likely to occupy the attention of researchers interested in criminal careers for the foreseeable future. We further explore issues of heredity versus environment in the final chapter. For now, we return to our focus on longitudinal research.

Three landmark longitudinal studies

In the pages above three landmark studies have been introduced for at least three purposes. Firstly, the Gluecks' study indicates the long history of longitudinal research in criminal careers. The pioneering work of the Gluecks, although developed somewhat outside the main criminological tradition of the time, remains impressive, particularly with the enhancement provided by Laub and Sampson's new empirical research in terms of a further follow-up and their innovative methodological analysis of the original data.

Secondly, the Cambridge Delinquent Development Study is the longest and most influential study in England and Wales with again some recent work on the cohort when they were nearing 50 years of age providing strong evidence of the importance of maintaining contact if analytical links between various stages of development are really going to be probed.

Finally, the Dunedin study provided a major analysis of gender similarities and differences. While other studies were beginning to do likewise, the Dunedin study moved the game from choosing samples on the basis of their known delinquency (i.e. the Gluecks' study) or a community where delinquency was most likely to occur (i.e. the Cambridge Delinquent Development Study) to a sample from a capital city.

We believe that the above three studies have been particularly influential in understanding criminal careers. However, there are other studies which are currently available. We briefly describe three of these below. The first is derived from the Home Office Offenders Index.

The Offenders Index contains records for every offender who has been convicted of a *standard list* offence in a court in England or Wales since 1963. Broadly speaking, the 'standard list' consists of all the indictable offences plus the more serious summary offences. An offender's record contains all convictions from each court appearance that resulted in a conviction for at least one standard list offence. Thus, although 'lesser' encounters with the criminal justice system, such as cautions or warnings, are not included, and neither are convictions for non-standard list offences in general, the Offenders Index forms a coherent criminal record for over six million 'more serious' offenders.

The Offenders Index Cohorts developed by the Home Office consist of six data sets. These data sets contain the complete criminal records as found on the Offenders Index for all offenders with a date of birth falling in four pre-selected weeks of the years 1953, 1958, 1963, 1968, 1973 and 1978, giving an approximate one-thirteenth sample of the population of offenders in each of the relevant years. Convictions on the Offenders Index go back to 1963 and so, with the age of criminal responsibility being 10 years, the full range of the 'official' criminal career is captured for all offenders in the six cohorts. The total numbers of offenders in the six cohorts is 58,407 (47,740 males and 10,667 females). While the Home Office has published some important studies using the cohort data (e.g. Prime *et al.* 2001), it has been more rarely used by academic researchers but there are exceptions (e.g. Francis *et al.* 2004a, 2004b, 2007; Soothill *et al.* 2003, 2004, 2008a, 2008b).

Unlike the Police National Computer, the Offenders Index is not an operational tool for the criminal justice system but has more of the characteristics of a research database. There have been plans to amalgamate the two databases (Francis and Crosland 2002).

The second example focuses on Scotland. The Edinburgh Study is a longitudinal programme of research on pathways into and out of offending for a cohort of around 4,300 young people who started secondary school in the city of Edinburgh in 1998, when they were aged around 12. Children for all school sectors are included (mainstream, special and independent). A census method was employed, resulting in 89 per cent coverage of the eligible school population within Edinburgh. Information has been collected over six annual sweeps from a range of sources, including questionnaires completed by cohort members, school records and files held by police juvenile liaison officers, the Scottish Children's Reporter Administration and the social work department. Response rates among the achievable population have been uniformly high which is a remarkable outcome. Important material is emerging from this study (e.g. Smith and McVie 2003; McAra and McVie 2007), but the burden of collecting data has perhaps slowed down the process of publication. Nevertheless, the Edinburgh study should continue to be a rich source in future years.

The third example is from Denmark. While we hear much of carefully constructed studies from the United States, such as the famous Pittsburgh Youth Study (e.g. Loeber *et al.* 1998), we fail to recognise the possibilities emerging in some northern European countries where much information on their populations is routinely collected. Hence there is scope for working with national cohorts. In Denmark, for example, various population-based registers – medical register on vital statistics (cause of death), education statistics (grades etc.), income compensation benefits (social benefits), national inpatient register, national psychiatric register and so on – can be added to the national criminal registers. Hence, a national cohort study of all boys born in Denmark in 1966 (n = 43,403) accumulates a rich amount of data, so that it is possible to identify a wide range of significant risk factors for, say, violent criminal behaviour (Christoffersen *et al.* 2003), becoming rapists (Christoffersen *et al.* 2005) or drink-driving offenders (Christoffersen *et al.* 2008).

One serious shortcoming of most cohort studies is that they are based on persons being born at a certain time (usually a particular year) and at a particular location (a locality, such as Camberwell for the Cambridge Delinquent Development Study or a nation for the Christoffersen studies). It is a shortcoming because, although there is much current attention upon immigrants, those born outside the location and who then move into it are usually excluded from consideration. Certainly in the Danish studies, immigrants are excluded because 'information about their adolescence and family background was considered likely to be inferior to that known of the native-born population' (Christoffersen *et al.* 2003: 370).

Policy implications

The longitudinal studies outlined in this chapter have undoubtedly contributed a great deal to our understanding of criminal careers. Inevitably, individual studies will all have their own particular policy implications related to the level of analysis that they operate at and in terms of what they set out to explain. So, for example, the Cambridge study has clear implications for risk-focused prevention programmes and early interventions into the lives of those deemed to be 'at risk'. Meanwhile, the Dunedin study paves the way for further work on understanding the differences in rates of offending between males and females. While the emphasis on the life-course persistent type may encourage an individual-blaming approach to offending, emphasising the importance of understanding gene × environment interactions will hopefully go some way to overcome this.

Moving from the specific to the general, we can identify some broader policy dilemmas with longitudinal research as a whole. One concerns the time taken to obtain research results and whether by the time they are published they will be relevant to the policy concerns of the day. Ministers and other officials increasingly require immediate responses to their policy-related questions, and researchers are frequently asked to come to swift and certain conclusions on the basis of rapid evidence assessments (REAs). In this respect, it is arguable that while longitudinal studies may well be the gold standard in understanding individual offending trajectories, they are perhaps only part of the solution to providing policy-relevant information on criminal careers.

A final point here is that while longitudinal research, by its very design, encourages a focus on the individual, we believe that there is also a pressing need for studies to take more account of generational differences and the related issue of social change. For example, a cohort born in 1953 may experience very different societal conditions from a cohort born in 2003, and indeed quite different criminal justice interventions. Thus the social context is crucial to understand if we are to move away from a purely individualistic focus to a more dynamic analysis of criminal behaviour over time. Interestingly, an emphasis on social context raises the question of whether the policy implications from a study in one country are applicable in a different country. This chapter has discussed a range of longitudinal research from across the globe but studies that have crossed international borders or that have been conducted in different countries simultaneously are very rare. This remains a challenge for future research.

Conclusions

This chapter has focused on longitudinal research, highlighting different types of research design as well as some of the strengths and limitations of this kind of research. There has been a particular focus on three pioneering studies and some of the key findings from these pieces of work have been outlined. So does longitudinal work represent the 'Great Solution' to understanding criminal careers? We maintain that it is certainly part of the solution, and any attempt to understand individual offending behaviour across the life course undoubtedly requires longitudinal work. That said, the length of time taken to produce results means that it often necessary to draw on findings from other types of research design in understanding certain aspects of a criminal career.

It is important to reiterate here that methodological questions and choices are often intrinsically related to theoretical questions. In turn the theories that we use to make sense of the world often have clear policy and practice implications. It is important to try and unite theory and data in order to provide the most convincing evidence.

Theory without evidence is often no more than ideas. Equally, data without theory may have no explanatory framework and may simply be a collection of figures.

So what does the future hold for longitudinal research? David Farrington has recently outlined some of the possible future directions for work in this area, emphasising the need to follow up people to later ages as many studies do not look beyond 30. Curiously, the long-term follow-up of the Glueck men to the age of 70 years was a fluke following the discovery of the data in the basement of Harvard University Library. The Gluecks did not originally intend for the men to be followed up that far.

Interestingly, Farrington also comments on the need for future research to do more on risk factors and life events for males versus females and for different racial and ethnic groups. While we know that Moffitt *et al.* have produced some pioneering work on the issue of gender, there has certainly been little work on the potential impact of race.

The neglect of race is perhaps curious. Race and ethnicity are rarely even mentioned. Studies such as the Cambridge Delinquent Development Study simply lacked a racial mix – they were recruited from a working-class area that was predominantly white. Also birth cohorts recruited locally will usually miss the influx of immigrants born elsewhere but who alter the racial mix of an area. Similarly, researchers whose studies are based on official records soon recognise either the unreliability or dearth of the appropriate information.

Nevertheless, what has been done is fairly unequivocal. Reviewing various studies, Piquero *et al.* (2003: 421) note that 'most of the studies report relatively large black/white ratios and strong associations between race and participation'. However, self-report comparisons of race prevalence tend to produce a rather different picture with black/white differences being less evident, although Piquero *et al.* (2007: 422) report that 'analysis confined to more serious offences suggests that the black/white ratio is larger, especially at younger ages'.

The apparent discrepancy between 'official' participation and 'self-report' participation has tremendous implications for criminal careers research. It means that the criminal career *process* in terms of the interactions with social control agencies, for example, should command much more interest than it currently attracts. Psychologists tend to focus on the official perpetrators without much thought as to how they got there, while sociologists – whose work is currently less central to criminal careers research – have traditionally focused on the reactions to crime; that is why some groups are more likely to be 'processed' than others. This is a debate that was central to the sociology of deviance in the 1960s and 1970s and urgently needs to be resurrected.

If we return to Farrington's suggestions for future research, he also emphasises the importance of comparing risk factors for early onset, persistence and desistance, etc. We can begin to consider this agenda item in the subsequent chapters on these topics. As we shall see, Monica Barry (2006) also emphasises the need for more links to be made between theories of onset and desistance in criminology. In her view, they have been considered separately for too long when they need to be understood in parallel as part of a process. Hence in having separate chapters we might, in Wordsworth's words, 'murder to dissect'. However, the importance of emphasising the overall process must not be overlooked.

Chapter 4

When does it all start?
Onset of a criminal career

There are three foundation stones for understanding criminal careers. Onset is the first and persistence and desistance are to follow. This chapter focuses on the key issue of onset, which refers to the beginning of a criminal career. While this sounds simple enough, defining the concept of onset is not always straightforward and there is, in fact, no universal consensus among researchers on exactly how we measure the 'start' of criminal behaviour. Some studies focus on official criminal records to identify age at first arrest or age at first conviction as the defining 'moment' of onset. Others use self-report data to consider the age when individuals first report breaking the law or 'getting into trouble'. To add further confusion, it can be difficult to make international comparisons in this area (at least between studies based on 'official' data), as the age of criminal responsibility (and therefore the age at which one can be officially convicted of a crime) varies widely across the globe.

Some of the complexities surrounding the measurement of onset will be explored below, as we outline a range of data and evidence on what is actually known about the beginning of a criminal career. We focus particularly on data from a relatively new Home Office self-report survey (Budd *et al.* 2005), and from interview studies with young offenders in Scotland (Barry 2006) and from young people in care who enter the criminal justice system (Taylor 2006). In policy terms, understanding issues related to onset is clearly of crucial importance, for if we can begin to understand exactly how and why individuals first become involved in crime, we may be better placed to direct policy programmes aimed at preventing this occurring in the first place.

The Home Office Crime and Justice Survey 2003

It is important to highlight from the outset that the actual onset of criminal behaviour may vary considerably between individuals. This is evident in the first results of the Home Office Crime and Justice Survey (C&JS), which provides some valuable information on the average age of onset. The C&JS is a new longitudinal self-report survey that was first used in 2003 (Budd *et al.* 2005). (Annual sweeps of the survey were also carried out between 2004 and 2006, although the published results do not provide the same level of detail in relation to onset.)

Broadly, the C&JS provides information on the self-reported offending of the general population between the ages of 10 and 65. It is different from the more familiar British Crime Survey (BCS) which focuses on victims, in that it is capturing a younger spectrum of the population as well (that is, including those under the age of 16) and focuses specifically on experiences of offending. The survey also asks children and young people about personal victimisation as they are not covered in the BCS, so it is not simply about personal offending behaviour.

Age of onset is measured in the survey by asking those who have ever committed a specific offence at what age they had committed it. However, the authors do make a number of cautionary points about this measurement.

- Respondents may have committed offences not covered by the C&JS.
- Because respondents were asked to recall the past, they may have forgotten relevant incidents.
- Age of onset estimates are influenced by the age of those interviewed. For example, a 10-year-old can only have an age of onset up to the age of 10, while a 65-year-old can potentially have an age of onset up to the age of 65. Therefore, if only 65-year-olds had been interviewed, a later age of onset would have been estimated. (Budd *et al.* 2005: 47)

While bearing the above points in mind, according to the 2003 survey, which was based on a random sample of about 12,000 people living in private households in England and Wales, the mean (average) age of onset for offending is 15. When we look at the gender division it remains at 15 for males but is slightly higher at 16 for females. Despite this average age, there is, as one might expect, a lot of variation in the age of onset between individuals, and the survey found that just over 10 per cent first offended before the age of 10 and a fifth offended at age 18 or older. So there are some quite distinct offending trajectories here that become somewhat obscured when we talk about the average age.

Previous research has suggested that earlier onset of problematic or antisocial behaviour is associated with escalation into more serious and prolific offending and so it is important to identify the age of onset. Indeed, it is also associated with the duration or length of a criminal career (see Chapter 8). In fact, the Home Office data shows that among active offenders who were classed as serious and prolific, the mean age of onset was as low as 11. This relates back to Terrie Moffitt's (1993) developmental taxonomy that we considered in Chapter 2, and specifically her distinction between 'adolescence-limited' and 'life-course persistent' offending. Moffitt notes that life-course persistent offending is generally more serious and tends to start at a much earlier age than adolescence-limited offending. So the links with these survey figures are quite evident.

Age of onset by offence type

As well as variation in age of onset, the Home Office Survey also highlighted variation in the age of onset by offence type (see Table 4.1).

Table 4.1 shows the age of onset by offence type in the Crime and Justice Survey (and is based on those who reported committing each offence). Most of the figures are shown in percentages. The figures show that there is considerable variation between offences. For example, if we consider the mean (average) age of onset under the category of 'Other theft' we can see that shoplifting (theft from shop) and theft from school are the offences to start earliest. The mean age of first offence for both of these was 13. In fact, as Table 4.1 shows, of those who had shoplifted at some point 21 per cent had done so before the age of 10.

At the other end of the scale in terms of age of onset is drug selling, which starts relatively late. Here we can see that under the category of 'Drug offences', 19 years is the mean age at first offence for selling drugs. This figure goes up to age 20 for the selling of Class A drugs. In relation to other offences, 'Theft from the workplace' also had a later age of onset with a mean age of 22 years, but this is not particularly surprising given occupational patterns and the fact that many people are not in work until their late teens and early twenties.

Table 4.1 Age of onset by offence type (based on those who had committed each offence)

Percentages	Under 10	10–11	12–13	14–15	16–17	18–19	20–25	26 or older	Mean age	Base n
Burglary										
Domestic burglary	6	8	10	28	19	2	8	4	16	62
Commercial burglary	9	8	23	28	14	8	2	2	14	224
Vehicle-related thefts (including attempts)										
Theft of a motor vehicle	1	3	7	33	21	17	6	5	17	262
Attempted theft of a motor vehicle	1	3	6	36	26	18	2	2	16	107
Theft from a motor vehicle (outside)	3	7	19	27	18	13	4	4	16	343
Theft from a motor vehicle (inside)	2	11	15	31	12	11	6	1	15	122
Attempted theft from a motor vehicle	3	4	13	31	19	18	2	-	15	111
Other thefts										
Theft from person	10	14	18	23	4	8	10	2	15	88
Theft from work	<0.5	1	1	4	19	16	32	16	22	1,254
Theft from school	13	14	26	22	9	5	4	1	13	1,173
Theft from shop	21	16	25	21	5	3	3	2	13	1,355
Other theft	18	25	18	13	10	6	6	3	14	660

										Base n
Criminal damage										
Damage to a motor vehicle	2	7	12	20	13	12	12	14	19	459
Other damage	9	11	22	23	11	7	6	3	14	765
Assault										
Assault with injury	10	9	11	17	11	10	12	11	17	1,904
Assault – no injury	10	10	12	15	9	8	14	11	17	1,715
Drug offences										
Sold Class A drugs	–	–	1	8	22	21	28	13	20	139
Sold other drugs	<0.5	<0.5	2	15	23	24	23	7	19	413
Any offence	14	13	14	14	8	6	8	7	15	4,174

Notes:
1. Source: 2003 Crime and Justice Survey, weighted data. Taken from Budd *et al.* (2005).
2. 'Don't knows' included in the base. A small number gave age between zero and four. These have been treated as 'don't know'. Means based on those who gave age so base is somewhat lower than indicated in Base n column.

The overall 'feel' of the figures is important and the relatively high proportion of people who had committed some offences at a very early age is noteworthy. However, we move on now to consider in more detail one of the most common first offences.

Shoplifting as the initial offence of choice

It is perhaps not surprising that shoplifting often emerges as the most common initial offence that young people are involved in. Thus it often represents the start of a criminal career. Shops are very easily accessible to children and young people, particularly on the way to and from school. Furthermore, the offence can provide immediate gratification. This is not only because one gains the goods that are stolen for free, but also because of the visibility of the offence in that peers are often there to see whether an individual has managed to steal something successfully.

A recent qualitative study by Monica Barry (2006) in Scotland confirms the Home Office findings above – that shoplifting is frequently the initial offence of choice for individuals when they start offending. Clearly shoplifting can be both the first and last offence for an individual (see Box 4.1 in relation to the early experiences of

---

Box 4.1   The 'criminal career' of GMTV newsreader, Fiona Phillips

At five she had a reading age of eleven. At six, she won a national poetry competition. By the time she got to comprehensive school, though, she was going off the rails – smoking at eleven ('Ten Sovereigns, 23.5p'), drinking at 13, in trouble with the police in her early teens. 'We had a shoplifting thing going. Until I got caught. I've still got a pair of knickers from BHS. They've got a little sailor's wheel on. Red, white and blue.' Does she still wear them? 'I did until recently – the elastic's no longer elastic.'

The police caution devastated her parents. 'I'll never forget the look on my poor mum's face. Whenever anything happened to me, she'd say, "Not my Fiona, my Fiona wouldn't do that." ' She never stole again.

But she continued to mess around. She only passed one O-level. The funny thing is, she says, she was always conscientious. She did paper rounds and paid her way, but she couldn't be bothered with schoolwork. The failure hit her hard. She went back to college, retook her exams, qualified as a radiographer, eventually did a degree in English and studied journalism.

Source: 'Queen of the couch', *The Guardian*, 24 November 2007.

---

the GMTV newsreader, Fiona Phillips). However, it may also signal the start of a long and serious criminal career. In her book *Youth Offending in Transition*, Barry (2006) interviewed 40 young people, and the results revealed that shoplifting was the initial offence for 10 out of 20 males and 15 out of 20 females in her study.

Obviously it is important to think about offence seriousness when one considers involvement in shoplifting, and this can vary a great deal between individuals. At one extreme, individuals may try to steal valuable electrical goods from a shop. More common though are attempts to steal easily concealable items like batteries and razor blades, both of which have been described as 'hot products' in their time (cf. Clarke, 1999). 'Hot products' refers to items that are most likely to be stolen by thieves. In Home Office crime reduction language, they share a number of common attributes that make up the acronym CRAVED. According to Clarke (1999), 'hot products' are:

Concealable
Removable
Available
Valuable
Enjoyable
Disposable

While batteries and razor blades may be 'hot products' for many shoplifters, when we think about how common shoplifting is among children, it is important to bear in mind that often only very minor things are 'craved'. At any rate, 10-year-old shoplifters are unlikely to have started shaving so they, at least, may not be after blades! They are far more likely to look for age-specific items to steal, such as chocolate.

It was just maybe a couple of cream eggs or a couple of bars of chocolate and going out to your mate and going 'look what I've got, whey hey' (Carol, 29, cited in Barry, 2006: 47)

As the quote above highlights, shoplifting can involve the theft of quite minor items (even if it is commonly the initial offence of choice for individual offenders). We continue our focus on Monica Barry's (2006) work now, by considering some of the specific factors that have been identified with the onset of offending behaviour. During Barry's interviews, she reports that respondents offered various reasons as to why they had started offending and what influenced them at that time. The main factors described were divided into four key categories of relational, personal, monetary and practical, and each of the categories provides some useful insights.

Relational factors influencing onset

According to Barry (2006), relational factors were the most prominent explanatory factors in her study, although personal and monetary factors were almost as important. She notes that a few young people (mainly young men) were influenced by their siblings who were offending and that this provided them with the rationale and motive for offending themselves. For example, Martin (aged 24) commented: 'My big brother ... the two of us, we were like a team, you know ... we can take on armies' (cited in Barry 2006: 47).

However, while a few young people emphasised the influence of siblings, the great majority emphasised that they felt the need to follow the crowd and to be seen to be sociable by joining in with friends. Several mentioned the sense of belonging they gained when involved in offending with their peers. Related to this point, several respondents mentioned difficult family relationships and commented that their family upbringings had not been a source of support or encouragement for them. Consequently they often turned to friends for company and social identity.

Barry notes that, for many, 'the initial impetus to offending was to form friendships and gain attention' (2006: 52). However, there was an interesting gender dimension here in that she found that the young women tended to be more influenced by relationships than friends *per se*, even if these relationships involved abuse or offending. For five of the young women, having a boyfriend who was offending was a crucial stimulus to beginning offending, not least when these boyfriends were encouraging them to take drugs and 'training' them to offend. Barry goes on to make the interesting point that for the young men in the study, being involved in a relationship was sometimes an impetus to *stop* offending. Yet for the young women, relationships were often the impetus to *start* offending (2006: 53).

Personal factors influencing onset

The second set of factors that Barry talks about are personal factors.

This category includes reasons for offending such as fun, excitement and to relieve boredom. Interestingly, in Barry's study these particular 'adrenalin-related' reasons were wholly the preserve of young men. The young women were more likely to suggest that personal trauma of abuse in the past or present was a trigger to their starting offending. Anger or depression resulting from abuse or bereavement was cited by eight females and just one male as an influence on their propensity to start offending. Owen captures something of this point when he notes, 'I wanted to sort of like hurt people the way that I was hurt' (Owen, aged 18, cited in Barry 2006: 54).

An additional personal factor influencing onset was simply getting older. Respondents noted that, as they got older and felt more mature, they stopped feeling like a child and simply began to make their own choices and follow their own initiative on how to behave and what routes to follow through life. No longer feeling like a child gave individuals the opportunity to develop autonomy and increased self-identity (Barry 2006: 56).

Monetary factors influencing onset

The third set of factors that Barry describes are monetary factors. She notes that 'the need for money (either for survival, consumables, drugs or alcohol) was often cited as a reason for starting to offend' (2006: p.56). However, gender differences were apparent here too. Whereas the young men tended to want money for consumables, many of the young women started to offend because of their need for drugs, either for themselves or because of encouragement from their partners who used drugs. Vicky, for example, highlights how the need for money can arise from drug dealing.

> You need to buy in bulk when you're dealing because you need to make the profit, so I didn't have the money to do that, so I started shoplifting and any money I got I was just buying a bag, two bags [of heroin], whatever I could get. (Vicky, aged 27, cited in Barry 2006: 56)

Barry notes that the power gained from offending is often dependent on access to economic capital, and many of the sample came from poor backgrounds and were conscious of the poverty in their area and in their family. Inevitably this had an impact on them citing monetary factors as important in terms of the onset of their offending.

Practical factors influencing onset

With respect to practical factors, Barry notes that while funding the purchase of alcohol and drugs was cited by some as a reason for offending, several respondents also suggested that *the effects* of one or other of these substances also made offending more likely. For example, young people talked about having 'Dutch courage' after lots of alcohol which made it more likely that they would start a fight or commit a breach of the peace. One young woman in particular noted how much braver she felt on drugs and reported feeling so 'invisible' when on amphetamines that she was convinced nobody would catch her shoplifting.

Success at offending was also seen as a practical factor that encouraged young people to continue offending. Offending was seen as something they could do relatively easily without getting caught, and getting away with it was part of the attraction. Many of the sample implied that their offending generally went undetected, suggesting at least some expertise on their part or incompetence on the part of law enforcers.

Several respondents also noted that the poverty of their area, or negative images associated with it, were also important factors. For example, if you came from an estate with a particularly bad reputation, respondents noted it was almost expected that you would get in with the 'wrong crowd'.

A final important factor associated with onset of offending was school exclusion and truancy, and this frequently emerges as an important factor in research. This is for the simple fact that if you are not in school, you are likely to have a lot of time on your hands and so offending becomes a possibility. This is a reason why school involvement is regarded as a protective factor against offending for some individuals. It does not necessarily matter whether you are good at school or not (although educational attainment is another kind of protective factor) – but the very fact that you are in school during the day means it is less likely you are walking the streets and mixing with others who have also been excluded or are truanting.

So these are some of the key factors that young people in Barry's (2006) study gave for starting offending. They also highlighted a number of advantages and disadvantages associated with offending, some of which are closely related.

Advantages and disadvantages of starting offending

By far the most commonly cited advantage of offending was money, regardless of whether it was associated with the reason for starting offending. Interestingly, women were more than twice as likely as men to see money as an advantage for starting offending, partly, Barry found, because of their greater need for drugs. However, she also says this was because of the way that looks and body image were part of the females' youth culture at a time when sexual relationships were becoming more important. Thus young women may have used the money for hair and beauty products in a way that males of similar age may have been less likely to.

Barry further notes that, for many, having money through offending enabled them to 'keep up with the Joneses' and in this respect access to money was very much a status symbol rather than a necessity.

Other advantages included the buzz that young people got from offending. For example, one young woman alluded to the links between drug use and excitement. Speaking in relation to the buzz, she says that cannabis, ecstasy and speed 'stops life being a bore' (Sam, aged 23, cited in Barry 2006: 63).

More young women than men also mentioned the relational advantages of offending, in particular where offending was seen as a means of keeping in with a group of friends or as a way of generating a circle of friends (2006: 64). Young people's reputation as an offender – either in gaining money or being seen to be 'hard' – was also important to several respondents early on in their offending.

In terms of the disadvantages of starting offending, the majority of respondents spoke of the practical inconvenience of getting caught. While several suggested that they did not really think about getting caught when they actually started offending, in retrospect they felt that involvement in both the Children's Hearing system (the study took place in Scotland) and the adult criminal justice system was a major disadvantage. Again there were gender distinctions here too though, and it appeared that young women were much more aware of the stigma attached to crime. This relates to arguments within feminist theory that suggest that females involved in crime are often regarded as 'doubly deviant', not only because they have broken the legal code but also because they have transgressed the 'feminine' code (Brown 1998) and have gone against stereotypical notions of what it means to be a woman.

In terms of letting people down, and particularly family, both males and females felt that this was a serious disadvantage of starting to commit crimes. Some commented that, in retrospect, they felt that they had not only let their parents down, but had also let themselves down.

So these are some of the advantages and disadvantages that young people attributed to starting to offend. Interestingly, several of the respondents in the Barry study had spent time being 'looked after' in residential care. As Barry indicates, researchers have shown that being in the care of the state can have the effect of labelling the child as either 'troubled' or 'troublesome'. While being 'in care' – or, to use the legal terminology, being 'looked after' – is often associated with early involvement in crime, recent research (Taylor 2006) highlights that the relationship between 'care' and crime is not straightforward.

Young people in care

In the book *Young People in Care and Criminal Behaviour* (2006), Claire Taylor[1] argues that society holds a popular perception that routinely links looked-after children with criminal behaviour, and it is frequently assumed that such children are troublemakers and far more likely to be involved in crime. Children in care may be placed in various types of placement including with foster families, in children's homes and in secure accommodation; children in the latter two types of provision are often perceived as having particularly challenging needs. Certainly official figures do reveal that, as a group, children in care are disproportionately likely to receive a caution or conviction and are over-represented in the prison population. Yet Taylor's analysis highlights that the links between care and crime are often more complex than the official figures suggest. Her work seeks to dispel the myth that looked-after children will inevitably and obviously have worse outcomes than all other children.

In terms of the headline figures, care-leavers are clearly over-represented in our prisons. Over 40 per cent of children in custody have been in the care system at some point during their lives (Hazel *et al.* 2002), compared with more than a quarter of adult prisoners (Social Exclusion Unit 2002). With respect to the offending rates of looked-after children, official figures reveal that these children are over two times more likely to receive a caution or conviction than their peers. According to the most recent government data, 9.5 per cent of children looked after for a year or more, and who were aged 10 or over, had been convicted or subject to a final warning or reprimand during the year. This compares with a figure of 4.1 per cent for all children (Department for Children, Schools and Families 2008a).

The data on offending rates shows us that looked-after children do, indeed, come into contact with the criminal justice system at a disproportionate rate to their peers. So how do we go about explaining these figures? Certainly some looked-after children have been in trouble with the police before entering the care system. Furthermore, many of the risk factors associated with admission to care, such as low educational attainment and early family disruption, are also the risk factors for offending behaviour (cf. Farrington 1986a). However, and this is a *very important point*, this does not mean to say that all children in care will go on to offend or that there is an inevitable and obvious relationship between being in the care system and later the criminal justice system. In fact, when we look at the figures on reasons for entering the care system, in the year ending 31 March 2008, a mere 5 per cent of children entered care principally because of their own behaviour (Department for Children, Schools and Families 2008b).

So this leads on to thinking about where the onset of their involvement in crime might occur for those who enter care having not previously been in trouble with the police. Here we need to focus on the care experience itself. If children are not offending before they go into care, but have a disproportionate likelihood of gaining a criminal record while in care, then what exactly is going on during their care experience? In fact, when we look at the residential care experience in particular, and the experiences of those who live in children's homes, then we can see that there are aspects of this that have been shown to be criminogenic. For example, peer pressure, bullying and a lack of staff continuity in children's homes have all been linked to creating an environment where it can be far easier for young people to get arrested than not (Taylor 2006).

Interviews with young people who have been involved in the care and criminal justice systems are instructive, and the following extracts come from Taylor's (2006) study on the care–crime connection, focusing particularly on the residential care experience.

Onset in residential care

Donnie was interviewed in prison when he was 19. He had been in and out of jail for the previous two years and went into care when he was 14. He described being in trouble before going into care and had been kicked out of two schools but notes that, in terms of his involvement in criminal behaviour, this only really got started when he entered the residential care environment. In his words:

> Basically I got all my criminal convictions from when I was in care ... I was just going out and getting in trouble with everyone else, getting in trouble with assault charges, theft charges, burglary charges ... I just went straight downhill. (Donnie, aged 19, cited in Taylor 2006: 84)

So Donnie paints a picture of being involved in regular trouble with a gang of others once he entered care.

Gemma, who was 18 and also interviewed in prison, felt particularly strongly about the fact that she would not have ended up in jail if it were not for being in care nearly all of her life. She had been in the care system since the very young age of 3 because of abuse at home. As she says:

> Because I wouldn't be mixing with the environment what I was mixing with in care ... going out robbing people, taking drugs and that ... I didn't have a clue about any of that until the kids' homes. People showed me things like that and I didn't have a clue. (Gemma, aged 18, cited in Taylor 2006: 88)

Stories like these sadly seem to confirm stereotypical views that residential care is often rife with kids getting into trouble, breaking the law and being influenced by other residents who are offending. For several respondents these kinds of experiences directly impacted on the onset of their official criminal career. Certainly it is important to acknowledge that these sorts of experiences do exist. However, there are other very important reasons why looked-after children are more likely to end up with a criminal record.

Prosecution of minor offences by looked-after children

One important factor to consider is the routine prosecution of minor offences like criminal damage in children's homes. This has emerged as a particular problem in recent years, and there is increasing evidence to suggest that residential care staff may rely on police involvement as a means of controlling behaviour. One inevitable consequence of this is that looked-after children can be unnecessarily criminalised for behaviour that would be highly unlikely to result in an official intervention if a person were living at home with his or her parents. Indeed, as Nacro observes:

Because the threshold for calling the police to deal with looked-after children can be low, some enter the criminal justice system earlier and for less serious offences than their peers. This situation widens the gap between the number of reported offences by looked-after children, and that by children generally. (Nacro 2005: 34)

Of particular concern is the policy that many local authorities have had of routinely reporting to the police any incidents of criminal damage and assault in care homes. While such policies may well exist to protect staff and the general home environment, they also need to be used with caution, and there must be clear agreement about what actually constitutes 'criminal damage' and 'assault'. As Chris Stanley notes, 'magistrates were seeing children in court for having thrown a cup across the room. They were saying "we do not know what to do with these children". Court was not the solution for them' (Stanley 2006, cited in McCormack 2006: 19). Comments from care leavers in the Taylor study highlighted many of these concerns.

For example, Tracy had never been in trouble with the police before going into care at 15, yet she left residential care with two assault charges on her record. She describes one assault on a member of staff which resulted in her receiving a fine:

> I was messing about in the kitchen ... and I wouldn't get down off the side, I was looking for something ... And I just got down and I was like in a hyper mood and I pushed the door to get out the way and it just hit her on the shoulder ... she took me to court. (Tracy, aged 16, cited in Taylor 2006: 89)

As one of us has argued elsewhere (Fitzpatrick, forthcoming), it is highly unlikely that birth parents would respond to this sort of behaviour in the same way, by taking a child to court. The low threshold described is incredibly worrying for looked-after children, not only because it means that this very vulnerable group may be discriminated against, but also because of the wider policy climate. We are living in an age where many young people are appearing before the courts and custodial rates for children are unacceptably high. There is great concern about net-widening generally (cf. Jamieson 2005), and the fact that young people entering the criminal justice system today are at increased risk of receiving a custodial sentence (cf. Smith 2003). For all these reasons, the situation looks particularly bleak for young people in care (Fitzpatrick, forthcoming).

In fact, the Home Office has at long last recognised that these are very real issues, noting in a recent study that: 'Police are too often used as an agent of control, called out too frequently for what they perceive to be "care" issues, and forced to arrest young people for want of any alternative' (Home Office 2004: 8–9). Clearly such issues need to be urgently addressed. Given that children are receiving custodial sentences for more and more minor offences, it is clear that the actions of carers who routinely prosecute children in their care may contribute, however unintentionally, to increasing the population of these children in prison.

To sum up the key findings from Taylor's (2006) study, there are some important messages. On the one hand, it can be argued that certain sorts of care experience, particularly those associated with some of the worst features of life in a residential setting, can create, promote and intensify criminal behaviour. So care experiences associated with bullying, peer pressure and a perceived couldn't-care-less attitude on the part of disillusioned staff are often associated with criminal behaviour in residents. In particular, the routine prosecution of minor offences in some residential homes can contribute directly to the onset of a criminal career (cf. Fitzpatrick forthcoming).

Yet, despite this finding about residential care, there are other types of care setting too of course, most notably foster care. Indeed, one finding that has not been emphasised here is that certain types of care experience, particularly those associated with stability, security and a quality relationship with a foster carer, can, in fact, help to protect against offending behaviour. In this sense, a care experience has the potential to divert the onset of a criminal career. In other words, there is a range of different pathways that young people may take through the care system, only some of which will lead them on to the criminal justice system.

Three studies – three lessons?

In focusing simply on three studies to introduce concerns about onset, there are many omissions. In addition, it is important to emphasise that each of the studies is based on self-report data, which have a number of potential limitations. For example, respondents may lie, exaggerate or be unable to accurately recall specific details retrospectively. Nevertheless, whatever the limitations, the importance of the three studies presented in this chapter needs to be underlined.

1 *The Crime and Justice Survey* produced some important evidence about the ages of onset. The average age of onset for offending is identified as 15. However, focusing on an average may produce as much distortion as insight. In other words, averages tend to mask variation and the recognition of variation is important. However, there is little doubt that early onset is often a crucial factor in offending. Indeed, Piquero *et al*. stress in relation to the Cambridge Study of Delinquent Development that 'those individuals who exhibited an early onset were more likely to have longer criminal careers, accumulate more offences, and be convicted of many more different types of offences than their late-onset counterparts' (2007: 73). However, it is also evident that adult-onset offenders provide a substantial minority of all offenders – for example Carrington *et al*. (2005) estimate that 45 per cent of males and 36 per cent of females are adult-onset offenders. So childhood is not necessarily the crucible that generates offending.

2 *The Barry study* identified the insights that can be gained from qualitative interviewing, in this case by probing the *experiences* of 40 young people. She provides a framework to help us to understand why they had started offending and what had influenced them at the time. The four key categories of relational, personal, monetary and practical factors have a strong resonance in seeming likely candidates for influencing young people beyond the 40 young people identified by Monica Barry to interview in Scotland.

3 *The Taylor study* on 'looked-after' children challenges some long-held stereotypes. One of the challenges is to question the supposed link between looked-after children and criminal behaviour. Rather than embracing the commonly held assumption that such children are troublemakers *before* they arrive into the care system, it is more appropriate to recognise that the care system may substantially contribute to their subsequent difficulties. Once into the system, they are then much more likely than their peers to receive a caution or a conviction. However, the important point is that there is not an inevitable relationship about being in the care system and ending up in the criminal justice system. It depends again on the care *experience* itself. The clear message is that individual-blaming in such cases is both inappropriate and wrongly focused, for one needs to challenge the system if matters are to improve.

The messages emanating from the three studies of the wide variability in terms of the age of onset, the variety of influences which impinge on youngsters and the relevance of the system in which the experience takes place are important ones. However, the focus has largely been on children and young persons. What of the large numbers of people, mostly men, who enter the criminal justice system for the first time in adult life?

Onset of crime in adulthood

Although less has been said on adults entering the criminal justice system for the first time, there are similar issues to consider. We are not aiming for completeness in coverage but simply trying to assess whether we can point to some important messages. In order to do this, it is useful to turn to the three classic longitudinal studies we identified in the last chapter and which to a greater or lesser degree match the gold standard of criminal career research.

Of course, they are all very different in both conception and design. However, this is useful in probing whether there are some common patterns emerging. Interestingly, they emanate from three different continents and gain their participants in three different eras. If patterns of criminality are unchanging, then one would expect very similar results. However, if patterns are different, then different questions emerge. In addition, if there are differences, we need to question whether these differences are 'real' or simply an artefact of different research designs. We may also want to question whether it matters that the social conditions for the three studies are somewhat different. For instance, is a difference in school-leaving age relevant? Is it relevant that the age of criminal responsibility varies across time and place? So what are the specific lessons about onset that we can learn from these major studies?

Lessons from the three 'classic' longitudinal studies

Table 4.2 displays the findings on onset which are embedded in recent publications relating to the three studies. Two immediate things are quite striking. Firstly, they are, in fact, difficult to compare, for they don't all tackle the issue of onset in quite the same way. So, for example, the definitions of onset and the way that it is measured are quite different. Laub and Sampson (2003), reporting on the Gluecks' data on onset, talk specifically about age at first arrest, noting that the mean age for this was 11.9. In contrast, Piquero *et al.* (2007), reporting on the Cambridge study, talk about age at first conviction,

Table 4.2 Comparison of the findings from the three classic longitudinal studies in relation to onset of crime

	The Gluecks' study (Laub and Sampson 2003)	Cambridge Delinquent Development Study (Piquero *et al.* 2007)	The Dunedin study (Moffitt *et al.* 2001)
Definition of onset	Age at first arrest	Age at first conviction	Age of conviction onset Age of conduct disorder onset Self-reported delinquency Arrested as juveniles
Average age	Mean age = 11.9	Mean age = 18.12 Median age = 16 Mode = 14 Hazard = 14	Mean age of conviction: Boys = 17.7 Girls = 17.9 Mean age of conduct disorder diagnosis: Boys = 14.7 Girls = 15.2 Mean age of self-reported delinquency: Boys = 13.3 Girls = 13.7 Mean age of juvenile arrest: Boys = 13.5 Girls = 13.7

but measure this in four different ways – providing figures for the mean, mode, median and hazard. Noting that the mean age of 18.12 in their study may seem high compared with other research findings, they comment that this may be explicable, in part, by the fact that some men in the Cambridge study were first convicted as adults, even in their 30s, and this has the effect of stretching out the mean. Thus, in their view, 'the median is particularly useful here because it avoids the distortion of a few very high-onset values' (Piquero *et al.* 2007: 63).

In contrast to the Cambridge study, Moffitt *et al.* (2001) found in the Dunedin study that adult-onset antisocial behaviour was extremely rare. In fact, they suggest that the findings regarding adult-onset are an artefact of official measurements. ' "Adult-onset" offenders cannot be defined for study with any certainty unless self-reported data are available to rule out juvenile onset prior to subjects' first official contact with the judicial system' (2001: 85). The authors further argue that, for both males and females, onset measured by conviction data will lag three to five years behind onset measured by self-report studies. Interestingly, in the Dunedin study, Moffitt *et al.* use the mean age of onset as their one key measurement, but define onset in four different ways by focusing on age at first conviction, age at first arrest, age of conduct disorder diagnosis and age of self-reported delinquency. In addition, their work adds a valuable gender dimension to the analysis, which complicates matters further while providing a fuller overall picture.

Putting all such complexities on one side for the moment, one striking point is that there seem to be more similarities than differences and the figures are not vastly different where they are comparable. For example, the mean ages of onset for first arrest in the Gluecks' early work and in the Dunedin study are no more than two years apart, ranging from 11.9 to 13.7. Similarly, the mean ages of onset for first conviction in the Dunedin study and the Cambridge study range only from 17.7 to 18.12. Finally, the gender analysis in the Dunedin study highlights that the mean age of onset for males and females is incredibly close. Indeed, the authors note that 'the overall pattern, regardless of measurement source, was for Dunedin study males and females to onset antisocial behaviour within 2 to 6 months of each other' (2001: 86–7). Moffitt *et al.* conclude that because they found no other published studies, this pattern of sex similarities awaits replication checks.

Having briefly considered some of the similarities and differences between the three classic longitudinal studies, we move on now to outline some of the key policy implications relating to the topic of onset.

Policy implications

As we indicated at the beginning of this chapter, understanding onset is of crucial importance to policy. Indeed, a greater knowledge of 'how', 'why' and 'when' individuals *start* offending may enable us to better develop policies aimed at preventing this occurring in the first place.

In very broad terms, onset-related research highlights the need to deal with the root causes of crime at the structural level. For example, poverty and a lack of social capital emerged as key themes associated with starting offending in the Barry (2006) study. Thus policies that seek to reduce poverty, unemployment and community deprivation are all relevant to preventing the onset of crime. In this respect, the work of the UK government's Social Exclusion Unit is important, as is its Neighbourhood Renewal programme that aims to improve community services in areas that struggle economically.

Criminal career research also tells us much about the average age of onset, and while this may vary between studies, in broad terms we know that many individuals will begin offending during the teenage years. Thus general strategies aimed at providing support and guidance to the general teenage population may be useful. For example, the Connexions service in the UK is a universal school-based service that is intended to provide personal advisors to 13- to 19-year-olds. Part of its remit is to reduce truancy and improve behaviour.

A recurrent research finding is that those individuals who exhibit an early onset tend to commit many more offences over the life course and are therefore most likely to become persistent offenders. Thus intervening swiftly with the very youngest offenders would seem to be an important goal, not simply in terms of punishment but in terms of providing support and guidance for dealing with their behaviour. While there is a danger that concerns over early starters becoming the chronic offenders of the future will lead to overly punitive interventions, it is important to emphasise for the purposes of policy that research also tells us that the majority of offending is 'adolescence-limited' (cf. Moffitt 1993). Thus there is a complex balancing act to be achieved in terms of intervening in the lives of young offenders, while also ensuring that we avoid unnecessarily bringing them into the justice system, with its potentially labelling and stigmatising effects that often follow an individual into their adult life.

A related and more specific point concerns the routine prosecution of children in some residential care homes. Work by Nacro (2005) has highlighted that the development of local protocols between children's home staff and the police, outlining how best to respond to disruptive behaviour in particular circumstances, has the potential to divert young people from unnecessary involvement in the justice system. Such policies may well serve to reduce the onset of official criminal careers among children looked after by the state.

Conclusions

This chapter has highlighted a range of important issues relating to understanding onset and the early development of criminal careers. Of particular note is that onset may be defined and measured by different researchers in very different ways. Age at first arrest, age at first conviction, age at first conduct disorder diagnosis and self-reported delinquency are all used to produce insights about the start of a criminal career. While this can make research findings very difficult to compare, our discussion of the lessons from the three classic longitudinal studies highlights that age-related findings are often surprisingly similar. This is despite the fact that these three studies were conducted on completely different continents in very different time periods. While we argue in Chapter 9 that it is crucial for research on criminal careers to take account of social context and social change, there are clearly some consistencies in research findings across time and place.

As we have emphasised above, another consistent research finding is that early onset offending tends to be associated with longer and more serious criminal careers. Indeed, Moffitt et al. (2001) introduce a gender dimension here in arguing that it is males who are far more likely to be life-course persistent offenders. The issues of persistence and desistance throw up many complexities of their own, and we use the following chapter to explore why some individuals do persist in criminal behaviour while others actively seek to desist.

Note

1 Now Claire Fitzpatrick – the 2006 book was published under her maiden name of Taylor.

Chapter 5

Continuity and change in a criminal career: persistence and desistance

In this chapter we deal with two of our three foundation stones for understanding criminal careers – persistence and desistance. As with onset, there are a number of problems to deal with, including those relating to definitions and being clear about exactly what we are talking about. There is no universal consensus over how to define persistence and desistance, so again it is crucial to understand the different definitions that researchers use in order to make sense of their findings. There are also methodological issues to consider. For example, how do we find the evidence of what we are talking about? In addition, identifying the link between theory and the evidence is an important feature to be grappled with. We begin this chapter with a focus on persistence and the continuity of a criminal career.

What is persistence?

If we consider official conviction data, persistence seems to be a fairly unusual phenomenon, for most people who are convicted seem to have only one court appearance. Indeed, of the 11,068 convicted persons in the 1953 Home Office cohort, 50.2 per cent of males and 74.3 per cent of females have only one appearance (Prime *et al.* 2001: tables 5a and 5b). So, for most, one court appearance is the end of the story. Some, mostly males, go on to appear on many occasions. Of those males convicted at least once in the 1953 cohort 16.4 per cent have a second court conviction but no more, while a further 22.5 per cent have three or more. In contrast, for females, the figures are

12.3 per cent and 5.4 per cent respectively. This difference shows the importance of considering males and females separately.

In definitional terms, the issue is when should one regard such behaviour as 'persistent'? Certainly it is not always clear about whom commentators are referring when they speak of 'persistent offenders'. It seems to be a term that we all readily acknowledge but the boundaries are vague. In most respects one can think of such a decision as fairly arbitrary for there is no theoretical point at which one can say with any degree of precision that a person has moved from a state of not being persistent to a state of being persistent in one's criminal behaviour. Hence, one can pick on an operational definition that simply suits one's purpose or one's data. For this reason there are various operational definitions.

According to Hagell and Newburn, 'no two definitions of persistence will lead to the identification of exactly the same individuals' (1994: 98). However, whatever the differences of definition, the focus on 'persistence' often reflects the same underlying concern, namely that a group of the offending population is convicted of disproportionately more crime than the rest of the offending population. Interestingly, the figures are similar across various countries. In the classic Philadelphia cohort study, Wolfgang *et al.* (1972) showed that 6 per cent of the males (18 per cent of the offenders) accounted for 52 per cent of all the juvenile arrests. In the Cambridge study in Delinquent Development, 7 per cent of the males accounted for around half of all the convictions up to the age of 50 (Farrington *et al.* 2006b).

A concern with those offenders who commit disproportionate amounts of crime is certainly reflected in current government policy in the UK. For example, a recent joint inspection report into persistent and prolific offenders makes reference to 'the habitual, persistent, prolific, recidivist or repeat offender' (Home Office Communications Directorate 2004: 7). The report notes that '(h)owever they may be defined, and exactly what they are called may be debated exhaustively, the fact is that relatively few offenders commit a large proportion of all crime' (2004: 7). The joint inspection report uses the following definition of a core persistent offender:

> Someone who is 18 years or over and has been convicted of six or more recordable offences in the last 12 months. (2004: 11)

The report notes that there is a separate definition of persistent young offenders (PYOs):

A PYO is a young person who has been dealt with by the courts on three or more occasions, and commits another offence within three years of last appearing before a court. (2004: 11)

The two definitions above have different qualifying ages (18 and over or up to 17), different definition periods (twelve months or three years) and different persistence tests (six recordable convictions or three previous sentencing occasions). They are therefore not directly comparable and highlight a further area of complexity in revealing that 'persistence' may be defined in different ways at different ages.

Gender differences among persistent offenders

In considering whether there are changes over time in the numbers and proportions of persistent offenders, Soothill *et al.* (2003) provide a useful gender dimension by focusing on females as well as males. Using data from the Home Office Offender Index up to 1999, they define a 'persistent' offender as having convictions for standard-list offences on at least four occasions over a maximum of 11 years.

Soothill *et al.* (2003) estimate that, at the end of 1999, there were around 640,000 males and 54,000 females aged 46 years or under in England and Wales who had been 'persistent offenders' at some point in their lives. These figures represent 4.7 per cent of the males and 0.4 per cent of the females aged 10 to 46 in the population. This figure is not static and the study identifies certain trends and patterns that characterise the present body of 'persistent offenders'.

1 Both male and female offenders who are first convicted at a young age are much more likely to become persistent offenders than their older counterparts. Hence there is merit in trying to target young offenders in attempting to break the offending cycle.
2 Male offenders are at much greater risk of becoming persistent offenders than females.
3 The proportion of female offenders who become persistent is increasing, and females are becoming increasingly more like males in terms of their likelihood of becoming persistent offenders.

Interestingly, if we think about how to link some of the findings above with Moffitt's (1993) 'life-course persistent' offender (discussed in Chapter 2), we can see that Soothill *et al.*'s findings seem to both support and extend work on this criminal 'type'. For example, while point number 2 above supports Moffitt *et al.*'s (2001) findings in the Dunedin study, point number 3 seems to extend our understanding by suggesting that a change over time has been occurring for females. There is clearly a need for further analysis in this area.

Soothill *et al.* observe a number of more general patterns arising from their data. They argue that, despite fears to the contrary, the numbers of new convicted offenders are declining among the younger age groups and there is a similar decline in terms of the numbers who become 'persistent offenders'. However, declining numbers mask another problem – while numbers are falling, those who are convicted for the first time aged 10–14 are much more likely to become 'persistent offenders'. In their view, this probably reflects the success of a cautioning policy over the years, which leaves those in the court arena dealing with a more intractable problem. (Having said this, in recent times there have been increasing concerns that the tide has turned again, with increasing numbers of young people being unnecessarily criminalised for minor offences (*see* Nacro 2008).)

In contrast, the story in terms of older offenders (that is, those aged over 20 years) is much more dismal. For male offenders, the numbers of new offenders seems to have stabilised among those aged in their 20s, for there is certainly no evidence of a fall commensurate with the younger age groups aged under 20 years. Furthermore, there is some evidence of a rise in the numbers of new convicted offenders among those aged 30 or over. However, there is not the same sort of concern that the numbers or percentages of 'persistent offenders' among the older age groups are also rising.

Curiously, among females, a different pattern seems to be emerging. Generally, among the older age groups of females, the *numbers* of new offenders are falling. However, the *proportions* of female offenders becoming persistent offenders among each age group are increasing according to birth cohort. In exploring the issue of persistence and continuity in a criminal career, the work of Soothill *et al.* (2003) highlights the crucial need for future research to address changes among female offenders, as well as differences between younger and older offenders.

Persistence is important but only a minority of offenders, in fact, persist. We suspect that most offenders stop offending or at least are no longer involved in the criminal justice system. Stopping or what is known as desisting is another conundrum to probe and so now we move on to the prospect of ending a criminal career.

Defining desistance

Desistance refers to the end of a criminal career, which sounds fairly straightforward in theory. However, in practice, the definitional pathway is arguably even more difficult than defining persistence, and attempts to define desistance are many and varied. So what exactly is this phenomenon that we hope to understand?

As Shadd Maruna (2001: 22) notes in his book, *Making Good*, 'the criminal career literature traditionally imagines desistance as an event – an abrupt cessation of criminal behaviour'. Indeed, desistance is often related to the language of 'burnout' and there is a belief among some commentators that it represents a key moment in time or a termination event. For example, Farrall and Bowling describe desistance as the 'moment that a criminal career ends' (1999: 253). As Maruna (2001) observes, in this version of desistance, a person quits crime in the same way as someone resigns from a decent job. As a result, there has been a focus in criminology on the notion of 'turning points' or 'conversion experiences' that can cause people to take the decision to simply give up crime or give up their job (Maruna 2001).

Unfortunately, the danger of pursuing the career metaphor is particularly evident here. As Maruna (2001) argues, the career metaphor misses a fundamental fact about criminal behaviour, and that is that it is sporadic. As he notes, 'termination' takes place all the time. In Maruna's example: 'A person can steal a purse on a Tuesday morning, then terminate criminal participation for the rest of the day. Is that desistance? Is it desistance if the person does not steal another purse for a week? A month? A year?' (2001: 23).

David Farrington (1986b: 201) has warned that 'even a five-year or ten-year crime-free period is no guarantee that offending has terminated'. Yet, as Maruna points out, most researchers who use terms like cessation and termination seem to imply that there is a permanent change. Yet, in his view, such a change can only be determined retrospectively – for example after the ex-offender is deceased. But even taking the apparently safe option of equating desistance with death has its problems.

How do we measure desistance?

So what does all this mean for how we *measure* desistance? Even if we do decide only to study desisters who are dead, we still have no real understanding of how to measure the termination moment – or the moment of truth when desistance occurred. Even if we know conclusively that the purse-snatcher in the previous example never committed another crime for the rest of his (or her) life, we still have the problem of not knowing when desistance actually started. Of course, an added problem once people have died is that we cannot ask them anything!

An alternative approach that Maruna (2001) discusses is to model the termination point as the moment when the person *decides* to quit the life of crime. Here the emphasis is on the decision. Research on the decision-making process is often referred to as the rational choice model of desistance (cf. Cusson and Pinsonneault 1986). Many of the reasons that former offenders give for why they quit offending are often quite convincing. Answers typically include 'I burnt out/hit rock bottom,' 'It was time to do other things' (Maruna 2001: 23). In fact, we suspect that this type of process will be more likely for some offenders and not others – but more of that later.

What Shadd Maruna (2001) does so successfully is to make the crucial point that deciding to desist and actually desisting are two very different things. This is supported by the evidence. Interviews with offenders highlight that individuals often have every intention of changing their behaviour, particularly during a spell in prison, but actually changing their behaviour after release is often easier said than done. Indeed, an Oxford University study of recidivism (Burnett 1992) revealed that when researchers asked a sample of prison inmates whether they wanted to go straight, over 80 per cent responded yes they were sick of the life of crime and would love to desist. Yet, 20 months after being released from prison, almost 60 per cent of the sample reported reoffending. Clearly there is a distinction between understanding the rationality of decisions that crime does not pay, and understanding the *process* of going straight and *staying* that way (Maruna 2001: 24).

As a result of all this, Maruna argues that rather than defining desistance as a termination event, it is far more productive to regard it as a 'maintenance process', with the emphasis on 'the long-term abstinence from crime among individuals who had previously engaged in persistent patterns of criminal offending' (2001: 26). Thus the focus here is not on a key moment or on a transition or a change, but rather on the *maintenance* of crime-free behaviour in the face of life's obstacles and frustrations.

Understanding desistance as a 'maintenance process' implies an ongoing work-in-progress, which crucially emphasises the process of *going* straight or *making* good. This emphasis on process is quite distinct; it raises questions about 'how' people manage to move away from a life of crime. This is very different from regarding desistance as a termination event where the focus is very much on the outcome. Criminal career researchers using statistical analysis to chart offending behaviour over time frequently reduce desistance to a one-off outcome but have little that is meaningful to say about how that outcome is achieved. So in many ways the definition of desistance that we are likely to find most convincing will be dependent on whether our interests lie in *process* or *outcome* or, to put it another way, whether our interest is in understanding *when* desistance occurs or *how* it occurs. Conceptually these are quite different ideas, with very different methodological implications.

Maruna is interested in trying to understand the mindset or self-perspective of the offenders in his study. This is why he uses a qualitative research strategy and bases his work on life-story methods and participants' narratives of their lives. Maruna's (2001) work in *Making Good* is based on the Liverpool Desistance Study which examined the narratives of 20 active or persistent offenders and compared these with the narratives of 30 ex-offenders who were actively trying to desist. The persistent offenders are included in the study in order to provide a contrast and a point of comparison to those individuals actively seeking to give up crime. In presenting his findings, Maruna suggests that the overarching theme among the persistent offending group was that they appeared to be reading from what he terms a 'condemnation script'. He argues that such a script is characterised by various factors.

Condemnation scripts and persistent offenders

Firstly, there is the notion that individuals perceive themselves to be 'doomed to deviance'. 'The long-term persistent offenders in the sample said that they are sick of offending, sick of prison and sick of their position in life. Several talked at length about wanting to go legit or at least doing something different with their lives' (Maruna 2001: 74). Yet they also said that they felt powerless to change their behaviour. This powerlessness was attributed to various things including drug dependency for some or, for others, poverty, a lack of education or skills, or societal prejudice against ex-cons. Many of the group suggested that they did not want to offend but felt they had no choice.

So Maruna characterises the narrative of active offenders as a condemnation script. The condemned person in the story is the narrator (although they also reserve plenty of condemnation and blame for society as well). Active offenders largely saw their life scripts as having been written for them a long time ago. They see their negative present very much as following on from their negative past. Many begrudgingly seemed to accept the labels that society had applied to them. So one 28-year-old male said 'I'm a thief, but if there was some other way I'd do that ... I guess I'm just a thief, no more, no less' (2001: 75). These sorts of comments reflect the fact that such individuals often perceive their identity in solely deviant terms and there is little evidence of any agency in their narratives. Forty years earlier Howard Becker (1963: 32), making use of Everett Hughes' (1945) distinction between master and auxiliary status traits, noted how 'some statuses, in our society as in others, override all other statuses and have a certain priority' (ibid: 33). He saw the status of deviant (depending on the kind of deviance) as this kind of status – 'one receives the status as a result of breaking a rule, and the identification proves to be more important than most others' (ibid.). The difficulty of shifting from that master status of 'thief', 'criminal' and so on is why Becker's work still has a contemporary resonance.

This brings us on to what Maruna describes as 'escaping the burden of choice'. Maruna argues that intentionally failing at things or committing acts that will result in yet another prison sentence can enable individuals to avoid the burden of responsibility about making choices in their life. The blame can be passed on to society. Interestingly, even when active offenders in the Liverpool Desistance Study were optimistic about their futures, they still saw little personal control over this outcome. They seemed to regard themselves as very passive onlookers with respect to the direction of their lives. The pursuit of happiness was something that they might have wanted, but again did not feel they had a great deal of control over.

Finally, Maruna suggests that the scripts of persistent offenders in the sample actually reflect conventional wisdom about offenders. These individuals saw themselves as victims of circumstance who did not have the ability to change their lives around. Often they found refuge in alcohol and drugs. The irony, according to Maruna, is that they may just be right about their poor prospects. The opportunities available to offenders without any training or education are usually very bleak. Certainly as a society in general we are often very ready to condemn and judge those with a criminal past.

Redemption scripts and desisting offenders

Unlike the active offenders, the long-term offenders who were actively trying to desist from crime had a lot to explain in Maruna's work. The participants in the Liverpool Desistance Study had each spent around a decade selling drugs, stealing cars and sitting in prison. Yet they were classed as in the process of going straight, and their narratives were characterised by what Maruna describes as 'redemption scripts'. Thematically, the narratives of desisting offenders differed from those of active offenders in quite fundamental ways.

Firstly, Maruna describes the establishment of the core beliefs that characterise the person's 'true self'. Here the emphasis is on the 'real me', with participants emphasising that deep down they are fundamentally good people.

In addition, there is an optimistic perception of personal control over one's destiny (some people might say this optimism is a useful illusion, but nevertheless it still exists in the narratives of individuals trying to desist). Maruna describes how individuals seek to find some reason or purpose for the long stretches of their lives when they have nothing to show, and often note that if it weren't for X (say going to prison) then they would never have realised Y (that there are more important things in life than money) (2001: 98). Here the belief is that a person's mistakes can make them stronger. Thus prior criminal experiences are turned into a strength in the redemptive script.

Also evident is the desire to be productive and give something back to society, particularly the next generation. The desire among reformed deviants to help others in this process is a well-documented phenomenon. The classic example is the recovering drug addict who wants to become a drugs counsellor. In the Liverpool Desistance Study, three of the participants had found full-time paid work as counsellors or in social work. Yet a further eleven were doing additional work in this regard or hoped to become full-time counsellors or youth workers in the future. Certainly there is a recognition that those with previous personal experience of prison, of offending, of drug addiction are often particularly well placed to support other people who are trying to change their lives round.

So the redemption script is characterised by people making good out of the bad and finding meaning and purpose in their lives, putting the previous negative experiences to some positive use. Maruna notes that this sense of optimism and self-efficacy is very necessary if desistance is to be sustained. By highlighting something of the maintenance process that enables people to desist, Maruna successfully calls into question the 'myth of the bogeyman' whereby deviants are regarded as fundamentally different from the rest of us.

Interestingly, Maruna also raises the question of how far society believes that offenders are able to change. Certainly there is a general belief that people can change. The proliferation of self-help books and manuals in society telling us we can lose weight overnight or change our lives in a few easy steps shows that there is a shared belief that we are able to change our own lives round for the better. In short, there is clearly a general belief that lives can be transformed. Yet, as Maruna notes, we do not always extend this belief in the ability to change to those whom society has labelled as criminal. We address this issue further in Chapter 8.

Anyway, Maruna's work certainly tells us something about 'how' desistance can be maintained by offenders. Other research focuses less on process and more on the 'why' questions – that is, looking at the specific reasons and motivations that individuals give for desisting. We now return to one of our classic longitudinal studies discussed in Chapter 3 – Laub and Sampson's (2003) *Shared Beginnings, Divergent Lives* – which attempts to explain some of the reasons for desistance and persistence in the lives of offenders.

Why do some people desist?

In their re-analysis of the Gluecks' data in the USA, Laub and Sampson (2003) traced the 'Glueck Men' up to the age of 70 and highlighted that going to reform school was a key turning point for many of the respondents in their study. The Lyman school was a reform school for boys, where young people who had been offending were sent. Although this was intended to be a deterrent against further delinquency, many of the sample reported that the Lyman school provided an important setting in which to acquire discipline and structure in their lives, particularly when this had been missing at home. It was also seen as a place where they could perform tasks that they would be rewarded for. This was in sharp contrast to many of their school and family experiences where achievements, praise and rewards tended to be rare (Laub and Sampson 2003: 129).

Military service was another key reason put forward in the study, as several of the men had completed a successful tour of duty. For some, this was a key turning point, giving them a sense of belonging and shared goals. Laub and Sampson note that 'the timing of the military experience for this cohort of men, who were raised during the Great Depression, is crucial as well' (2003: 132). As they point out, the military in the 1940s was a very different experience from today. In particular, patriotism and pride in the armed forces were abundant throughout society during the Second World War era. Yet perhaps of even more significance is that the military provided clothes, shelter, meals and discipline to men who had very little and who came from very deprived backgrounds.

Unlike the persistent offenders in the study, the desisters all had stable marriages, with divorce or separation being noticeably absent from their life stories. The significance of marriage was illustrated particularly well by Leon. He had been married for 49 years when he was interviewed at the age of 70. He said 'if I hadn't met my wife at the time I did, I'd probably be dead. It just changed my whole life ...that's my turning point right there' (2003: 134). Earlier Laub et al. (1998) found that the quality of marriage, as opposed to marriage per se, was associated with desistance from offending in early adulthood. So Laub and Sampson continue to emphasise the importance of a good marriage and the social capital that can result in this. Interestingly, they note that what has received less attention in the criminal career literature is the role that marriage can play in restructuring routine activities, as well as the direct social control that spouses may provide.

Laub and Sampson (2003) also talk about the importance of employment. The men in their study who desisted from crime showed marked stability in employment. It is argued that processes for the impact of work are similar to those of marriage, in that work can change routine activities and can provide direct social control. Employment can also change a person's sense of identity. The authors note that while stable work was not necessarily self-defined as a major turning point among the men, it did play an integral role in the process of desistance from crime.

So these are just some of the issues that Laub and Sampson touch on when examining why offenders may choose to desist from crime. They also highlight that in order to understand desistance, we need to examine both individual motivation and the social context in which individuals are embedded (2003: 145). According to Laub and Sampson, the process of desistance operates simultaneously at different levels. So we can examine desistance at the individual level, the situational level and the community level. Furthermore, desistance operates across different contextual environments, including the family, work and the military.

91

Having talked about desistance, Laub and Sampson then turn their attention to the challenge of trying to understand the lives of the men in their study who continued to be persistent offenders, repeatedly committing offences well into middle age. They define persistence as being arrested at multiple phases of the life course and ask why is it that some people never appear to move away from a life of crime?

Why do some people persist?

In considering why some people continue to offend persistently throughout their life, Laub and Sampson draw on the case study of Boston Billy in their work. They highlight the lack of positive turning points in Billy's life and suggest he had 'little opportunity or ability to engage successfully in the traditional pathways away from crime. He did not serve in the military, he did not have a steady job that he was willing to invest in (or an employer to invest in him), and he did not have any strong ties to a wife' (2003: 160). Furthermore, being sent to reform school seemed to have little effect on him.

Laub and Sampson also point to the initial attraction and excitement of crime as helping persistent offenders to sustain their behaviour. Again in the case of Billy's narrative, it was clear that crime was an attractive alternative to conformity. It was viewed as very exciting. Laub and Sampson note that at the age of 68 Billy was asked what he remembered most from his adolescence. His response was being shot at by the police and getting away when he was 16 years old. Many years later, they report that he was able to describe this scenario with great animation (2003: 165). As Laub and Sampson note, narratives such as these suggest that researchers should be paying more attention to the attractive elements of crime, highlighting that crime can be, and often is, a lot of fun for offenders.

Like many persistent offenders, Laub and Sampson note that Boston Billy had a serious problem with alcohol that contributed to a sense of losing control over his life. Yet one of the most striking aspects of his life history was the amount of time he had spent in prison. He had spent roughly 32 years experiencing what Gresham Sykes (1958) calls the 'pains of imprisonment'. When asked why prison had not been a positive turning point in his life, he responded that '... prison toughens you up to a point that you don't care' (2003: 168). He went on to talk about the 'universities of crime' phenomena related to prisons where people go in for one sort of offence and end up learning how to commit all sorts of other offences. For example, he described learning how easy it was to commit a robbery, whereas he actually went into prison for stealing cars.

So these are some of the reasons that the persistent offenders in Laub and Sampson's follow-up study gave for why they continued to persist in offending, often into their mid-50s. A lack of positive turning points through life, the excitement of crime, alcohol abuse and the 'criminalising' effect of prison all emerged as important factors in explaining persistence. In addition, there were some powerful narratives about desistance that suggest that reform school, military service, marriage and employment are key issues in explaining why some individuals desist from offending behaviour.

However, the study also raises some important methodological issues that need to be confronted. These relate particularly to issues of time and space. Firstly, can we be confident that a study whose members were recruited into the sample so many years ago can really tell us much about the issues that confront offenders today? Secondly, one also needs to recognise that these offenders were a very special group of offenders in the sense that they were 'captured' in one of two Massachusetts correctional schools – the Lyman School for Boys in Westboro and the Industrial School for Boys in Shirley.

Of course, one cannot provide a definitive answer in terms of whether the results of a particular study are generalisable to all eras and to all countries. The likelihood is that there will be some almost universal truths (that is, messages that occur in many, if not most, studies) and some findings which are bounded by the particular historical era or by some peculiarities of the sample. However, one way of finding out is to consider some other studies.

When 'going straight' is 'curved'

In her book *Straight to the Point* Julie Leibrich (1993) describes the results of an interview study with 48 randomly selected former offenders in New Zealand. All had been conviction-free for about three years and were therefore identified as trying to give up crime. Her work was funded by the Department of Justice in New Zealand. Leibrich's work is slightly unusual for a government-sponsored book in that it is set in a dramatic framework like a play in which twelve people appear as actors telling the stories of their lives.

The views of the people in the study on desistance are by no means black and white. This is illustrated in a quote by Jake:

> They either go up and be straight or they can be crooked and come down ... Or they come half way. I'm half way ... I'm an honest thief ... I don't see myself as a hood, a rogue, anything like that. (Jake, cited in Leibrich 1993: 38)

As Jake's quote shows, Leibrich found that 'going straight' is often curved, and that the people she interviewed did not fall into neat categories such as 'straight' or 'crooked'. Again her work, which espouses a qualitative approach, highlights the problems with statistical analyses that accept categories, such as desistance, uncritically. This should not come as a surprise as this chapter has tried to highlight some of the complexity associated with desistance and has explored some of the meanings behind behaviour that may be associated with going straight.

Benefits and costs of desisting

Most respondents in Leibrich's study felt that that there were benefits associated with stopping offending and some mentioned more than one. Feeling good about yourself was the most common response, mentioned by twelve people. This was consistent with the finding that a major persuader to going straight was developing a sense of self-respect (this links in with Maruna's (2001) emphasis on 'redemption scripts' which we discussed earlier). Less hassle from the police was mentioned by seven people, with respondents commenting they did not want the police constantly knocking at their door or hanging around where they lived keeping an eye on them.

Six people felt that a better life was a major benefit of stopping and five spoke of the relief of having a clear conscience which, in turn, was related to being able to sleep and not having to go through the emotional stress of constantly wondering when you were going to get caught. Other responses included getting respect from others and feeling safer. Just four respondents could not think of any benefit from stopping offending.

Grace emphasised the feel-good factor associated with stopping shoplifting, as well as noting that it was nice not to be watched:

> I just feel good ... I used to feel as if everyone was watching me ... I feel better about myself. I honestly do, there's no two ways about it, and it's a nice feeling. It's a nice feeling when

you know, you know you're taking things and you're going to pay for them and doing the right way you know. (Grace, cited in Leibrich 1993: 206)

Meanwhile Joan highlighted the importance of a clear conscience and being able to sleep:

Just my conscience and you know being able to sleep. I didn't like doing it at the time and it did end up in sort of quite an emotional strain and so, there's that benefit that you're not going to have that emotional strain again. (Joan, cited in Leibrich 1993: 207)

It is worth noting here the contrast between Joan's comments that she did not like offending at the time and the earlier comments made in reference to Laub and Sampson's work and the case of Boston Billy. Recall Billy at the age of 68 remembering his adolescent crime and giving the clear impression that he got a buzz out of offending, perceiving crime as fun, exciting and attractive. While just two cases make a very limited source of comparison, the emotional strain of offending evident in Joan's comments compared with the apparent carefree attitude of Billy perhaps hints at a gender difference which may be worth considering.

In terms of the costs of stopping offending, only one-third of the respondents could identify any costs. Four mentioned the loss of goods or income. Two mentioned the loss of friends, loss of marriage or the loss of pleasure from doing drugs. The inconvenience of getting home was mentioned once (possibly this refers to not getting taken home in a police car all the time!). Cultural compromise, loss of honour and loss of home and child were also all mentioned once. Interestingly 24 respondents stated that there were no costs associated with stopping offending.

In her work, Leibrich introduces the idea of a balance sheet, with offenders weighing up the worth of offending. Again this hints at some kind of rational choice calculus but, in her case, there is also an emotional component in the calculations. She says that at some point in their offending career, people appear to weigh up the relative costs and benefits of offending and going straight. Indeed, she suggests that perhaps it is when the balance sheet declares going straight to be a better option that the decision to desist can actually take place.

Policy implications

In terms of the policy implications of Leibrich's work, there is clearly a need to help offenders feel that the balance sheet is weighted towards going straight being a plausible and desirable option. In the UK, much policy attention has been directed at persistent offenders in an effort to reduce the relatively small number of individuals who commit disproportionate amounts of crime. For example, the Prolific and Other Priority Offenders (PPO) Strategy was launched in 2004 and aimed to replace work previously carried out under the Persistent Offender Scheme. The new strategy has three strands: Prevent and Deter, Catch and Convict, and Rehabilitate and Resettle. Activity within the first two strands includes early identification of children perceived to be at risk of becoming persistent offenders and the punishment of those who have actually committed offences. While there are concerns here about the potential for stigmatising and shaming young people, the third strand – Rehabilitate and Resettle – seems to have a more obviously supportive function.

The emphasis on creating positive 'turning points' for offenders in the criminal career literature (e.g. Laub and Sampson 2003) highlights that there is certainly a need for rehabilitation programmes that seek to help offenders to change their behaviour. For example, education and welfare courses in prison settings have the potential to help develop skills and confidence for when offenders leave prison or young offender institutions and so encourage the idea that alternative routes away from crime are a real possibility.

In the UK a number of educational initiatives exist aimed at encouraging prisoners to reform. For example, young offenders may be encouraged to take qualifications in core subjects like English and Maths. In addition, courses in anger management, and drug and alcohol rehabilitation are often provided to enable offenders to try and deal with behaviour that may contribute to their offending behaviour. Similarly, those serving community sentences may be required to attend training programmes or courses in an effort to encourage them to desist from crime.

Yet, if one thing is evident from the work presented in this chapter, it is that the process of 'going straight' and *staying* that way is certainly not straightforward. As Maruna (2001) argues, it may be most helpful to view desistance as a 'maintenance process' and an ongoing work-in-progress rather than a one-off event in an individual's life. In addition, research suggests that policy interventions aimed at helping to rehabilitate or resettle offenders may have a very different impact at different points in an individual criminal career.

Over 40 years ago in the late 1960s, Soothill (1974) conducted an experiment in which 450 prisoners were offered the services of a newly formed employment agency for ex-prisoners (APEX). Their success (or otherwise) in avoiding a reconviction was compared with an appropriate control group from the same two prisons who were not offered this placing service. So this study achieved the 'gold standard' of having a randomly selected treatment and control group. Disappointingly, almost identical proportions of the two groups were reconvicted after one year. While this was deemed as another example of the popular cry at that time of 'nothing works' (cf. Martinson 1974), there is much to learn from this experiment. Just finding a job may not be sufficient. Of course, ex-prisoners are mostly untrained and unskilled and so the jobs found for them were probably thought by some ex-prisoners to be an unattractive alternative to crime. More importantly, expecting people who have been immersed in crime to be rehabilitated without help and support in changing their view of the world is not likely to succeed.

Interestingly, in the early 1970s, this same organisation, APEX, offered their services to offenders seeking white-collar employment; with more qualifications and experience to work in the white-collar field there was some scope in finding employment options that were perhaps more attractive than crime. Unfortunately, in this experiment, there was no control group, so the results could not be compared with what normally happens without the intervention of a specialised employment agency for ex-offenders. Nevertheless, again there are lessons to be learned. The first analysis of the results (Soothill *et al.* 1997) suggested that the impact of placing effort, irrespective of whether an employment opportunity was actually found, was, in fact, an indirect measure of an ex-offender's general motivation to stay out of trouble. In other words, the amount of placing effort seemed to be measuring *the ex-offender's willingness* to remain in contact with an agency seeking work on their behalf and the actual placing outcome seemed curiously irrelevant. *Being willing* to remain in contact, often for a long time, perhaps reflected their general interest to reform on this occasion.

Importantly, those with three or more previous convictions, who could so easily be written off as 'unreformable', had an interesting variety of outcomes with some offenders seemingly being much more successful than others. Why was this successful outcome emerging in particular for those with three or more convictions rather than for those with just one or two previous convictions? In short, it needs to be recognised that an intervention may have a different impact at different points in a life trajectory or, in this case, over a criminal career. As Soothill *et al.* outline, those with higher numbers of convictions may have been less likely to have their own social networks intact, and therefore high placing efforts by APEX may have had more of an impact on them (and reflected their own personal commitment to rehabilitation).

Emphasising that an intervention may have a different impact at different points in a criminal career is an important point in its own right. However, it also returns our attention to the need to understand the whole criminal career and not just distinct parts of the process.

Conclusions

There is a danger in seeing what we term as the three foundation stones for understanding criminal careers – onset, persistence and desistance – as rather distinct and with few links. This possibility needs to be examined. Interestingly, the work of Monica Barry (2006) seeks to make links between the processes associated with desistance and those associated with onset. Her view is that the component parts of onset, maintenance and desistance ought to be understood in parallel rather than separately. In particular, she suggests that criminological theory has been fairly limited to date in trying to make links between the processes associated with onset and desistance.

Barry (2006) notes that the 'literature on offending and desistance can suggest no common thread that enables an understanding of offending and desistance as parts of the same process' (p. 18). She argues that, on the one hand, the literature on onset focuses on factors such as self-control, social control and opportunities that meet young people's expectations for personal identity. On the other hand, she notes that the literature on desistance focuses predominantly on 'trigger points' during the life course which are likely to encourage desistance. Yet, in her view, they 'cannot account for desistance where no such trigger points exist' (2006: 18). So while many young offenders, particularly those from poor backgrounds, may not have opportunities such as stable employment or a home and family of their own, the majority of these young people will nevertheless stop offending.

Barry's (2006) key point is that 'because theories of offending and desistance cannot adequately differentiate over time between the three phases of onset, maintenance and desistance, there is little continuity between such theories' (p. 19). As a result, there is a lack of continuity generally in criminology between factors influencing onset and those influencing desistance. Barry's view is that structural constraints and societal factors tend to be seen as most influential in explaining young people's propensity to start offending. So, for example, Merton's strain theory very much emphasises the societal factors in explaining deviant behaviour.

Yet, on the other hand, Barry argues that it is individual determinants (or agency) that tend to be seen as most influential in explaining how young people desist from crime. Socio-political solutions are rarely addressed in the desistance literature. The emphasis is very much on the person, the individual, needing to change. For Barry, the fact that marginalisation in society is associated with onset but not necessarily addressed in explaining desistance is a serious anomaly (2006: 22). She believes it is one that requires further attention in criminology. Another way to think about the link between onset and desistance is to consider the issue in terms of the *duration* of a criminal career. However, Ezell (2007: 26–7) has noted that 'of all the dimensions of the criminal career approach, the study of the length of criminal careers has received less attention'. This is certainly an anomaly and we consider this issue in Chapter 8 when we ask 'When do ex-offenders become like non-offenders?' To complete the process, this is a notion that needs to be addressed. Before that, however, we consider two topics of interest to criminal career researchers. Firstly, the question of specialisation is considered in the following chapter. We then move on to explore issues relating to dangerousness, prediction and risk.

Chapter 6

Specialisation

Specialisation is a puzzle in criminal careers. From fictional representations of criminals that we see in films or on television or read about in books, we perhaps come to expect criminals to specialise. Further, when we hear about serial killers, bank robbers or drug barons in both fact and fiction, we do not get to know much about whether they are or have been involved with other criminal activities. However, the research evidence on the topic is much more ambivalent.

Certainly the simple idea of specialisation has generated some heat, with some researchers arguing that specialisation does not truly exist and others identifying a strong degree of specialisation in various groups of offenders. We will see that some theories of crime lead to the conclusion that specialisation cannot occur; other theories are more forgiving.

First, however, we need to clarify more exactly what is meant by the concept of specialisation for, as we have noted with some other topics, much confusion can develop from failing to take definitional issues seriously.

The concept of specialisation

So what is specialisation in criminal careers? Put simply, this is the degree to which offenders focus their behaviours on a single crime or a collection of crimes. A specialist offender might specialise in burglary. Or the offender might specialise within burglary, ignoring domestic homes and focusing efforts on commercial premises and breaking into shops. While specialist burglars might also involve themselves in other crimes to a greater or lesser degree their preferred offending will involve burglary.

The opposite of a specialist offender is a general or diverse offender who involves himself (the offender is usually male!) in all areas of crime with no discrimination, seeking opportunities for criminal behaviour where and whenever they arise. Indeed, within the criminological literature, the debate is nowadays concerned with diversity as much as specialisation.

At its most extreme, specialist offenders involve themselves almost entirely in a particular area of crime. Thus the topic of specialisation is closely connected with typologies of crime and the issue of whether it is possible to classify criminals into groups or 'types' defined by their preferred offending behaviour. We discuss this issue in further detail below.

Empirical work on specialisation has largely been based on arrest records or conviction records – however, self-report offending studies have also been used. Of crucial importance is the issue of measurement – how specialisation is assessed in a criminal career. We will see that the degree of specialisation depends on the categories of crime chosen. (For example, are we looking at specialisation within property offences, within burglary, within commercial burglary?) It also depends on the length of the criminal career. (That is, are we concerned with short-term specialisation or long-term specialisation, and does specialisation change over the life course?) Furthermore, the type of data that is chosen will also impact on the degree of specialisation. Interestingly, researchers have proposed both measures of specialisation and measures of diversity, as we discuss later.

Specialisation and typologies of crime

In the early days of criminology, the predominant view both of criminologists and the general public was that criminals specialise. Crime types were proposed that were based either on the nature of crime or on the nature of the criminal. One of the earliest typologies was proposed in 1851 by Henry Mayhew who, in his groundbreaking work on the London poor, identified over 100 different groups of criminal activity in London among 'those who will not work' (Mayhew 1851). Thus thieves were classified into stall stealers, till stealers, child strippers, drunken men stealers, etc.

This theme was echoed in the US: in 1908, the *New York Times* pronounced that 'Criminals are no longer general practitioners – the specialist has become even more of a necessity among crooks today' and described detailed specialist offending such as the 'pennyweighter' who replaces valuable goods in shops with inferior copies, 'wagon thieves' who steal from wagons, and the 'top-storey man' (Figure 6.1) who breaks into apartments from rooftops (*New York Times*, 24 May 1908).

Other books continued in a similar vein, proposing distinct typologies of offender. Henderson's *Keys to Crookdom* (Henderson 1924) describes 25 offender classes ranging from robbers, bandits and swindlers through to fraud mediums and grafters.

Meanwhile, a rather different focus on typologies was taking place in Europe at the end of the nineteenth century. Lombroso, in his text *The Criminal Man* (1876), proposed four different types of offender – the 'born criminal', the 'insane criminal', the 'occasional criminal' and the 'criminals of passion'. All types were atavistic – throwbacks to earlier human evolution, and could be distinguished from non-criminals by physical features. Ferri, a student of Lombroso, developed Lombroso's biological classification and proposed an anthropological offender typology with seven classes. These kinds of general typological classifications of offenders have continued to be developed. However, it is a tradition that somewhat ran out of steam in the mid-1970s when Don Gibbons, a major proponent of the approach, enunciated some dangers and difficulties, specifically the difficulty of assigning real-life criminal histories to theoretical classifications (Gibbons 1975),

Figure 6.1 The top-storey man as illustrated in the *New York Times* in 1908.

and enthusiasm tended to wane. Interestingly, Terrie Moffitt's (1993) work on 'adolescence-limited' and 'life-course persistent offending', which we discussed in Chapter 2, has contributed to a recent revival of interest in offender typologies, although her categories are not accepted uncritically (cf. Sampson and Laub 2003).

The idea of the specialist offender has always been bolstered by literature and this focus continues to this day. Popular Victorian novels described such characters as Raffles, the specialist 'gentleman safe-breaker' (Hornung 1899), while Simenon describes 'Alfred-la-triste', a professional safe-breaker, and films such as the Pink Panther follow the exploits of the jewel thief Sir Charles Litton. Biographies of individual criminals, for example the jewel and fur thief Peter Gulston (Scott 1996), add to the evidence that at least some offenders specialise. However, when Peeters (2002) notes that one Dutch prolific burglar was reluctant to talk about his arrest for indecent exposure, this illustrates how selective such biographies may be in the crimes they focus upon.

Specialisation and theories of crime

While the popular idea of specialisation is informed by literature, this is not always the case with criminological theory. Indeed, different theoretical explanations may have very different implications for the issue of specialisation and whether or not it actually exists. For example, Gottfredson and Hirschi argue in their general theory of crime, which was introduced in Chapter 2, that with self-control as the driver of criminality, there are no distinctions between crimes, and that specialisation cannot exist. Instead, they boldly assert that there will be 'much versatility among offenders in the criminal acts in which they engage' (Gottfredson and Hirschi 1990: 91). Interestingly, other theoretical approaches are less dismissive of the notion of specialisation, as the following two examples highlight.

Sutherland's differential association theory

This theory arose out of Sutherland's observations of Chicago neighbourhoods in the 1930s and 1940s, and was strongly influenced by Shaw and McKay's concept of social disorganisation (Shaw and McKay 1942). Sutherland noticed that within each neighbourhood, there was a conflict between a criminal culture and a non-criminal culture which competed for the attention of individuals. These individuals were therefore drawn to the specific culture that they more strongly associated with. The work was published at the end of the 1940s and identified nine propositions on the causes of crime (Sutherland 1949). The first four propositions stated that criminal behaviour is learnt, is learnt in interaction with other people, is learnt in intimate groups, and the learning includes both techniques of committing crime and motives, drives, rationalisations and attitudes. Additionally, Sutherland believed that the theory was appropriate both to juvenile delinquency in poor neighbourhoods and to illegal acts committed by people of high standing – the so called 'white-collar' crimes. Such differential association, Sutherland believed, would play a large role in the type of subsequent criminal activity carried out by the offender and would therefore impact on whether they became a pickpocket or fraudster. Thus differential association theory implicitly leads to the notion of specialisation and to offender typologies.

Labelling theory

In contrast to Sutherland's work, labelling theory is concerned primarily with the official process of becoming a criminal, and how individuals become labelled as an offender or delinquent through involvement in the criminal justice system. According to labelling theory, this process has several outcomes (Becker 1963). Firstly, society views the individual primarily as a deviant, and therefore the individual may be more likely to seek out delinquent groups for whom the social stigma of, say, a court conviction is not relevant. Secondly, the individual's self-image will also change; they will view themselves as a criminal, or perhaps more specifically as a thief or sexual offender, and therefore seek out further opportunities in a similar criminal enterprise. Thus labelling may contribute to specialisation or, indeed, the embracing of a 'master status' (see also p. 88).

Recent evidence on whether labelling leads to specialisation is inconclusive. Sherman *et al.* (1992) carried out a study of domestic violence offenders who were arrested and found a differential effect. For those employed, the effect of arrest (and therefore of being labelled as a domestic abuser) appeared to decrease subsequent episodes of domestic violence whereas for those unemployed the episodes appeared to increase. Thus for those with a work identity, labelling appeared not to have the serious impact suggested by the theory; in contrast, for those with no work identity the arrest appeared to increase specialisation in violence. More recent studies on domestic violence (Thistlethwaite *et al.* 1998; Ventura and Davis 2005) found that a conviction reduced the likelihood of a domestic violence conviction. In contrast, Taxman and Piquero (1998) studied drink-driving convictions and found that a conviction increased the risk of a subsequent drink-driving offence by 12 per cent; for first-time offenders the risk increased by 27 per cent. In other words, a convicted drink driver is more likely to have a future drink-driving conviction than an offender without a conviction.

Thus both labelling theory and differential association lead naturally to the conclusion that offenders are likely to specialise. The theories, however, do not suggest that offenders limit themselves to one particular offence, simply that they are more likely to involve themselves in one type of activity compared with others.

Measuring specialisation

To move the debate forward, it is important to develop good measures of specialisation which can be used to address and test theory. Does there seem to be evidence of specialisation or not? Can we produce specialisation measures for a criminal population? Can we also identify whether a particular criminal career is specialised or not? Over the past two decades, there have been two main approaches to measuring specialisation and versatility. Early work on specialisation constructed a measure called the forward specialisation coefficient. However, more recent work has focused on measures of diversity.

Before we examine the two measures in depth, care needs to be taken. It is clear that specialisation measures will depend on a number of factors. Most important are the number of groups into which crimes have been categorised. If crimes are divided into just three groups – property crimes, crimes against the person and other crimes – then there is a greater chance for specialisation to be demonstrated than if, say, 30 groups are used. Also important is the length of follow-up time of the criminal career and thus the length of time over which specialisation is measured. Offenders may, for example, choose to specialise in one type of crime for a short period before moving on to a different criminal activity – such offenders will be diverse over their criminal career, but will be short-term specialists. Other important factors are the characteristics of the sample (gender, age and social class mix), the nature of the offenders examined (for example, whether a complete cohort of offenders or a sample of prisoners) and whether self-report data or official records are used. All of these factors make it difficult to compare measures across studies or surveys.

The forward specialisation coefficient (FSC) was proposed by Farrington (1986b) and examined in more detail by Stander *et al.* (1989). It looks at transition proportions in moving from the offence type of one conviction (or arrest) to the offence type of the subsequent conviction. A typical table (taken from Stander *et al.*) is shown in Table 6.1 taken from a 10 per cent sample of 811 English prisoners in 1972.

The figures in the table give the observed proportions of those moving from one conviction type (given in the left column) to the next, averaged over the first eleven convictions. Thus 0.064 (or 6.4 per cent) of those with a principal conviction for theft (given that they are convicted again) will be next convicted of violence. In contrast, 0.538 (or 53.8 per cent) will have a next conviction for theft and will remain unchanged in their offence group. Thus the interest is in the diagonal of this table – does the figure of 53.8 per cent represent more than might be expected given the fact that theft is so common? Certainly the figure of 0.500 for a repeat sex offence looks large – this suggests that half of those who are convicted for a sex offence as their main offence will be next convicted of a subsequent sex offence. The forward specialisation coefficient estimates the proportion of observed repeat offenders of a particular type that is above what is expected from a theoretical table with random patterning of offences (technically speaking, a table with no dependence of an offence on the previous offence). It usually takes a value between 0 and 1, with

Table 6.1 The (average) transition matrix for English prisoners

Conviction t-1	N			Conviction t			
		Violence	Sex	Burglary	Theft	Fraud	Other
Violence	253	0.221	0.004	0.217	0.340	0.028	0.190
Sex	120	0.075	0.500	0.117	0.208	0.017	0.083
Burglary	1,237	0.060	0.013	0.411	0.370	0.034	0.112
Theft	2,437	0.064	0.019	0.210	0.538	0.056	0.114
Fraud	254	0.055	0.004	0.169	0.406	0.311	0.055
Other	650	0.086	0.017	0.200	0.395	0.035	0.266

Note: The figures here are based on the first 11 transition matrices.
Source: Stander *et al.* (1989).

0 indicating no specialisation and no relationship between the two sequential offence types and 1 indicating complete specialisation. Negative values are also possible and, if present, indicate a tendency to switch into a different offence. Table 6.2 gives the specialisation coefficients averaged over the first eleven offences.

We can see that all specialisation coefficients are positive (see column 2 on 'Average FSC'), and Stander *et al.* (1989) report that most of the individual FSC values are statistically significant (see column 4). This indicated that there is a tendency for offenders to be convicted of the same type of offence again. Those for sex offending are particularly large, with an average FSC of 0.45. In other words, of those offenders not expected by chance to commit another sex offence, 45 per cent of them do. This indicates specialisation.

The FSC measures the likelihood of staying within the same offence group when moving from one conviction to another but has been criticised in a number of different ways. First, it deals with movement from one conviction to the next conviction – these convictions might be close together in time and separated only by days, or alternatively they might be separated by years. Thus there is no concept of time in this measure. The time between convictions will also vary from offender to offender in producing this summary measure. Recently, Armstrong (2008) addressed this issue, showing that trends in specialisation over arrest or conviction number are more likely to be changes in specialisation over age. Secondly, there are problems where offenders are convicted of more than one offence

Table 6.2 Summarising forward specialisation coefficients (FSCs)

Offence type	Average FSC		Number of FSCs significant out of 11	
Violence	0.15	(0.13)	9	(5)
Sex	0.45	(0.27)	11	(6)
Burglary	0.21	(0.17)	11	(9)
Theft	0.14	(0.15)	10	(9)
Fraud	0.27	(0.24)	11	(9)
Other	0.15	(0.12)	9	(6)

Note: The figures in parentheses show the results for the 209 prisoners with 12 or more convictions.
Source: Adapted from Stander *et al.* (1989).

at the same conviction. The rule here is to determine the principal (or most important) offence – sometimes counting rules are constructed by governments for this purpose. So, if there are two offences to consider, for example, the rule may be that the offence receiving the severest sentence will be called the principal offence. If the offences are awarded the same sentence, then the offence which could in theory receive the longest sentence will be considered the principal offence, and so on. Thus someone convicted of burglary and rape would have a principal conviction for rape if it received the more severe sentence and the burglary conviction would not be counted in the analysis. If the previous conviction was for burglary, then this offender would be viewed as non-specialist. However, one can be more sophisticated in measuring transitions. Hence, moving from a burglary conviction to a burglary and rape conviction could be viewed as specialisation from other viewpoints.

There are other potential problems with this measure which were identified by Piquero and his colleagues (1999). First, the measure depends too much on the ordering of convictions. If two offenders are considered, each with five convictions for theft and five for burglary in the space of a year, an offender whose five burglaries come before the five thefts in the conviction history would be regarded as more specialised compared with an offender whose conviction history alternated the thefts and burglaries. Finally, the FSC is an aggregate measure of specialisation which relates to specific populations; it does not provide a measure of individual specialisation. Thus we cannot estimate how specialisation changes over time for an individual, or indeed what proportion of individuals have high specialisation throughout the life course. Because of these problems, the diversity index was proposed.

The diversity index is a measure of individual specialisation over a fixed period of time. It was originally proposed by Simpson (1949) as a measure of species diversity, and was first used in criminology by Piquero *et al.* (1999) and subsequently by an increasing number of recent studies. The idea of the diversity index is simple. Within a fixed period of time, the proportion of each type of offence committed is determined. For example, if there are $k = 6$ offence types, then the sum of the squares of these six proportions is formed and subtracted from one – this forms the index, which we call D. D has a minimum of zero (no diversity or perfect specialisation) and a maximum of $k - 1/k$, where k is the number of offence types. For six offence types, the maximum is 5/6, or 0.83, whereas for ten offence types the maximum is 9/10 or 0.9 – thus the maximum diversity increases with the number of offence types. Simpson (1949) points out that the index can also be interpreted as the probability that two events chosen at random from within the time period will belong to different groups.

The problem with the diversity index is that there is no concept of diversity above chance – it is simply a measure of absolute diversity – although the expected diversity based on the average proportions of each crime type can easily be calculated for any sample. To summarise, the strength of the diversity index is that it measures diversity over a fixed time period rather than from offence to offence. However, the issue of what values might be expected by chance has not been addressed.

The evidence for and against specialisation

The views on whether specialisation exists have varied over the years. We have seen already that the debate has been polarised, with some researchers maintaining that specialisation does not exist (cf. Gottfredson and Hirschi 1990) and others presenting evidence to the contrary. Interestingly, researchers studying particular types of offending, such as sex offending and homicide, have had no doubt that specialisation exists for a proportion of offenders and have developed their own research.

In the 1970s, researchers began to look at existing datasets searching for specialisation. Klein (1971), in looking at the criminal records of 800 gang members in Los Angeles, identified the existence of cafeteria-style delinquency. What this means is that gang members engage in a wide variety of different offences getting into any and every kind of trouble; Klein used a vivid picture of selecting from a cafeteria menu of crimes to illustrate this. This finding was reinforced by Hindelang (1971) who also found no evidence of specialisation in a non-gang sample of 763 adolescents. Early major longitudinal studies such as the 1945 Philadelphia Birth Cohort Study were also examined; Wolfgang et al. (1972) focused on sequences of offences and found little evidence of specialisation. In 1984, Klein reviewed 33 separate studies on specialisation and found that 21 were supportive of diversity, eight were ambivalent and only four had clear evidence of specialisation. The 33 studies used a variety of statistical methodologies and a variety of different data sources (self-report data, court records, police records) and, while all four of the studies supporting specialisation were self-report studies using factor analysis, there were also self-report studies using factor analysis which found no evidence for specialisation. Certainly it is worth pointing out that all of the studies in the Klein review involved juvenile offending. As we shall see, there may be different patterns in adult offending.

Such work lends empirical support to the work of Gottfredson and Hirschi which, as we have seen earlier in this chapter, theorises that specialisation does not exist.

It is noteworthy that Kempf (1987) effectively challenged Klein's notion of 'cafeteria-style delinquency' when she pointed to the existence of specialisation in the 1945 Philadelphia Birth Cohort Study. She used her own work suggesting the presence of offence specialisation to lend support to the emphasis on crime-specific explanations by Clarke and Cornish (1985) in their espousal of rational choice theory. However, Kempf did say that her work should not be considered as conclusive evidence of crime specialisation because not all data limitations were overcome. First, only criminal behaviour that was brought to the attention of law enforcement officials was identified, and it is likely that various crime types have a differential chance of arrest. Allied to this, it is also plausible that especially skilful offenders, perhaps specialists, are better able to avoid police contact. Second, the limitation to five categories in the analyses was perhaps unable to discern unique behaviour in patterns hidden within the crime classification. So, for example, drugs offences are combined with perjury and loitering. Third, while the patterns seemed to hold when, say, race and gender were separately controlled, the analyses failed to provide for all potential controls such as socio-economic variables.

Other studies give a similar nuanced view. Blumstein et al. (1988) identify a higher degree of specialisation among adult offenders compared with juveniles. The Stander et al. (1989) study referred to earlier identified specialisation particularly among sexual offenders; Albrecht and Moitra (1989) identified specialisation in property offences and in traffic code violations.

The most recent work on specialisation has used diversity to measure specialisation. For example, Sullivan et al. (2006) calculated diversity measures on self-report data using ten categories of offending. They found that there was strong evidence for short-term specialisation when looking at the diversity measure on a month-by-month basis. Indeed, they state that 'short-term specialisation is not a methodological artefact but rather a reflection of an enduring empirical reality'. They point to the need for a more careful analysis of specialisation which moves away from saying that 'there is no specialisation' and instead asks the question 'when does specialisation exist and for whom?' They also make the pertinent point that measures for aggregate groups do not necessarily generalise to individuals. In other words, there may be specialist individuals in a sample which are hidden by aggregate measures of specialisation.

Developing this work, McGloin *et al.* (2007) looked at the relationship between specialisation and variables measuring local life circumstances and frequency of offending. They found that in the prediction of short-term diversity, increasing frequency of offending is associated with increasing diversity; also short-term increases in drug and alcohol use were associated with increasing diversity.

The focus of this section so far has been on the general run of offenders and the degree of specialisation which an individual exhibits. However, can we find specialist behaviour in subsets of offenders? Perhaps specific types of criminal behaviour are more specialist than others. We therefore turn our attention to two specific types of crime of increasing concern in society – sex offending and violence.

In most western countries sex offending has been on the political agenda in recent years. In England and Wales, a plethora of legislation such as the Sex Offenders Act 1997, the Crime (Sentences) Act 1997, the Children (Protection from Offenders) Regulations 1997, the Crime and Disorder Act 1998 and the Sexual Offences Act 2003 have focused fully or in part on sex offending. What started as something resembling a moral panic about the sexual abuse of children has now widened its scope considerably.

In the last decade there has been a tendency for sex offending to be set apart from other types of offending, creating what has been called a kind of criminal apartheid (Soothill and Francis 1997). So, for example, Marshall (1997), in a commentary in preparation for the introduction of the sex offenders' register in England and Wales, made two interesting observations – first, that 'reconviction rates for sexual offenders are low in comparison to other types of offenders' and, secondly, that 'it is unlikely that these [reconviction rates] are an accurate representation of reoffending levels'. Thus sex offenders may exhibit low specialisation based on official data, but may be sexually reoffending to a greater extent than is known about from criminal records.

Sex offenders have increasingly been thought of as a special kind of offender, who are in need of special treatment in prisons and for targeted monitoring on release. The implied orthodoxy is that sexual offenders tend to specialise and therefore need to be assessed and monitored through appropriate risk scores such as STATIC-99 (Hanson and Thornton 1999). Evidence for this comes mainly from two sources. Firstly, studies have taken place on the risk of recidivism of treated and untreated sex offenders. Hanson *et al.* (2002) reported on 38 studies and found an overall risk of recidivism of 12 per cent for treated sex offenders compared with a comparison group risk of 17 per cent for untreated sex offenders. Secondly, there are comparative studies between sex offenders and non-offenders in their risk of sexual reoffending. Hanson *et al.* (1995), for example, compared child molesters to non-sexual offenders (defined as those with no sexual offence in their entire criminal history) and found a long-term sexual recidivism rate of 35 per cent for the sex offenders compared with only 1 per cent for the non-sexual offenders. Thus the evidence is that while not all sex offenders sexually reoffend, some do, and the risk of a sexual offence is far higher if there has been a prior sexual offence than if there has not been. Soothill *et al.* (2002) carried out a case control study on serious sexual assaulters (rape and serious indecent assault) which supported this view. They found that the risk of a first-time serious sexual assault offence increased 19-fold if the offender had been previously found guilty of attempted rape, and increased 26-fold if the offender had been found guilty of unlawful sexual intercourse with a child under 13. More recent work has questioned the assumption of specialisation, and has seen both specialisation and generality in the careers of sex offenders. We return to this idea in the next section.

Studies on the specialisation of violent offenders are also increasingly topical. The issue of whether violent offenders are special and whether they can be distinguished from frequent offenders has generated some controversy. Research results are mixed with some studies reporting no difference and others identifying specialisation. For example, Piquero (2000) in a small-scale study found that frequent violent offenders are indistinguishable from frequent non-violent offenders and there is no tendency to specialise in their future careers. In contrast, Deane *et al.* (2005) report that violent offenders are more likely to engage in further violent offences than non-violent offenders. In examining the risk of armed violence, unarmed violence, group violence and causing serious injury offences, there is a significant and positive effect of the number of prior violence offences. Their conclusion is supported by recent evidence from Osgood and Schreck (2007: 274) who 'found substantial levels of specialization in violence, and considerable stability in specialization over time'. As with sexual offending, the consensus appears to be moving towards the idea that specialisation exists.

Why do such studies report such different results? We take the view that different researchers are conceptualising specialisation differently. Measuring diversity or forward specialisation coefficients provides two such methods of specialisation, but we have also seen that recent research is examining whether prior offending of a specific type predicts future offending of the same or related type. Thus, rather than a black-and-white view of the 'complete specialist' versus the 'complete generalist' which appears to characterise some theoretical debates, the focus is shifting to risk and prior offending.

Current debates in specialisation

Much of the debate up until now has focused on the degree of specialisation of the individual offender and whether specialisation exists in an individual. We have seen that different studies have come to somewhat different conclusions, with perhaps a shift in view towards the existence of short-term specialisation, and that specialisation exists for sex offenders and violent offenders and for particular specialist types of crime such as corporate crime.

We now focus on two recent developments on the topic of specialisation, but we also take a brief glimpse at an issue that has not yet been fully confronted.

The first takes a developmental approach, with the idea that individuals specialise in a particular activity at a particular period of their criminal life course before moving on to a different activity as they age. The second debate will suggest that the concept of specialisation is more complex and that many offenders, while generalist in their overall offending, will specialise in the detailed nature of their specific offending.

The brief glimpse at the issue which has not been confronted is the notion that specialisation itself is changing. Dick Hobbs – see Box 6.1 – makes two important points. He notes how – for some at least – 'crime is normal, and a part of everyday life'. However, more importantly for our present discussion, he notes how 20 years ago when he began his research, anyone carrying a gun was a specialist. Sadly, nowadays, we are beginning to learn how much more pervasive a gun culture is within parts of British society. In short, criminal specialisation can change, just as the nature of normal occupations can change over time. We come back to this in Chapter 9 when we suggest that societal changes are currently overlooked by those interested in criminal careers, but that comes later.

Box 6.1 '[Crime] is normal, and a part of everyday life' – but specialisation is changing

Professor Dick Hobbs, who has examined gun crime, bouncers, drug trafficking and the night-time economy (Hobbs 1988, 1995, 2003) says, 'I want to get away from the idea that crime is an extraordinary activity. It is normal, and a part of everyday life.' This is a view formed after a childhood spent in the East End of London and an academic career dedicated to talking to others about their lives in a big city. However, he stresses that this is not to say that the nature of crime and violence has remained constant. When he began his research 20 years ago, anyone carrying a gun was a specialist. 'He was known as a shooter, and these weren't random acts', he says. 'It was someone who would use weapons as part of their job.' If guns were used in a vendetta, it demonstrated a major step up – a step across the line – whereas now, he says, guns are more likely to be used simply because there are more of them around. The kind of violent feuds once associated only with professional criminals now seem to be taking place between children, he says – something he blames not only on the greater availability of weapons, but on a youth culture which, dominated by consumerism and by the US, encourages young people to carry them.

But, according to Hobbs, what has really transformed the nature of crime since he began studying it is the dominance of drugs and the instant and enormous fortunes they offer. Drugs, he says, have taken away any notion of criminal specialisation. 'Anyone can have a whip-round, take a cheap flight to Amsterdam and become an international drugs smuggler. Hijacking a lorry, robbing a bank, breaking a safe, or whatever, is impossible because of the levels of knowledge you'd need. Now, it's a complete and utter free for all. It's very democratic.'

Where once villains needed to come from the right criminal family and to serve an apprenticeship of several years to learn their safe-breaking or bank-robbing craft, the underworld has become more diffuse, fluid and multicultural, he says. While criminals have always had a streak of entrepreneurialism, crime itself has now gone from a craft to an international business. Just as city analysts seem to take in their stride the risk of getting things wrong, so the smugglers make realistic assessments about the risks of getting caught – which, on the whole, are not that high.

Source: Adapted from 'Professor of the underworld', *The Guardian*, 12 August 2008.

Developmental or lifestyle specialisation

The developmental approach to specialisation takes as a starting point the idea that offenders proceed through a series of sequential stages in their criminal career. One of the first proponents of this idea was Don Gibbons, who termed this 'role-career analysis'. He identified 21 classes of criminal behaviour, including the professional thief, the joyrider, naive cheque forger, the aggressive rapist and the male homosexual (Gibbons 1973). Gibbons's idea was to make these groups wide enough in definition to encompass changes in detailed offending within a category. Thus the joyrider might start off by breaking into cars, then progress to stealing cars, before graduating to selling and processing stolen cars.

While this provided an important step forward over the fixed typologies proposed by others, Gibbons's model assumes that once an individual is on a career path, they will stay on that career path for the rest of their offending history. Thus it does not allow for offenders changing career at life stages.

Shover (1996), in a book on persistent thieves, suggested another model. Rather than rigid specialisation, he suggested a model of short-term specialisation where offenders become involved in a particular type of offending and exclude all other types. Experience allows offenders to build up skills in this type of offending and this becomes more attractive and successful.

Francis *et al.* (2004b) took this idea and looked for short-term patterns in offending types. Unlike Shover, who was focusing on types of theft, the conceptual model of Francis *et al.* was that of lifestyle specialisation. Thus while some offenders might focus on one particular offence over the short term, others would focus on a group of offences. These might be across traditional offence categories – thus burglars might commit criminal damage or sexually assault an occupant of a house if the opportunity arose, and car thieves might also break into cars, drive without insurance and steal from cars. Thus offenders specialise within particular periods of time, some offenders focusing on one offence, some on two and others being versatile across a range of offences (but still avoiding some).

Recent work by Soothill *et al.* (2008a) illustrates the idea. They looked at the criminal convictions of 16–20 year olds for six birth cohorts of offenders. They used a probabilistic clustering technique called latent class analysis to identify distinct conviction types within these five-year offending windows – separately for males and females. They found 16 clusters for male offenders and five female clusters.

Nine of the clusters were specialist and involved only one type of conviction. These included shoplifting, possession of an offensive weapon and drugs offences. Three were dual-offence lifestyles, such as fraud and forgery with theft, but with little chance of violence. A final set of clusters were versatile in their offending behaviour, but three distinct versatile groups were identified with different offence combinations.

In their original paper, Francis *et al.* (2004b) acknowledge that offenders can move between clusters as they age. Thus, from looking at movements between ages 16–20 and the next age group of 21–25 for the 1953 birth cohort, they identified that 6 per cent of those involved in vehicle theft alone move onto more aggressive property offending and car crime compared with 6 per cent who stay in the same cluster and 69 per cent who have no convictions in the later period. Transition percentages such as these could be used to look at long-term criminal lifestyle specialisation, with the latent classes identifying short-term patterns of specialisation and versatility.

Concurrent specialists and generalists

Another more nuanced view of specialisation has been recently suggested. It is best illustrated by an analogy from sport. We can confidently say that, if people play sport at all, they are more likely to dabble in a variety of different sports rather than specialise in just one sport. However, there are, on the other hand, some people who do just concentrate on one sport. Even more confusing, though, is that those who do seem to specialise in playing a particular sport – premier league footballers, professional tennis players or cricketers and so on – may still play other sports on occasions as well. We would perhaps be reluctant to call these 'specialists' (as they do play other sports) or 'generalists' (as this seems to go against common sense). In short, perhaps the specialist/generalist dichotomy masks a more complex picture. We explore this concern below by focusing particularly on sex offending.

The term 'sexual offenders' rather suggests that they are a homogeneous and coherent group. There are dangers in both theoretical and policy terms in believing that this is the case where the evidence may indicate otherwise. Secondly, to talk of 'sexual offenders' suggests that they are somehow distinct from the general run of offenders. In fact, while some may be, there are many others whose sexual offending is just another type of behaviour they are displaying within a broad criminal repertoire.

Obviously one way to resolve all this would seem to be to distinguish between 'specialists' and 'generalists' in the ways that the reviews discussed in the previous section have tried to do. However, just as in thinking about sport, we contend that the distinction is too simplistic and one needs to make some further conceptual decisions. Indeed, we suggest that what plagues criminology in relation to the specialisation debate is the insistence that offenders *either* specialise *or* are versatile. In a paper in the *British Journal of Criminology*, Soothill *et al.* (2000) suggested that they can do both. This becomes understandable when one appreciates that in relation to sex offending (and the argument can be extended to any kind of offending), there are essentially two levels of analysis – analysis of their participation in crime in general and, within their sexual offending career, the analysis of *specific* kinds of sex offending. At one level, therefore, offenders may or may not specialise within their general criminal career while at a more specific level offenders may or may not specialise in specific kinds of sex offending within their sexual criminal career. These two levels may act quite independently in so far that an offender could be a specialist at one level and a generalist at another.

Two examples may help. An offender may be convicted of a wide range of offences as well as sex offending and so can be regarded as a 'generalist' at the more global level while, when he is involved in sexual offending, it is always related to committing indecent assaults against males – and so in this more specific level he can be regarded as a 'specialist' in terms of the type of sexual offending he commits. The opposite may also happen. An offender who only commits sexual offences can be regarded as a 'specialist' in sexual offending at the more global level but, in relation to his sexual offending, he may be involved in a variety of sexual offences and so can be regarded as a 'generalist' at the more specific level. Only two other possibilities remain. Thus a person who is only convicted of rape with no evidence of any other types of offences can be regarded as a 'specialist' at both levels, while an offender who is involved in two or more types of crime (e.g. robbery, sexual offending, fraud, etc.) and also involved in various types of sexual offending can be regarded as a 'generalist' at both levels.

It may all sound a bit confusing so a return to the sporting analogy may help to chart the way. In brief, a person may play many sports but, when he plays football, he has the favoured position of centre forward. Thus a person can, indeed, be regarded as a versatile sportsperson (that is, he or she plays many sports) *and* a specialist centre forward at the same time.

A consideration of the similarities and differences in the criminal histories of persons committing very different kinds of sex offences has been curiously neglected. However, at the more global level there is evidence that sex offenders are treated as 'specialists'. As Simon has pointed out, 'offenders who commit sex crimes are also treated as specialists by the legal and mental health systems' (1997: 41). In other words, that is their stereotype. In fact, this is implicit in the Sex Offenders Act 1997. However, as Simon also points out, 'although there are a few specialists, the majority of criminal offenders are generalists who exhibit wide versatility in offending' (ibid.: 35), while stating in relation to sex offenders that 'many studies unwittingly find that offenders who commit crimes are not specialists' (ibid.: 43).

The concept of specialisation coexisting with generalisation has also been addressed by Lussier (2005), although he did not address the idea of specialisation at different levels of crime aggregation. He suggested instead that specialisation and generalisation should not be thought of as at opposite ends of a single spectrum but rather as two separate concepts. While specialisation in sex offending tends to be measured by the importance of prior sexual offending in predicting future behaviour, generalisation tends to be measured by the existence of other offences in a sexual offending history. He points out that both concepts can coexist – and that an offender can be both a specialist and a generalist.

Specialisation and policy issues

Why are we bothered about specialisation and why has so much research effort been focused on this topic? In brief, criminal justice policy may be directly affected by whether offenders are thought to specialise. We turn to Armstrong (2008) who, in a recent issue of *Crime and Delinquency*, discusses why specialisation is so important.

Armstrong contrasts two scenarios in his paper. If offenders specialise then knowledge of past offence types in a criminal career can be used to predict later offence types. He also refers to the idea of type-specific treatment policies and suggests that specialist programmes such as enhanced sentences for particular offences or sex offender treatment programmes will have a 'disproportionate effect' on the targeted offences. In contrast, if offenders are versatile then there is no predictive value in knowing the number or type of offences in a prior criminal career.

Armstrong then goes on to discuss the policy implications of trends in specialisation. For example, if specialisation increases over the life course for persistent offenders, then targeting policies on reducing violence to those later in life would have a disproportionate effect on reducing violent crime.

Whether specific programmes are put in place for particular offences, of course, is not just a research question. Reassuring the public can often drive policy as much as research evidence. Thus programmes for dangerous offenders on release from prison are probably as much to do with reassurance as the idea that these offenders are specialist and dangerous throughout their life. Research evidence from criminal careers studies can help to move the balance towards what works rather than what is thought to be politically expedient.

Conclusions

This chapter has attempted to address the contentious issue of specialisation within offending. We have argued that, while there are genuine problems still to confront, recognising the importance of the most appropriate ways of defining and measuring specialisation is the first crucial step on the journey of understanding the concept of specialisation.

Recognising the links between theories of crime and one's understanding of specialisation is a further necessary development which has been stressed in this chapter. In fact, some theoretical approaches invite and embrace the notion of specialisation – we pointed to the pioneering efforts of Sutherland in this respect – while other approaches more readily dismiss the notion following their theoretical speculations – we pointed to the popular work of Gottfredson and Hirschi as not countenancing ideas of specialisation.

In policy terms the notion of specialisation (or not) is undoubtedly important. If there is specialisation, then efforts relating to both prevention and rehabilitation can be more targeted. However, if offenders tend to be generalists, then specific targeting may be wasteful of resources.

We maintain that there have been some recent advances in this area. In fact, one advance is to recognise that the issues are not simply technical ones of measurement, although accurate measurement is always a help. In various ways at both the conceptual and empirical levels there is much to suggest that it is worth embracing more complexity. Indeed, we suggested that, in thinking about two levels of analysis, the two levels may act quite independently in so far as an offender could be a specialist at one level and a generalist at another.

Another dimension to consider more systematically is that of time. Why should a person be either a specialist or a generalist throughout their lives? A promising development is perhaps to think in terms of 'short-term specialisation' which can eventually change in various ways or, indeed, continue. Certainly there is scope in this area for continuing to draw together conceptual, theoretical and empirical work. There has been progress but we still have some way to go.

Chapter 7

Dangerousness, prediction and risk

There is a widespread perception that we are now living in a 'risk society'. The term, first coined by Ulrich Beck, a German sociologist, implies both that society is increasingly concerned with risk and its assessment and also that society is increasingly organised in response to risk (Beck 1992). Indeed, with the complexities of new technologies (such as genetically modified crops), he states that risk is becoming harder to assess.

Coupled with this changing focus on risk by western society comes a magnifying fear of everyday life and an intolerance of risk combining to form a view in society that all risks can be avoided given enough effort by the state. Frank Furedi in his book *Culture of Fear* identifies the new world as a 'world of risky strangers' with uncertainties about the future of the world influencing behaviour between strangers (Furedi 1997). In the criminological domain, for example, there are repeated calls for a zero-tolerance approach to detected child abuse crime, with long prison sentences being called for and subsequent monitoring on release.

Policy-makers are therefore seeking to minimise risk in all spheres of life, reacting to the greater intolerance in society towards certain aspects of risk.

This chapter focuses on what the study of criminal careers can contribute towards the assessment of risk and dangerousness. We will investigate three forms of risk in crime and what methods can be used using criminal careers to predict risk. Our focus here is on *risk of offending* – the likelihood of an individual committing or recommitting a crime. Our aim is to determine whether risk factors exist which can predict whether someone is likely either to commit a crime for the first time or to reoffend given that they have already committed a crime.

We will first consider *reoffending* and will examine two different types of risk – the risk of any form of reoffending and the risk of dangerous or serious reoffending. We will then consider what can be done to assess the risk of a *first offence* either of a particular type such as homicide or the risk of a person starting a criminal career. There will thus be some overlap with the previous chapters on onset and desistance.

Of course, there are other forms of criminological risk. Victimisation risk is an increasingly important topic, and researchers have found that both community factors (such as social lack of cohesion and residential instability) and individual factors (such as personal lifestyle and being a prior victim) influence the risk of being a future victim (Sampson and Wooldredge 1987; Sampson and Lauritsen 1990; Farrell *et al.* 1995). Situational victimisation risk instead focuses on the circumstances and surroundings of the person – perhaps identifying dark streets and walking alone as pertinent risk factors for a violent attack. However, neither of these forms of criminological risk is strictly appropriate to criminal careers research, as information on offender histories is not relevant. Finally, an additional form of risk is the risk to the offender of getting a prison sentence and we will touch briefly on this aspect of criminal careers towards the end of the chapter.

Risk and prediction

The concepts of risk and prediction can be thought of as two sides of the same coin. A *risk* is a chance or probability that some event (usually undesirable) will happen in the future. Thus we can talk about the risk of a cyclist in the UK having an accident in the next year or the risk of a sexual offender reoffending in the next five years on release from an English prison. Good risk statements should include some element of location (risks for cyclists in the Netherlands may well be lower than in the UK) and some indication of a future time horizon (the next year, the next ten years, etc.). However, these are sometimes left implicit, leaving the reader to judge what the statement means.

A prediction usually relates to a particular person and uses the risk measure to make a judgement about an individual experiencing the negative event. This prediction may, in turn, be acted upon and some judgement made about the individual based on the prediction.

We can focus our discussion on risk and prediction of reoffending. This risk, strictly speaking, is the probability or chance that the offender, who has already offended once, will offend again in the future within some time horizon. Alternatively, there may be a risk score which identifies broad categories of risk. For example, the risk score might identify an offender as belonging to one of five categories: 'highly unlikely to reoffend', 'unlikely to reoffend', 'equally likely to reoffend or not', 'likely to reoffend' and 'highly likely to reoffend'. A prediction of reoffending, in contrast, is using that risk probability or score (and possibly other information) to make a judgement as to whether one particular person will reoffend. Less commonly, a prediction might estimate how many of a group of offenders will reoffend. Thus a prediction might be made that a male sex offender in Scotland released from prison who has three prior sexual convictions has a 40 per cent chance of reoffending with another sexual offence in the next five years. Based on this prediction, a decision might be made on the form of post-release supervision needed by the offender.

Such work is therefore often quantitative. Our contention is that *all* criminologists need to enter this territory for otherwise the appreciation of their discipline is incomplete. We were struck recently by Peter Wilby's (the former editor of *The Independent* newspaper) claim that 'most journalism training courses do not have modules on how to handle numbers' (see Box 7.1). It is arguable that the same is true of many criminology courses.

Using criminal careers to assess risk of general reoffending

Our approach will be to start by considering risk and prediction for the general offender in reoffending before giving a more specific focus on serious crime and dangerous criminals. We will concentrate on work carried out by the UK Home Office in developing the Offender Group Reconviction Score (OGRS). This work, carried out by Copas and Marshall in the early 1990s, was an attempt to estimate the probability of reconviction in a two-year follow-up period given details on prior criminal history (Copas and Marshall 1998). The original purpose of the work was to aid probation officers in writing pre-sentence reports. Using the Offenders Index and both prison and court data, the researchers were able to include 14,000 offenders combining both those released from custody and those starting a non-custodial sentence to build a statistical model. Given the criminal conviction history, the age and the gender of the individual, the model produced a numerical risk score which lay between 0 and 100. This score could be interpreted as the estimated percentage of offenders who would be reconvicted out of a group of offenders with identical age, gender and criminal background. This produced the 'offender group' reconviction score. The score could also be interpreted as an estimated chance of an *individual* being reconvicted.

Copas and Marshall found five predictors were important in predicting recidivism. Four of these were straightforward: age of offender (with risk decreasing with age), gender of offender (males more likely to be reconvicted than females), type of offence (with burglary, motor theft and theft having the highest risk, and sexual offending the lowest risk), and the number of youth custody sentences (with the risk decreasing with increasing custody periods). However, the fifth, later known as the Copas rate, caused some controversy. The fifth predictor took a ratio of the total number of prior court appearances to the length of criminal career in years, giving a 'court appearance' rate. However, Copas and Marshall found that this raw

---

Box 7.1 Journalists are not very good with figures ...

[Many newspaper] stories depend on statistics ... In five recent issues of the *Daily Mail* I counted 19 stories that relied almost wholly on statistical data. They revealed, for example, that women treated for early signs of cervical cancer are at 'double' the risk of contracting full-blown cancer 25 years later; the UK population will rise to 81 million by 2074; people who try to stop thinking about chocolate eat more of it; more than 1.2 million people have been on sickness benefits for more than five years; the sex lives of 'up to' 15 million Britons are affected by stress; and eight out of 10 dog owners are 'relaxed' compared with three in 10 of those who do not own pets.

Journalists are not very good with figures. The great majority come from an arts or social studies background. I studied maths at A-level (I failed) but most of my colleagues will not have grappled with a differential equation since their early teens. Basic statistical concepts – confidence intervals, standard deviation, probability and so on – are alien to them. Most journalism training courses do not have modules on how to handle numbers. Literacy is considered essential for reporters – or at least their subeditors – but not numeracy.

Source: Peter Wilby, 'Damn journalists and statistics', *The Guardian*, 5 November 2007.

---

ratio worked better if a transformation was used and suggested that adding a constant of five years to the length of the career and taking the square root of the ratio produced better predictions.

The reaction to this innovative measure can be seen in Box 7.2. *The Independent* newspaper led the witch-hunt, with a leader complaining of a 'fiendishly complicated sum' which was impossible to use and stating that the 'Home Office's new method is about as discriminating

---

Box 7.2 The first Offender Group Reconviction Score and newspaper reaction

Notation	Covariate
x_1	Age in years
x_2	Gender, coded 1 if female and 0 if male
x_3	Number of youth custody sentences
x_4	Total number of court appearances
x_5	Time in years since first conviction
x_6	Type of offence

$$Y = 31 - x_1 - 3x_2 - x_3 + 75\sqrt{\left(\frac{x_4}{x_5 + 5}\right)} + x_6.$$

The *Independent* leader comment July 24 1995:
It's a fiendishly complicated sum. Those who try to use the equation will certainly find it more difficult than filling in a *Cosmopolitan* questionnaire on 'Is your man a psychopath?'...

All very impressive. The 'Offender Group Reconviction Scale' could eventually be turned into a Christmas board game, renamed Go to Jail! Yet close examination of the proposal reveals that the Home Office's new method is about as discriminating as a policeman's truncheon at a football riot.

Daily Mail comment 25 July 1995:
But dismayed probation officers argue they don't need A-level statistics and a calculator to work out that a young criminal put in custody with a list of previous convictions will probably offend again. 'Any rookie probation officer will tell you a stable relationship, a stable address and training or work is the best way of turning people around,' Mr Fletcher said.

as a policeman's truncheon at a football riot'. More predictably, the *Daily Mail* the next day followed *The Independent's* lead. Rather than criticising the mathematics, they put the probation officers' point of view. Harry Fletcher both belittled the formula as containing a set of obvious factors and identified a set of other, more personal factors such as a stable relationship, a stable address and work or training as being far more important.

The reaction to this risk score is interesting. On the one hand, *The Independent* was able to scoff at the 'advanced mathematics' of a formula involving a square root and thus dismiss the relevance of the work; on the other, the *Daily Mail* presented an argument which was essentially about deskilling of the probation service and reflected both their legitimate views that knowing the offender was more valuable than a mathematical score and also their fears that their work would be reduced to that of form-fillers. We will see in a later section that these criticisms echo a criminological debate between the relative value of actuarial and clinical predictions.

By 1999, the controversy had died down and a more sober assessment of the OGRS score could be made. The Home Office came to the conclusion that the OGRS was generally a very good predictor of recidivism, but was poor among certain age groups, particularly in the most important age group of 13 to 17, but also for those over 50. This led to the development of a revised score OGRS2 (Taylor 1999) and a reoffending-based OGRS3 (Francis *et al.* 2008).

Actuarial and clinical risk

The OGRS score is an example of an *actuarial risk* measure. Actuarial measures use summary measures of criminal career data on a large set of offenders together with other information about the age, gender and circumstance of the offender to estimate a risk score. The offenders are followed up for the required period of time and each offender is then identified as a recidivist or not. This risk score estimate is made though the application of statistical modelling methods such as logistic regression or other score building models. The performance of the measure can be assessed by dividing the set of offenders into two – using one part of the data to build the risk score, and the second part to assess how well the measure performs.

Clinical risk assessment, on the other hand, takes the judgement of professionals such as probation officers or parole board members to make a relatively informal judgement on the likelihood of an offender to reoffend. Although these professionals will have access to the same information on past criminal career history, they will also take into account a whole set of personal factors such as degree of remorse, demeanour, family support, stable residential status, etc. to determine risk (Milner and Campbell 1995).

Both measures would tend to be used at the start of some process, for example in considering release from an indeterminate prison sentence or in pre-sentence reports presented to the court. Which of these two approaches appears to give better predictions? An important study by Grove and Meehl took 136 separate studies – a mix of clinical and actuarial studies. In general, the clinical studies had a great deal of extra information available compared with the actuarial studies (Grove and Meehl 1996). Their study came to two important conclusions. Firstly, in studies which compared practitioners, there was little agreement between them. Secondly, despite using less information, the actuarial studies were either equal or superior to clinical risk assessment.

However, there have been criticisms of the actuarial approach (Quinsey *et al.* 1998: chapter 9). Firstly, it can categorise whole groups of individuals as high risk, even though it is recognised that personal circumstances will mean that some individuals are at low risk within a high-risk group. Furthermore, actuarial measures fail to take account of intention of the offender to desist from crime. There are also other criminological arguments which need to be considered – that actuarial risk measures focus on the individual to the exclusion of other causes of crime, notably economic and social deprivation (Young 1999a). Nevertheless, actuarial measures are perceived by many as providing a reliable estimate of risk and are increasingly used in daily criminal justice practice. Woods and Lasiuk (2008) suggest that for dangerous offenders, current practice relies increasingly on some combination of a structured clinical judgement and actuarial measures.

Serious repeat offending and risk

Interest among criminologists has tended to focus on high-frequency and low-tariff crimes, while there has been much less focus on serious crime (that is, low frequency but high-tariff crimes) which can, indeed, be life-threatening to the victim. Thus murder is a comparatively rare activity while shoplifting is a frequent event; for the former offence the tariff or sentence is high, while for the latter offence the tariff is low. However, the risk assessments for criminologists and criminal justice practitioners are very different for the two types of offences. The question asked about a person convicted of shoplifting is more likely to be whether he or she is likely to be reconvicted for an offence within two years and there is rarely much interest in the type of offence for which the person is likely to get reconvicted. In contrast, for murderers, the basic question for parole boards and the like is perhaps more specific – is he or she likely to murder again or, at least, commit another serious offence. At present, among criminologists, there is little engagement with this latter type of question, although psychiatrists and psychologists often have to embrace the reality, either implicitly or explicitly, of being asked this sort of question by parole boards. Tidmarsh (1997), for example, describes the reality of risk assessment in a parole board setting for rarer, serious cases. In other words, the consequences of making a wrong decision, that is a released murderer murdering again, are horrendous; of course, this is the case for the victim(s) and their loved ones but the consequences are also unpleasant for the ill-fated psychiatrist who may have contributed to the fateful decision. It is quite evident that an easier parole decision is not to release someone, for offenders and offender-patients can rarely challenge the decision of not being released and being held in custody unnecessarily. In terms of psychiatric patients who subsequently kill after release there is the potential pillory of the so-called Homicide Inquiry Reports,[1] but also, on occasions, the massive public outcry which is orchestrated on the pages of the popular press. In the UK, for example, the stranger killing of Jonathan Zito by Christopher Clunis, who was a 23-year-old diagnosed with schizophrenia, was instrumental in changing attitudes in government towards psychiatric patients.

The other type of decision – that is, not to release – may also be wrong: in other words, the person may be perfectly safe to be released but the 'easy' decision is to take no risks. As mentioned above, the latter decision is more difficult to challenge and the evidence of 'failure' (that is, a person being incarcerated unnecessarily) rarely becomes public. The exception is if there is a legal case reported in a newspaper but, until a person is actually released, there is no real evidence to show that the decision was wrong or inappropriate. As we shall see in the next chapter, even the person who has never been convicted of a crime and has led a totally blameless life still presents a risk of being convicted of a crime for the first time, so there is no such thing as a 'risk-free' decision in assessing the likelihood of a crime. It is perhaps no wonder that criminologists do not want to enter such difficult waters and are more content to worry about the more shallow waters of less serious antisocial behaviour.

False positives and false negatives

In considering probabilities and risk, Box 7.3 moves us away from criminology to the health issue of breast cancer. The aim is to introduce the issue of false positives and false negatives in a wider framework and as part of the general language of risk. This example is sadly often close to home – a mother or a sister or another relative may learn that she has a positive mammogram. So what are her chances of having breast cancer? The figures in Box 7.3 are not real but simply illustrative. However, with the figures provided, very few of our students produce the correct answer to the probability or likelihood of the person with a positive mammogram having breast cancer.

Box 7.3   Considering probabilities and risk

Example: A female friend aged 40 with no other symptoms is told that she has a positive mammogram. Does this mean that she undoubtedly has breast cancer? You typically get this type of information:

The probability that a woman of 40 has breast cancer is about 1 per cent. If she has breast cancer, the probability that she tests positive on a screening mammogram is 90 per cent. If she does not have breast cancer the probability that she nevertheless tests positive is 9 per cent.

What then is the probability that our 40-year-old woman friend with a positive mammogram has breast cancer?

The correct answer is 10 per cent. In other words, about nine out of ten women who are told their mammogram is positive will eventually be found not to have breast cancer. We have translated the problem into 'natural frequencies' instead of percentages. 'Think of 100 women. One has breast cancer, and she will probably test positive. Of the 99 who do not have breast cancer, nine will also test positive. Thus, a total of ten women will test positive.' Now, of the women who test positive, how many have breast cancer? Easy! Ten test positive of whom one has breast cancer – that is, 10 per cent.

Source adapted from Gigerenzer (2002)

The correct answer is 10 per cent. In other words, the nine out of ten women who are told that their mammogram is positive and will eventually be found *not* to have breast cancer are *false positives* (that is, the positive mammogram gave a false prediction).

However, the story has an additional twist. The example in Box 7.3 rather suggests that the screening procedure is successful in identifying cases of breast cancer (albeit that nine out of ten do not have the condition). But some people will be told that they do not have breast cancer when they do. Of every 1,000 women tested ten will have breast cancer, and the test will be positive for nine of these ten women. In other words, the test will fail for about one in one thousand women. This can either be because the screening test does not identify all types of breast cancer or that the technician has failed to interpret the text data correctly. Mostly one hears in newspaper reports about the latter rather than the limitations of the machinery but both 'mistakes' are possible and such cases are known as *false negatives* – that is, people are told that they don't have breast cancer when they do.

So now that we know about false positives and false negatives, how does this relate to crime and deviance? 'False positives' are those individuals whom a criminologist (or some other professional) predicts will commit crime or, more usually, the prediction is that the person will be convicted of a crime within a certain period but, in fact, turns out not to be so. In contrast, 'false negatives' relate to those cases where a prediction is made that a person will *not* be convicted of a crime but turns out to be so.

While the same principles underpin the prediction of serious and more trivial crime, the stakes are much higher in relation to the former. The public are more fearful and the dangers are, indeed, more dire. In turn, the proposed solutions can be more draconian and the consequences of failure can be more painful.

Is the problem here related to the concept of risk? The answer is no. Most risk scores will give a statement or probability of an event happening rather than an absolute statement that an individual will certainly commit a crime. However, criminal justice professionals may act on a statement saying that X is very likely to commit a further crime or has an 80 per cent chance of reconviction in the next two years and mentally turn this into an absolute statement that X is bound to commit a crime. Conversely, statements of low risk are turned into absolute statements that X will never be reconvicted. Risk probabilities are never estimated to be either 0 or 1; life is never certain. False positives and false negatives occur when predictions and diagnostic tests are read as absolute statements of fact rather than as evidence with uncertainty.

With the understanding that risk statements are never absolute statements of future truth, we need to examine the meaning of what exactly is dangerousness and dangerous behaviour. Is there a general agreement about whom we should be protected against?

The dangerous offender and dangerous behaviour

While there has always been a recognition that a society needs to control danger, however defined, the use of the concept of dangerousness has really only emerged as a phenomenon over the past three decades. Greater intolerance towards risk combined with media moral panics has led to a focus on the need to control the dangerous offender, and particularly the child sexual offender. The Home Office is now piloting 'Sarah's Law' – a toned down version of the US 'Megan's Law', under which worried parents can find out if those in contact with their children have sexual convictions. There is increasing concern from police and children's charities about making such information public (Sare 2008).

Starting in the 1980s, these debates have tied the concept of dangerousness in more closely with changing conceptions of punishment. There developed a recognition that serious offenders and non-serious offenders needed to be distinguished, leading to a twin-track view of sentencing. For the non-serious offender proportionate sentencing was thought to be appropriate, but for the serious offender, public protection would also need to play a role in sentencing behaviour (Kemshall 2003).

In this debate, there was often confusion as to what constituted a dangerous offender. For many in the criminal justice system, dangerousness was equated with persistence and repeated recidivism as well as victim damage. Thus persistent offenders became 'dangerised' along with sexual and violent offenders (Kemshall 2003: 83). In the UK, the issue of dangerousness was clarified by legislation in the 1990s. The Criminal Justice Act 1991 identified dangerous offenders as predominantly sexual, violent and drug offenders, who needed preventative sentencing to reduce 'serious harm' to the public. This was coupled with a reduction in the use of custody for those involved mainly in minor property offending. Serious harm was defined in the Act to be 'death or serious personal injury, whether physical or psychological', coupled with a likelihood for recommitting such offences in the future. Following this the 1997 Crime Sentences Act introduced mandatory life sentences for second conviction of a range of violent and sexual offences, including robbery with a firearm and possession of a firearm.

There is a recognition among some criminologists that dangerous offending is broader than such violent offending – it may be much more insidious and hidden. So, for example, if a developer clears polluted land and dumps the soil close to a housing estate, would we be thinking of locking up the individual responsible for life? Would we think that there is any danger of such persons becoming recidivists and doing something similar in the future? Such arguments identify the covert danger to the public in terms of health which may affect a larger number of people.

However, we return to the legislative view of dangerous offending. Given the focus on violent, sexual and drugs crime, what tools are there to predict dangerous recidivism?

Predicting recidivism for dangerous offenders

The research literature on risk of violence and sexual offending is extensive. Most work, however, has focused on the risk of violence among psychiatric inpatients, or among those with psychosis or more generally among the seriously mentally ill – see Woods and Lasiuk (2008) for a review. These, however, are special groups of individuals which exclude the majority of offenders. Instead we focus here on the risk of dangerous reoffending among dangerous offenders.

For violent offenders, the VRAG or Violence Risk Assessment Guide (Quinsey *et al.* 1998) is currently the most used actuarial prediction tool. Following a specific violent offence (known as the index offence), VRAG predicts the risk of violent recidivisim. However, it was developed from patients detained in secure hospitals and, although it is used for more general violent offender populations, care needs to be taken in interpreting the outcome. A wide variety of items make up the scale. From the criminal history of the offender, there is the non-violent offender history prior to the index offence, the age of the offender at the index offence, the sex of the victim and the most serious victim injury at the index offence. There are also items relating to the family history (separation from either parent before age 16), the psychiatric history of the offender, the marital status and an alcohol abuse measure.

The VRAG has been criticised for failing to give guidance on management and for ignoring other possible risk factors (Litwack 2001). This has allowed other measures to be developed which have combined actuarial measures with clinical assessments. The HCR-20 (Webster *et al.* 1997) is one such structured clinical instrument which allows clinical factors such as attitude and motivation to be included with historical actuarial items.

For sex offender recidivism there are again many risk assessment tools. Predominant in the UK is the Risk Matrix 2000 (Thornton 2000) used by both police forces and probation officers. This measure was developed from a sample of prison releases and so is concerned primarily with the more serious sex offender. Items appearing in the risk assessment include age, prior sexual convictions, prior general convictions, gender, presence of stranger victims and marital status. In contrast, the RRASOR and STATIC-99 are the most widely used tools in the US. STATIC-99 is a ten-item scale which seems to do particularly well in predicting predatory offending (Barbaree *et al.* 2006). It has, however been criticised as being difficult to use and thus prone to user error.

Risk of first offending

Rather like the familiar refrain of the Jesuits – 'Give me a child for his first seven years and I'll give you the man' – some criminal career researchers have increasingly pointed to the importance of intervening early in people's lives in order to prevent future offending behaviour. However, this approach poses a number of challenges and is certainly not accepted uncritically by all (see Goldson 2007), as we discuss later.

Over the years David Farrington has become a leading figure in the development of the 'risk-factor paradigm', focusing on the identification of risk factors for the onset or development of criminal behaviour in individuals. Farrington has identified a number of risk factors associated with criminal behaviour, many of which have arisen from his work on the Cambridge Longitudinal Study. These include individual factors (e.g. impulsivity), family factors (e.g. parental discipline) and peer and school factors (e.g. anti-bullying programmes). Highlighting such risk factors has led to the idea of risk-focused crime prevention, which involves implementing programmes to reduce or counteract the various risks (see Farrington 2007).

It could be argued that, in order to be the most effective, a number of preventive strategies should be implemented as elements of a larger coordinated programme targeted on different risk factors. An example of such a larger programme is the *Communities that Care* model developed by Hawkins and Catalano (1992). The 'community' could be a whole city, a small town, or even a neighbourhood or a public housing estate. The menu of strategies listed by Hawkins and Catalano (1992) includes prenatal/postnatal programmes, pre-school programmes, parent training, school organisation and curriculum development, teacher training and media campaigns. As an example, Project Northland in Minnesota (Perry *et al.* 1996) intervened in a cohort of early adolescents through a multi-faceted menu of social-behavioural curricula in schools, peer leadership, parental involvement/education, and communitywide task force activities, with the aim of preventing or reducing early alcohol use. Results were successful, with the intervention group reporting less alcohol use than the control group.

On the one hand, the justification for risk-focused prevention programmes seems to be persuasive. Farrington and others have argued that there are enough positive results to justify a greater emphasis in policy and research on developmental, community and situational prevention rather than on criminal justice measures. Certainly few would wish to deny that the promotion of healthy and law abiding behaviour is a preferable aim to the punishment of offenders.

Yet, on the other hand, there are a number of objections related to 'pre-emptive intervention' in particular and the labelling of individuals who have not yet committed a crime. According to Goldson (2007):

> Children and young people face judgement, and are exposed to intervention, not only on the basis of what they *have done*, but what they *might do*, who *they are* or who they are *thought to be*. In the final analysis perceived risk is not crime, yet terms such as 'potential offender', 'pre-delinquent' and 'crime-prone' are increasingly mobilised to legitimate formal intervention, intelligence gathering and the free-flow of information exchange within and between state agencies. (2007: 9, emphasis in original)

We later discuss some of the ethical issues associated with early intervention in more detail. For now, it is important to note that studies have tended to focus on the risk factors for the onset of general offending and antisocial behaviour. Hence the main focus has been on the early identification of individuals at risk of antisocial behaviour and on suggesting which kinds of intervention efforts may benefit such individuals. But is such a focus applicable to dangerous offending?

Risk factors for first dangerous offending

We now return to dangerous offending which we discussed earlier in this chapter. Can we determine risk factors for first dangerous offending in the same way that we can identify risk factors for the onset of general criminal behaviour?

Being able to identify such individuals and to take preventative action is a seductive idea. Following the murder of Jonathan Zito by Christopher Clunis in the early 1990s, the government became gripped by the idea that psychiatrists can identify who will be a killer and so lock them up before they strike. Until the Mental Health Act 2007, doctors could only incarcerate those whose illnesses can be treated. Over the past decade or so there has been an attempt by the Department of Health and the Home Office to ensure that people who are not able to be helped will instead be imprisoned. Cohen (2002) has maintained that the plain word for what the government wants is internment. Just as some governments hold individuals without trial because they think they may be terrorists but do not have evidence that would stand scrutiny in open court, so critics argued that there was a danger that some persons who were mentally ill would be imprisoned without trial because psychiatrists thought they may be violent one day.

During the controversy many psychiatrists and psychologists queried this approach. Munro and Rumgay (2000) found that of the mental health homicides considered by public inquiries, only 27 per cent were predictable. Tony Zigmond of the Royal College of Psychiatrists argued that even on the kindest of assumptions about the reliability of predictions 2,000 people would have to be incarcerated to prevent one murder. At worst, that figure rises to 5,000 (see Cohen 2002).

We now will present evidence that Zigmund is wrong. While recognising that around one-third of English homicides are committed by individuals with no prior convictions, we can indeed identify risk factors for first serious sexual offending and for first murder which substantially raise these risks.

We first consider sex offenders. Are they more likely to be convicted of homicide (that is, murder or manslaughter) than other members of the population? In work looking at this likelihood, Francis and Soothill (2000) found that, of the 7,401 males convicted of an indictable sex offence in 1973, 19 were convicted of homicide over the next 20 years – that is 1 in 400. They also calculated that the likelihood of males in the population of 1973 being convicted of homicide over the next 20 years was 1 in 3,000, so one can say that sexual offenders are seven times more likely to be convicted of homicide in the next 20 years than male members of the general population. Certainly that evidence shows that sex offenders are, indeed, more likely to be convicted for homicide than the general population.

However, it might be argued that sex offenders themselves are dangerous individuals, and it is not surprising that these offenders have a higher than average rate of homicide. So, following this early study, further work by the two authors and their colleagues looked at a wide variety of risk factors in the prior criminal history of male offenders. They focused on two specific dangerous offences: first murder and a first serious sexual assault against a female (rape and serious indecent assault). Because murder and serious sexual offending are both relatively rare, they adopted a case-control approach, matching each dangerous offender to a set of non-dangerous offenders and comparing their prior records. Thus, for murderers, each male murderer in England and Wales in the period 1995–7 was matched to up to four non-murderer offenders who offended at the same age and in the same police force area (Soothill et al. 2002). Both cases and controls needed to have a prior criminal history to allow risk factors to be identified.

The results of this analysis show that a wide variety of criminal career risk factors exist for both first-time murder and first-time serious sexual assault. For murder, the analysis showed that a kidnapping or blackmail conviction increased the risk of subsequent murder fourfold; arson, wounding, robbery, absconding from lawful custody and custody of the previous offence doubled the risk, and any custody multiplied the risk by one and a half times.

When the authors looked at specific types of murder, different risk factors became important. Thus a conviction for issuing threats to kill increased the risk of a domestic homicide over tenfold, but not for other homicides. In contrast, a conviction for robbery was a risk factor for stranger and acquaintance murders but not for domestic murders.

In terms of absolute risk, one out of every one thousand offenders will be subsequently convicted of murder. This risk decreased to one in every 250 offenders convicted of kidnap.

For serious sexual assault, the risk factors were even more striking. A conviction for cruelty or neglect of children multiplied the risk of serious sexual assault by nearly ten times; a conviction for kidnapping quadrupled the risk, and a conviction for arson or robbery doubled or nearly doubled the risk.

Combinations of these risk factors can be made, and the report presented risk scores for both murder and serious sexual assault. Thus robbery, arson and a custodial sentence at the last conviction would together increase the risk of murder eightfold, taking the risk from 1 in 1,000 to just over 1 in 125.

How can this be used? The problem of false positives is still large. For every 125 males convicted of arson, robbery and having a prior prison sentence, only one will go on to commit murder and the other 124 will not. On the other hand, the risk is relatively large, suggesting that some form of post-sentence monitoring might be valuable for high-risk individuals. The balance of public protection and rights of the offender always need to be in focus, and we discuss this problem in greater depth in the next section.

Policy issues and ethics in relation to risk prevention

At a conference in Korea in 1997, Uberto Gatti of the University of Genoa, Italy, raised some important issues which still need to be confronted (Gatti 1998). He introduced a theme which is only marginally touched upon in Farrington's presentations, namely the ethics of early psychosocial intervention, which constitutes the type of prevention which is more closely linked with longitudinal studies.

First, a distinction must be made between 'universal' and targeted programmes. The former are aimed at all children in a community while the latter are aimed at specific risk subjects. The former present fewer ethical problems and our discussion below refers to programmes which identify specific children within a community for special action.

One of the main ethical problems raised by early prevention programmes regards the risk of a *stigmatising* effect. The problem with targeted programmes, particularly with 'selective' types of intervention, is that definitions such as 'pre-delinquent', 'potential delinquent' and 'subject at risk of delinquency', etc. may constitute labels which are dangerous for the social development of children. Indeed Goldson (2007) has recently argued that early intervention encourages child criminalisation as opposed to crime prevention, and overstates the predictive capacities of developmental criminology. Similarly, evidence from the Edinburgh Study of Youth Transitions and Crime supports the view that repeated contact with youth justice agencies may be damaging to young people in the longer term. In reporting their findings from the Edinburgh study, McAra and McVie (2007) argue powerfully that 'the key to reducing offending may lie in minimal intervention and maximum diversion: doing less rather than more in individual cases may mitigate the potential for damage that system contact brings' (2007: 336–7). Clearly there is a need to seriously consider the potential labelling and stigmatising effects that may result from early intervention.

The point raised above by Goldson in respect of the predictive capacities of developmental criminology is also of crucial importance. Statements about risk and prediction are often discussed with great certainty by politicians eager to appear confident and definite in their knowledge. Yet, what is of crucial importance, and what is rarely the subject of debate, is that although we know a lot about the risk factors associated with offending behaviour, our powers of prospective prediction remain very limited. This is even acknowledged by leading proponents of the risk-factor paradigm. Commenting on the statistical barriers associated with labelling children as 'potential delinquents', Sutton *et al.* note:

> Research into the continuity of anti-social behaviour shows substantial flows out of – as well as into – the pool of children who develop chronic conduct problems. This demonstrates the dangers of assuming that anti-social five-year olds are the criminals or drug-abusers of tomorrow. (2004: 5)

Indeed, Farrington (2007) has further noted that while we are fairly skilled in retrospective prediction (looking backwards on an offender's early life and seeing that the presence of various risk-factors meant that delinquency was likely), we are far less skilled at prospective prediction (looking forwards into the future to accurately predict who will commit crime). This relates back to our earlier discussion of false positives and false negatives. Worryingly, the issues raised here are rarely acknowledged by policy-makers with intervention programmes targeted at pregnant mothers and early childhood experiences.

However, a balance needs to be struck. Research shows that home visitation of pregnant women does lower delinquency. For example, the Elmira home visitation study targeted pregnant women who were poor, adolescent or unmarried. The children of the randomised group receiving extended home visits both during pregnancy and up to two years after birth had fewer convictions, fewer instances of running away and fewer arrests (Olds *et al.* 1998).

An additional ethical issue to address is the one of confidentiality. The identification of certain important risk factors, such as a parental criminal record, again raises delicate problems both on account of the unwelcome intrusion into family life and on account of the risk of leaking confidential information. It needs to be recognised that confidentiality is not always easy to maintain when various institutions, such as schools and social services, are participating in the programmes. So in order to implement targeted prevention programmes, valid consent may need to be obtained from the individuals involved and particularly from their families. Further, a particularly delicate point concerns the possible use of *coercion* to participate in programmes should parents refuse to do so, and then what kind of coercion is exerted.

A final ethical problem is raised by the possibility that prevention programmes may produce *undesired side effects.* Here Gatti focuses on the results of what he describes as one of the most interesting and prolonged studies carried out in criminology, which analysed the long-term efficacy of a delinquency prevention programme carried out in Cambridge-Somerville. McCord (1978) reports how several years after intervention the results were surprisingly negative; in spite of all the efforts made and all the support for the children and their families, the subjects treated suffered a higher percentage of mental illness, early death, alcoholism, recidivism, failure at work, etc. during the course of their lives. While it is fairly easy to explain the lack of success of preventive intervention if the results show no difference between the treatment and the control group, it is much more difficult to explain the worse outcome of the treated subjects.

According to McCord (1978), a possible explanation for the negative results lies in the conflict created within the treated subjects between the values learnt from the family and surrounding environment and the values proposed by the social workers.

Another possible explanation is that the intervention might have induced the subjects to depend on outsiders, thus leading to upset and difficulty once the external support was removed.

A third explanation could be derived from the theory of anomie. The programme might have raised the subjects' social expectations without removing the structural obstacles to reaching such goals.

A further explanation is connected with the previously mentioned labelling theories: participation in a delinquency prevention programme may produce a stigmatising effect.

A final explanation, put forward by McCord (1992) herself, may be traced back to the compensatory model that underlies the Cambridge-Somerville programme. According to this model, appropriate treatment can make up for the deficit suffered by children brought up in a context of deprivation and risk. McCord (1992), however, feels that this concept might be totally mistaken in that, for example, a child neglected by his parents might actually be harmed by a programme that attempts later on to compensate for the original lack. In brief, the argument here is that if compensation for a deficit is offered too late, the results might be negative.

In summary, therefore, whatever the reasons, one needs to recognise that early psychosocial intervention on the basis of risk may not only raise important ethical issues but the outcome may not be what is expected or what is desired. Sadly, the old adage, 'The road to hell is paved with good intentions', can be active in the area of crime prevention.

Moving forward?

There have been those who have simply argued that 'traditional delinquency prevention efforts be abandoned' (Lundman 1993: 243), adding that 'prevention projects don't work, ... waste money, [and] violate the rights of juveniles and their families' (ibid.: 245).

However, Gatti argues that these conclusions are too radical, too simplistic and too pessimistic to be acceptable. Moreover, they seem to ignore recent research findings which have demonstrated the efficacy, even in the long term, of certain early programmes for the prevention of antisocial behaviour. Nevertheless, some of the problems that Gatti and others have raised cannot be overlooked. So how can we move forward?

The first proposal is that programmes should be reoriented towards promoting good psychosocial development rather than preventing delinquency. This orientation is justified by the fact that the predictors of delinquency have now been ascertained to be also predictive of numerous other disturbances, such as chronic unemployment, scholastic failure, poor interpersonal relationships, health problems, accidents, drug addiction, alcoholism, early initiation of sexual intercourse, etc. Indeed, the majority of programmes for the prevention of delinquency also measure, as criteria of success, other variables of social adjustment, such as success at school or at work, social relationships, family adjustment, and so on.

So if one looks at the measures when these programmes are evaluated, the aim of preventing delinquency seems to be just one of several aims to be pursued. Often, however, the prevention of delinquency is presented as the only or the main objective of intervention, perhaps with a view to obtaining a consensus – or, more likely, funds – by focusing on a problem that arouses intense social alarm and therefore finds easy acceptance on the part of financing authorities. So the argument is that if in fact the objectives to pursue are numerous (and that of reducing delinquency merely one of many) there is no reason why these programmes should be located in the symbolic area of crime. Of course, a cynic might say that this is simply a relabelling of the prevention programme with a new name.

Another proposal suggested by Gatti – which in effect comes to much the same as the previous proposal – is that of developing 'universal' projects aimed at all children living in a particular area or attending a particular school rather than pursuing 'targeted' programmes. One obstacle which is usually put up to this type of proposal is on the grounds of cost, in that generalised programmes tend to require high levels of funding. However, the screening procedure for the targeted programmes may be very costly and the rate of refusal to participate in data collection for screening may be higher among those very subjects who have the most serious problems.

So with Gatti's help we have focused on some of the important ethical issues which often seem to be neglected in considering the policy implications stemming from longitudinal studies. The successes achieved by these intervention methods vary widely – broadly, the results will rarely match the more extravagant claims of the enthusiasts and the harm done is unlikely to be as bleak as the harshest critics assert. Owing to the ethical implications which are sometimes overlooked, evaluating a risk-focused approach to prevention is more complex than most people realise. Certainly the message seems an amber light and one needs to proceed with caution.

Policy implications

Unlike other chapters where the 'policy implications' tend to be discussed towards the end of the chapter, in this chapter 'policy implications' have underpinned the whole discussion. Indeed, dangerousness, prediction and risk are terms which mainly have a purchase in the policy domain. Ever since Ernest Burgess conducted the first important prediction study in Chicago in the 1920s in relation to parole violation (Mannheim 1965: 146), prediction has developed as the hotline between criminologists and administrators. The concepts of dangerousness and risk are later manifestations of the same desire to control crime and offending behaviour. Indeed, if one can predict such behaviour, then the policy implications may appear to become clearer. Further, if one can identify who are the dangerous persons, then the story seems complete. However, our task here – and, indeed, in this chapter – is to emphasise a more cautionary tale. Caution needs to be on display both if prediction and its various surrogates work and also if they do not!

The latter is the usual concern for rarely do predictions and the like work as well as one might hope. Hence, the problem tends to be seen simply as a technical one of improving the mechanisms of prediction. Being captured by the technical tasks of improving prediction scores helps to characterise criminologists as mere technicians. However, there are other concerns.

Imagine that prediction scores fully work, that is one can actually predict who is likely to offend in the future, which offenders are likely to reoffend and so on. In this context there are at least two other dimensions to the 'policy implications' which need to be considered, as well as a missing dimension which needs to be developed. Briefly, these are the ethical, practical and theoretical considerations. While potentially interlinked they can be considered separately.

The ethical dimension has been strongly brought into focus in this chapter. If all the prediction activity actually works, what is one actually entitled to do? What is the appropriate balance between freedom and control within people's lives? To what extent is one entitled to intervene? The ethical implications should always be seen as a feature of 'policy implications' which need to be taken on board.

The practical dimension may be even less easy to stomach. One should not too readily assume that what one is doing in good faith may actually have a beneficial effect. The work of Joan McCord in relation to the outcomes of the Cambridge-Somerville study briefly discussed in this chapter provide evidence that there are dangers in making this assumption. In short, while one might be able to predict who is likely to commit crime in the future, it may not be so easy to work out what to do about it. Taking some kinds of action may actually be counterproductive and intensify the harm.

Finally, the missing dimension is, of course, the theoretical one. This is especially true in relation to thinking about risk factors, for example. In fact, thought is often the missing ingredient. The gap that is often missing in talking about risk is in understanding what the results exactly mean. This involves theorising about risk factors. One approach is to consider whether risk factors are indicative or causal.

In fact, risk factors can be either *indicators* (symptoms) or possible *causes* of antisocial behaviour. That is, certain kinds of behaviour can reflect *either* an antisocial tendency or be the *cause* of that antisocial tendency – or both. For example, both indicative and causal factors can be found in long-term variations between individuals if their antisocial tendencies are related to the use of drugs. Drugs may symbolise a lifestyle – thus are indicative – or the taking of forbidden drugs over a short period can cause more antisocial behaviour which takes place under the influence of the drugs – and so in that sense is directly causative.

The different policy implications are profound in terms of whether one is dealing with a causative or an indicative factor, but rarely are such theoretical issues discussed. Increasingly – and dangerously – prediction in criminology is seen as a separate science that deals with complex statistical issues. Of course, that is part of the task but, hopefully, this chapter has shown that there is much more in considering the 'practical implications'.

Conclusions

A focus on dangerousness, prediction and risk seems a very contemporary concern. There is often more than a hint that such issues need special skills. However, our clarion call is that such issues should not get divorced or separated from the mainstream of criminology. There should be a requirement of every criminologist to develop the ability to understand the principles of the technical matters under consideration. But the main message of the chapter is that there is so much more to consider than technical issues.

Earlier we focused on Barry's *cri de cœur* that there is a lack of continuity generally in criminology between factors influencing onset and those influencing desistance. This cry for continuity should be further widened. We neglect the ethical, practical and theoretical issues, which should underpin any discussion of the matters raised in this chapter, at our peril.

Note

1 Inquiries into homicide by people with mental health problems were made mandatory in 1994 through NHS Executive Guidance (Department of Health, 1994). More recently, the new National Patient Safety Agency was established to gather incident data anonymously, in an effort to advance learning from adverse events in the health service.

Chapter 8

Criminal careers for everyman – and woman?

Everyman is the central character in the most famous English morality play, which was first produced in the late fifteenth century (Evans 1970: 386). In the play Everyman is an unprepared sinner informed by Death of his imminent judgement day. As he faces his maker, he is deserted first by his friends and his family and then by his wealth; these are then followed by his strength, beauty and knowledge. All that is finally stacked in his favour in the divine audit are his good deeds. As Tim Adams (2006) notes, 'It is not a cheerful tale'. More recently, the famous American author, Philip Roth, has taken *Everyman* (2006) both as the title and the theme of his book which provides a powerful portrait of a dead man seeking absolution. However, while Roth may provide echoes of the fifteenth century morality play, nowadays Everyman more simply refers to 'everyone, without exception', 'every man Jack' (Evans 1970).

Everyman, as the theme of this chapter, embraces the notion that the study of criminal careers should consider everyone. In other words, criminal careers should not relate to a small segment of the population set apart from the rest. We need to recognise that we all have a chance of becoming criminals as well as recognising that criminals may have the chance to become non-criminals. We have addressed the latter issue in Chapter 5 on desistance, but we will also need to return to the topic here.

Expanding the potential boundaries of criminal careers reflects the supreme tension in criminology which derives from the work of the so-called founding father of criminology, Cesare Lombroso. He – both implicitly and explicitly – split the world into two constituencies –

those who commit crimes and those who do not. The world in these terms is comfortably black and white. Interestingly, those who have not committed crime seem reluctant to embrace the notion that they ever could commit crime. In fact, the evidence suggests otherwise.

Self-report studies, stemming from the pioneering work of Wallerstein and Wyle (1947) which involved adults over 21 years of age, suggest that most people have engaged in activity that is in contravention of the criminal law. Of course, some may lie when responding to self-report studies about involvement in crime – some may exaggerate their participation (false positives in the terminology introduced in Chapter 7) or deny their real participation (false negatives) – but the evidence is overwhelming that many more participate in crime than ever come to the notice of the criminal justice agencies. If driving offences are included, it would be tempting to suggest that everyone has committed an offence such as speeding at some point, whether caught or not. Furthermore, even non-drivers would perhaps not be averse to taking a notepad from work which is, after all, technically a theft. The magnitude of the offence is not the issue, but the point remains that a simple Lombrosian division between the criminal and the law-abiding is not a helpful one.

At the individual level persons are more likely to commit crimes at certain points in their lives – usually when they are younger – than at others. Persons experiencing financial difficulties are more likely to be involved in pecuniary crime than those who are not in financial difficulties. Arson for gain is more likely to be committed by a person whose business is failing rather than by a person whose business is doing well. Our claim is that nobody should be excluded from the possibility of crime. The study of criminal careers needs to embrace everyone.

'Criminal careers' is a seductive metaphor but, in trying to widen the horizons, current usage may not be helpful. Although there were earlier attempts, the more systematic study of criminal careers roughly started in the mid-1980s. Blumstein's two-volume book on criminal careers published in 1986 is a useful marker to a new era. Blumstein and his colleagues locate the use of the term firmly within the ranks of those who have been arrested for or been convicted of a crime. Interestingly, however, Blumstein and his colleagues do not probe the earlier uses of the 'career' metaphor.

Everett Hughes is normally credited with the introduction of the 'career' metaphor (Hughes 1958) which was originally developed in studies of occupations (e.g. Hall 1948). Certainly the term began to be used quite pervasively in the 1950s. Erving Goffman, for instance, writing originally in 1959, tells of the shift:

> Traditionally the term *career* has been reserved for those who expect to enjoy the rises [*sic*] laid out within a respectable profession. The term is coming to be used, however, in a broadened sense to refer to any social strand of *any person's* course through life. (Goffman 1978: 120, emphasis added)

Crime is a social construction and we can be interested in any person's participation (or not) in the activity. We would not dismiss interest in a person's health record just because they had remained healthy throughout his or her life!

In fact, Gofffman's analysis largely focused on the *moral* aspects of career – what he calls 'the regular sequence of changes that career entails in the person's self and in his framework of imagery for judging himself and others'. Goffman reminds us that material on moral careers can be found in early social anthropological work on ceremonies of status transition, so it has a long history. Shadd Maruna is perhaps the most recent exponent of this approach within criminology. As a keynote speaker at the 2008 British Criminology Conference, he intriguingly appealed to the claims of anthropologists when he stressed the importance of focusing on reintegration as a rite of passage. He talked of celebrating the end of a criminal career. The end of a criminal career means that the expectation is that a person will behave like a 'non-offender'. In fact, the 'non-offender' is the missing link in most, if not all, work on criminal careers. While the ultimate aim in most rehabilitation work is for offenders to behave like 'non-offenders', we need to understand more about so-called 'non-offenders'.

There are two sides of the same coin that we try to address in this chapter – the duration of a criminal career and the duration of a non-criminal career. The importance of focusing on 'non-offenders' is that they are the obvious comparison group for those who offend. It is only by introducing 'non-offenders' into the equation that we can really decide whether it seems likely that a criminal career has ended. Here, we propose to focus upon the question of 'when do ex-offenders become like non-offenders?' First, however, we need to focus upon the more traditional question of the duration of a criminal career. We need to understand what normally seems to happen in the lengths of criminal careers.

The duration of a criminal career

Earlier we suggested that another way to think about the link between onset and desistance is to consider the issue in terms of the *duration* of a criminal career. However, while duration may be part of the traditional approach, Ezell (2007) maintains that, of all the dimensions of the criminal career approach, the study of the length of criminal careers has tended to receive less attention. In fact, a focus on the duration of a criminal career has a long history, but the topic then became somewhat neglected. It was perhaps because the established longitudinal studies had not been in progress long enough to produce much definitive work on the likely duration of a criminal career. However, there has been a recent renaissance of interest in the topic. So, for example, an entire issue of a leading criminological journal, *Crime and Delinquency*, was recently devoted to the issue of criminal careers and three (Ezell 2007; Francis *et al.* 2007; Haapanen *et al.* 2007) of the seven articles explicitly referred to criminal career lengths in their title. Elsewhere (e.g. Piquero *et al.* 2003, 2004) there are detailed reviews on the existing criminal career length literature; there are controversies in this area, but there is also some consensus.

The consensus is that the lengths of criminal careers do vary but that most seem to be quite short. Career length tends to be associated with onset age such that younger starters tend to have longer careers (cf. Moffitt 1993). The type of offending may well make a difference. While the actual figures may vary from study to study, most of the principles remain the same – that is, a career of violent offending seems to be shorter than a career of property offending, for instance. Hence the pioneering work of Sheldon and Eleanor Glueck conducted in the 1930s whose material has recently been brought back to life by the careful re-analysis by Laub and Sampson, who have now traced the cohort's offending histories between ages seven and 70 and produced many results which are unlikely to be contested. These authors found that average career length of a sample of *persistent* offenders was 25.6 years, with average career lengths of 9.2 for violence, 13.6 for property and 11.4 for alcohol/drugs (Laub and Sampson 2003: 90).

Using data from six different cohorts born between 1953 and 1978 (see Chapter 3, p. 53–54 for further information on this data set), Francis *et al.* (2007) found that, in predicting criminal career length, the most significant variable is the age at first conviction. Gender is also very important, with females approaching a 40 per cent higher likelihood of stopping than males. Although gender differences are rarely charted, generational effects are even less so. In this study birth cohort is highly significant, with later cohorts much less likely to desist.

The authors strongly see this result in terms of a system change rather than a behavioural one with the move in the 1980s and early 1990s of introducing diversionary procedures (e.g. cautions, warnings, etc.) to try to prevent less serious offenders from appearing in court and hence avoid the stigma of a court conviction. Removing the less serious offenders from the court system means that the later cohorts consist increasingly of the more serious offenders who are less likely to stop after the first conviction. While the interpretation may be open to challenge, the important point to note is that there are changes over time that are identified by the calculation of the cohort effect.

While focusing on the duration of the criminal career may have been a neglected area, recent work has changed that. We now know quite a lot about the likely length of criminal careers. However, this cannot be said about our knowledge of non-offenders and their likelihood of becoming offenders. Before confronting this issue, we must first review why a new set of questions about criminal careers is coming to the fore.

Surveillance and human rights

There are currently tensions within society that are emerging in various forms. Put extremely, do we want to be a policed society or a free society? Of course, it is more complex than that. Those who are content with greater surveillance argue that this helps to safeguard and maintain our freedoms, while those who show concerns about greater surveillance argue that it infringes the freedoms which we hope to preserve. Our concern here is not to enter that wider debate, but simply to indicate how the debate has a bearing on the interpretation of criminal careers. It comes under various guises. In the last chapter, for instance, we raised some ethical concerns about the impact of early intervention in the lives of so-called potential criminals. Here we are more concerned about what happens at the other end of the process, namely, when it appears that an offender has stopped offending.

In brief, do ex-offenders ever deserve to be regarded in the same light as those who have never offended? If so, when should this happen – should it be after five, ten or 20 years? In other words, should there come a time when the slate should be wiped clean, so that an ex-offender no longer has to suffer the possible stigmatisation of a criminal conviction? The knowledge that a criminal conviction is still on record can affect ex-offenders at both the personal and public levels. Having a criminal conviction can affect one's image of self as well as one's official position in society in the sense that certain opportunities – including educational, work and even the opportunity to travel and enter certain countries – can continue to be blocked.

Box 8.1   What is the Rehabilitation of Offenders Act 1974?

The Rehabilitation of Offenders Act (ROA) 1974 applies to England, Scotland and Wales, and is aimed at helping people who have been convicted of a criminal offence and who have not reoffended since.

Anyone who has been convicted of a criminal offence and received a sentence of not more than 2.5 years in prison benefits as a result of the Act, if he or she is not convicted again during a specified period otherwise known as the 'rehabilitation period'. The length of this period depends on the sentence given for the original offence and runs from the date of the conviction. If the person does not re-offend during this rehabilitation period, they become a 'rehabilitated person' and their conviction becomes 'spent'.

For example, if a person receives a sentence of imprisonment or detention in a young offenders institution of between six months and 2.5 years, the rehabilitation period is ten years, or five years if the individual was under 18 at the time of conviction. For an absolute discharge the rehabilitation period is six months.

Sentences can carry fixed or variable rehabilitation periods and these periods can be extended if the person offends again during the rehabilitation period. However, if the sentence is more than 2.5 years in prison the conviction never becomes 'spent'. It is the sentence imposed by the courts that counts, even if it is a suspended sentence, not the time actually spent in prison.

Once a conviction is 'spent', the convicted person does not have to reveal it or admit its existence in most circumstances. However, there are some exceptions relating to employment and these are listed in the Exceptions Order to the ROA. The two main exceptions relate to working with children or working with the elderly or sick people. If a person wants to apply for a position that involves working with children or working with the elderly or sick people they are required to reveal all convictions, both spent and unspent.

Source: Website of the Criminal Records Bureau: http://www.crb.gov.uk/

Kurlychek and her colleagues in the United States suggest that 'many of these individuals will feel the consequences of their criminal justice system involvement years and years after that involvement occurs' (2007: 65). They produce a daunting list of so-called 'collateral consequences' of criminal involvement including such varied policies – which are certainly relevant in the United States – as restrictions on voting rights, access to firearms, loss of eligibility for public assistance such as housing and food stamps, and limits on educational loans. They suggest that one of the most concerning consequences, however, is restrictions placed on employment opportunities. As they also note, with 'the increase in computerisation of records, there has been a large increase in the number of employers using criminal background checks on a routine basis' (ibid.), and the situation is likely to get worse for ex-offenders. So what is the answer?

In the UK there have been earlier attempts to effect a satisfactory balance between safeguarding a society by providing access to information about a person's criminal past and providing the opportunity for a person to put this behind him or her. Thirty-five years ago the Rehabilitation of Offenders Act 1974 was enacted with the aim of helping people who had been convicted of a criminal offence and who had not reoffended since. Box 8.1 provides the circumstances in which a conviction can be regarded as 'spent' so that the convicted person does not have to reveal it or admit its existence. As Box 8.1 reveals, there are exceptions. If a person wants to apply for a position that involves working with children or working with the elderly or sick people they are required to reveal all convictions, both spent and unspent.

Revealing a conviction when applying for a 'protected' occupation does not necessarily mean that a person will be barred. In fact, there is much dispute about how one should judge the relevance of previous convictions. So, for example, a recent case that achieved national publicity highlights the issue. Under the headline 'Reformed burglar can study to be a doctor' (*The Guardian*, 8 August 2008), the report updates a continuing saga. The good news was that a teenager who had been told that he could not become a doctor because of a spent conviction for burglary had won a place at a top medical school. His case had reached the newspapers after earlier he had learned that his place to study at another top medical school had been withdrawn after the college learned of his conviction. The candidate had been awarded a four-month community service order for a burglary he had committed three years earlier when aged 16. Since then it was reported he had turned his life around, achieving top grades and volunteering at GP surgeries and charities.

When the candidate appealed against the college's rejection, the college said the conviction would not have had an impact on the vast majority of its courses but that it was relevant for medicine. Specifically it said, 'Medical practitioners hold a position in society, and must deal with vulnerable people. The public must have confidence in the integrity and probity of its doctors' (*ibid.*).

The medical school which eventually agreed to accept the candidate had also rejected him earlier. Interestingly, the deceit in dealing with the case was revealed when the candidate obtained information under the Freedom of Information Act indicating that the university had cited his conviction as a factor in initially rejecting him, despite publicly declaring that the decision was based on his academic record and experience. Integrity and probity – so demanded of ex-offenders – seem sometimes missing in the ways that some institutions deal with ex-offenders. In fact, it is perhaps difficult to believe that this candidate would have been successful without the intervention of a national newspaper to back his case.

Dealing with the more run-of-the mill cases, the provisions of the 1974 Act seem sensible and, in broad terms, it has worked. However, in the 35 years since this Act came onto the statute book, there have been massive societal changes which have already been mentioned; there are the contradictory pulls of a society wanting more protection from internal and external threats on the one hand, and a greater focus on human rights on the other. However, there are other issues. The increasing importance placed on data protection has further confused what is already a complex issue. Individuals are anxious to ensure that information on databases is secure, while at the same time there have been provisions, such as the Freedom of Information Act 2000, which enable greater and more widespread access to information on databases.

That is not all. While the 1974 Act seems sensible, the provisions were not constructed following a systematic review of the likelihood of persons with particular criminal histories going on to be reconvicted of criminal offences. However, as with the example of the teenage ex-burglar wanting to become a doctor, most of the problems relate to persons wanting to work with children and vulnerable adults. Under the Rehabilitation of Offenders Act 1974, an individual is entitled not to answer any question about his spent convictions (see Box 8.1). The Rehabilitation of Offenders Act 1974 (Exceptions) Order 1975, however, provides that a person may ask about an individual's spent convictions in order to assess the suitability of an individual to hold certain positions of trust/responsibility. The question of what sort of information should be provided – for instance, should 'soft' data or intelligence be provided for individuals working with young and/or vulnerable people – is both sensitive and complex. It cannot be dealt with here. Nevertheless, one can note that there are both empirical issues (i.e. what does research on criminal careers tell us about the likelihood of a further conviction? Also which offences are strictly relevant?) and policy issues (i.e. what should we do about effecting a reasonable balance between the protection of society and the rights of individuals?). Both these issues need to be confronted. The rest of this chapter focuses on this challenge in relation to what the study of criminal careers might be able to offer.

When do ex-offenders become like non-offenders?

Certainly this basic question has rarely been posed in such direct terms. However, in the United Kingdom the question was recently posed in the context of developments stemming from an instruction by the Information Commissioner's Office (Information Commissioner's Office 2007).

In November 2007 the Information Commissioner's Office (ICO) ordered four police forces to delete old criminal convictions from the Police National Computer (PNC). The ICO was concerned that the old conviction information was being held contrary to the principles of the Data Protection Act because the information was said to be no longer relevant and was excessive for policing purposes.

After investigating complaints from four individuals, the ICO issued Enforcement Notices to Humberside, Northumbria, Staffordshire and West Midlands Police. The police appealed each case to the Information Tribunal, which meant the information in question did not need to be deleted until after the appeal was determined (Information Commissioner's Office 2007). The Information Tribunal upheld the enforcement notices and dismissed the police appeals; at the time of writing, the case is now with the Court of Appeal. However, essentially the issue is when are past convictions of a particular vintage of no value in the prediction of future criminality? In other words, at what stage is the likelihood of an offender committing a future offence the same as for a non-offender?

It is at this point we need to consider in more depth the notion of a non-offender being drawn more centrally into the study of criminal careers. In short, we assert that we need to focus on the criminal careers of everyman and woman. To do this, we focus upon the evidence presented to the tribunal together with some relevant material published by Kurlychek and her colleagues (2006, 2007). The former uses the Home Office cohort study already discussed in Chapter 2 and which relates to England and Wales, while the Americans use two established longitudinal studies – the 1942 Racine birth cohort study and the 1958 Philadelphia cohort study. While there are some differences in terms of methodology and outcome, the results – perhaps unusually for criminological research – have quite amazing similarities, so suggesting that there may be 'truths' about criminal careers that are ready to be revealed.

Thinking about non-offenders

In working with offenders, prediction instruments and risk assessments have become part of a familiar discourse with increasingly sophisticated approaches. However, perhaps the answers emerging do not quite match up to what employers and others in the community really want to know. In brief, they – unlike criminal justice authorities who have, say, the responsibility of discharging prisoners into the community on parole – do not want to consider them as ex-offenders but they are interested in whether they can regard them with the same confidence as employing non-offenders. In brief, have these people entered the pantheon of the non-offending population? In confronting this issue, there are both conceptual and methodological issues to consider.

Conceptually there is a tension. The ex-offender might genuinely believe that a Damascene moment has occurred and that he or she will never commit another crime, but most members of a society, perhaps especially employers who may have had some bad experiences in employing ex-offenders, would not be convinced by such a straightforward declaration. Elsewhere we have argued that the journey towards rehabilitation – especially among those with several convictions – is usually much more hazardous and likely to be occasioned by set-backs. Interestingly, however, in all that discussion of desistance the notion of non-offenders is rarely addressed.

Non-offenders are normally regarded as those persons who have never come to the official notice of the police and other statutory authorities in relation to the commission of a crime. This is the vast majority of females and a sizeable majority of males. However, few would contend that all of these have never actually committed a crime. In this respect, as already mentioned, studies of self-reporting help. Further, we need to recognise that everyone has the potential to commit a crime. But what are their actual chances of committing a crime? Age and sex are usually good indicators. If you are female, you are much less likely to be convicted and being older helps too. However, local newspapers sometimes show how so-called pornographic Internet crime ('Father downloaded child porn pictures', *Lancaster Guardian*, 1 February 2008) has penetrated the older age groups; probably few would have expected that this 45-year-old father of two would be facing a sentence at the crown court. So, the first task is to recognise that the non-offender population to which ex-offenders might aspire is not necessarily as faultless as some might think. Indeed, the most upright person may reveal at a cocktail party the circumstances *in extremis* under which he/she would commit a crime and then perhaps drive off suitably (or, rather, unsuitably) inebriated.

Having established that the non-offending population is not perfect, how then can they be compared with the ex-offender population? The literature on the topic helps.

A recent article by Kurlychek *et al.* (2007) used police contact data from the 1942 Racine birth cohort to determine whether individuals whose last criminal record occurred many years ago exhibit a higher risk of acquiring future criminal records than do individuals with no criminal record at all. Their findings suggest that there is little to no distinguishable difference between these groups after about seven years. How did they reach this conclusion?

In their work they consider a data set of 670 males born in Racine, Wisconsin, in 1942 and followed until age 32 (in fact, they use data from the study conducted by Shannon (1982)).

Of the 670 persons in the birth cohort, 349 individuals had at least one police contact before the age of 18 (called the 'baseline offenders') while the other 321 individuals did not (called the 'baseline non-offenders'). As Figure 8.1 shows, their work indicates that the juvenile offenders and the juvenile non-offenders exhibit important differences in the likelihood of being caught for new offences early in their adult years. So, for instance, around one in three of the juvenile offenders had a police contact in the year after their seventeenth birthday. However, a vital point also to note is that the non-offenders – that is, those with no police contacts to that point – have just under a one in ten chance of being arrested in the year after their seventeenth birthday. At this juncture the two groups are quite a distance apart in their likelihood of being arrested in the next year. However, as one can see from Figure 8.1, gradually the two lines representing the

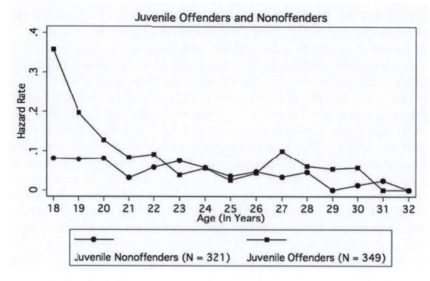

Figure 8.1 Conviction hazard rates through age 32: juvenile offenders and non-offenders
Source: Kurlychek *et al*. (2007).

two groups begin to converge. The crucial feature is the convergence between the groups by age 23. In their words – 'In any given year after the mid-20s, there appears to be little difference in offending likelihoods between juvenile offenders who have offended during early adulthood and those with no record at all' (2007: 72). In short, this 'buffer period' of around seven years since their juvenile offences is crucial in identifying the set of ex-offenders who have very similar likelihoods of any further crime as non-offenders.

These authors continue with the same logic in considering those offenders who were convicted in the early adult years (that is 18–20 years). Here the convergence seems to come later but certainly is accomplished by their late 20s.

The Kurlychek team produces some important benchmarks. However, the studies have some limitations. Take the Racine study as an example. While the focus on 'police contacts' seems appropriate, it does mean the inclusion in the 'baseline offenders' group of many who would not be involved in court proceedings. In fact, the Racine birth cohort divides almost 50/50 between 'baseline offenders' and 'baseline non-offenders' and, by including many (perhaps the majority) without convictions in the 'baseline offenders' group, the likelihood is that the overall subsequent police contacts will be lower than for a series based on court convictions. Nevertheless, the convergence pattern remains striking.

However, the most important limitation relates to the construction of crime statistics in the United States. In this study the police contact information 'was coded from the Juvenile Bureau and the Record Bureau of the Racine Police Department' (2007: 71), so offenders who move out of the area and then recidivate will not be 'captured' by this retrieval process. Hence, it gives the figures for local boys who 'make good' in the local area but masks the spectre of local boys going elsewhere and 'doing bad'. While it can be argued that there is scope for both the 'baseline offenders' and the 'baseline non-offenders' acting in this way, it would seem more likely to be an option exercised by those with something to hide.

Certainly the American studies produce some clues but in another cultural context, there may be differences. So, for example, what happens in England and Wales? The cohort studies produced by the Home Office provide the opportunity to probe this with the additional advantage of being a national series rather than the inhabitants of one small part of the United States.

Comparing the trajectories of non-offenders and convicted offenders

Figure 8.2 shows a diagram for England and Wales for the 1953 cohort that reproduces the type of plot deriving from the use of the hazard function employed by Kurlychek and her colleagues. Soothill and Francis (forthcoming) look at two periods of early convictions – aged ten but under 17 (the juvenile findings of guilt) and aged 17 but under 21 (the young adult convictions). In fact, using the data from the 1953 cohort the figure shows four trajectories – (a) those with no juvenile findings of guilt or convictions between 17 and 20 (solid line); (b) those with no juvenile findings of guilt but at least one conviction between 17 and 20 (dashed line); (c) those with juvenile findings of guilt but no convictions between 17 and 20 (dotted line); and (d) those both with findings of guilt at the juvenile court and with convictions(s) between the ages of 17 and 20 (dot dash line).

The first peak shows the likelihood of a new conviction after age 20 with over one in three members of the dot-dash line (that is, those with findings of guilt at the juvenile court and with convictions(s) between the ages of 17 and 20) having another conviction by the age of 21. In fact, at the age of 21, the four groups are in the order

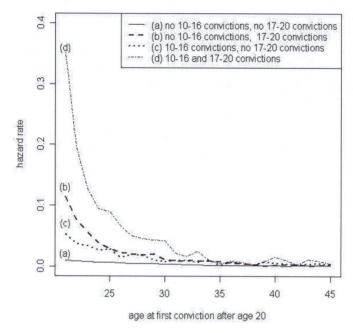

Figure 8.2 Conviction hazard rates for four groups using the 1953 Offenders Index Cohort Data

of (a) with very little likelihood of a conviction, (c) more likely with one in 20 having a conviction, (b) even more likely with one in ten having a conviction, and finally (d) with, as already stated, a one in three chance of having a conviction within that first year until 21. Gradually, however, there is a decline in the likelihood among groups (b), (c) and (d), while group (a) maintains its position with its members being most unlikely to be convicted. Eventually, the trajectories of (a), (b) and (c) seem to converge at around the age of 30 years – an age that is quite similar to that of the Racine data. In contrast, the eventual convergence of group (d) – a group whose members have findings of guilt or convictions as both a juvenile and as a young adult – with the other three groups happens at around 35 years.

It perhaps needs to be stressed that by the time the cohort reaches 35 years of age without a conviction after the age of 20, then the chances of a further conviction are then getting very small indeed. Essentially – looking at Figure 8.2 – the chances are that, at 35 years of age, there is around 1 in 200 chance for each of the group members being convicted for a further standard-list offence before the end of the next year.

One important point needs to be noted. Among the non-offending group, there continues to be a decline in the likelihood of any offending. In other words, the other offending groups are chasing an increasingly difficult target for, as they get older, the chance of being similar to the non-offending groups becomes harder. This is shown in Figure 8.2 where the chances of the non-offending group becoming criminally active as measured by a criminal conviction becomes less likely as they age.

Three emerging principles seem to stem from this work on the 1953 Home Office cohort:

1 All non-offenders have a risk of being convicted within the next year – from around 9 in 1,000 at the age of 21 years, around 6 in 1,000 at the age of 25 years, around 3 in 1,000 at the age of 30 years and around 2 in 1,000 at the age of 35 years.

2 The three groups with convictions between the ages of 10 to 20 years have very different likelihoods of a further conviction in the first few years after their twentieth birthday, but then they begin to converge.

3 While they get close, the three convicted groups do not finally converge with the non-offending group.

So what do we learn?

The particular focus of the Kurlychek *et al.* study was on 'the issue of the period for which a past criminal justice contact should be considered relevant to employment decisions' (2007: 66). In opening up the discussion about the non-offending population, they point to the dangers of assuming that this population will necessarily remain crime-free. Perhaps at this point an analogy is appropriate.

To continue to use an example from the treatment of cancer (see also Chapter 7), we can see some parallels. If a person is treated for cancer, then there is a concern whether or not there will be a further outbreak. The patient is monitored closely for perhaps five years after which it is thought that the person's chances of getting cancer again are about the same as anyone in the population of the same age and sex who has never had cancer. There are two points analogous to criminal careers. Firstly, everyone who has not had a cancer has a chance of contracting the disease. Different people will have differential risks – smoking, for example, does not help your chances – but everyone is at some sort of risk. Secondly, even the most successful treatment for cancer cannot provide the promise of a cancer-free life. The best that a cancer specialist can offer is for your chances to be similar to members of the currently cancer-free population. Similarly, in terms of criminal careers, the members of the non-offending population always have a risk of being convicted. Secondly, it is more appropriate to compare an ex-offender with a non-offender of the same age and sex and not with a saint.

We have stressed that the risk of being convicted declines with age. The results of the Soothill and Francis study indicate the expected outcomes of a comparatively high risk for all groups in their early 20s and a fairly rapid decline after that. After all, this is the story of the age–crime curve. However, this work says more. It suggests that eventually it does not seem to matter whether it was a finding of guilt *or* a conviction as a young adult which was their original downfall. If they continue to be free of crime by their late 20s, the likelihood of a further conviction is much the same and at this point gets closer to the target of the same likelihood as the non-offending population of the same age. However, if a person aged between 17 and 20 years, has both a juvenile finding of guilt *and* a conviction then such a person needs a few more crime-free years before the likelihood gets much the same as the other three groups. Nevertheless, by the age of 30 years – if they have avoided a conviction in the intervening ten years – they are all performing well in potential reconviction terms. But do the three offending groups really converge with the non-offending group?

Kurlychek and her colleagues talk of actual convergence and their diagrams suggest this happens. In contrast, Soothill and Francis (submitted) indicate that the three offending groups get close to the non-offending population but they never quite converge. Theoretically the latter result is perhaps less surprising. After all, all the adverse consequences – what Kurlychek and colleagues call 'collateral consequences' – don't suddenly disappear after around seven years. If there is a connection between the lack of employment opportunities, educational deficits and so on (which are disproportionately experienced by ex-offenders) and subsequent crime, then it is a surprise that the risk, compared with non-offenders, does in these various series approximate after seven years.

The individuals mentioned earlier whose cases were supported by the Information Commissioner's Office provide another type of evidence that – on account of their previous criminal record – they still felt stigmatised. Even after many conviction-free years since some comparatively minor infractions as youths or young people, they must have felt that their life chances continued to be diminished. Otherwise, why would they bother to take action? In other words, their criminal past, meagre though it apparently was, still caused them difficulties either at the private or public level. Indeed, perhaps for a minority with a criminal background their lifestyle becomes so diminished that they do, indeed, resort to bad and almost lost habits even after very many crime-free years. In short, is it reasonable to expect that they will, indeed, match the risk levels of non-offenders who do not have to battle against such stigmatisation? Hence, the puzzle is why the Kurlychek figures seem to produce a convergence between their 'baseline offenders' and their 'baseline non-offenders' while the series considered by Soothill and Francis – despite doing remarkably well – do not.

There could be several explanations but the main one is probably methodological. With the Kurlychek *et al.* series it is likely that more of their 'baseline offenders' than their 'baseline non-offenders' move out of the town and thus avoid the follow-up, while there are likely to be fewer such leakages in a national sample which was the source of the Soothill and Francis figures.

Policy implications

So what are the policy implications? Ultimately, it is a value judgement whether or when ex-offenders should be treated exactly like non-offenders. Certainly, using the findings of the Soothill and Francis study, it is quite a conservative position to say, for example, that it is time to wipe the slate clean after ten years if ex-offenders have managed such a significant crime-free period. By then, to answer the Kurlychek question, prior contact is no longer predictive of future criminality. In other words, this is the time that statistically ex-offenders become like non-offenders. Indeed, one perhaps needs to reflect that employers have – if ex-offenders have managed significant crime-free periods – more to fear from the non-offending population than from these ex-offenders. How does one accomplish this sleight of hand? In brief, there are so many more people in the non-offending population that they also supply more new offenders! In fact, one can calculate that 17 out of every thousand 30-year-olds who have had a conviction-free period during the previous ten years will be convicted in the next five years. Further, of those 17 persons 13 will have previously had no convictions at all and four will be from one of the three other groups with a conviction between the ages of 10 to 20 years. Whatever else, such calculations should help to preserve a sense of proportion in terms of the size of the problem.

Before implementing such a policy, one would need to try to meet the possible objections and to note some safeguards. Perhaps there are some offences which are so obnoxious or potentially harmful that we should never countenance their obliteration. But many of these are already covered by other legislation and practices. So, for example, sex offenders are subject to the sex offenders' registration scheme; those who murder are on licence for life. Perhaps there are other types of offences, even when committed as a young person, which need to be administratively tagged in some way, but the onus should be on those who wish to do so to show that they are predictive of future criminality or that knowledge of the crime needs to be retained for some reason. However, for the rest – that is, records for the vast majority of offending behaviour of youths and young persons who manage a sizeable crime-free period – we maintain they can be safely expunged. Of course, that was the rationale of the Rehabilitation of Offenders Act 1974 but, sadly, the spirit of that Act is currently being eroded. We need to remember that the greatest protection of the public is when ex-offenders become like non-offenders and we also need to be more welcoming when that transition happens.

As a keynote speaker at the 2008 British Criminology Conference, Shadd Maruna provocatively and powerfully argued for the importance of focusing on reintegration as a rite of passage. He appealed to the claims of anthropologists that there are some social and developmental transitions that simply cannot be experienced without the involvement of ritual and rites of passage, stressing that ex-offender reintegration may be one of these. Certainly, as he pointed out in his talk, 'the punishment process involves an inordinate amount of ritual behaviour, from the drama of the courtroom to the elaborate de-individuation processes involved in institutionalization' (Maruna 2008: 1). Curiously, however, when it comes to reintegration, 'all such rituals are typically foregone and efforts are made to make the process as stealthy and private as possible'.

Maruna's plea for a reintegration ritual seemed to produce the audience reaction of puzzlement and the rather ritualistic reluctance among many academics to embrace notions of change! However, Maruna is arguing that reintegration into society might mean something more than just physical resettlement, that is finding jobs and accommodation, which may not be sufficient conditions both to feel and to be seen once again as non-offenders. He suggests we may need to recognise much more about 'a symbolic element of moral inclusion involving forgiveness, redemption and reconciliation'. His message is that ritual may be required to foster such dynamics. Rather ambitiously, he concluded his paper by exploring what a reintegration ritual might look like.

There are, in fact, various possibilities. However, at this stage one need not get involved in such details. The first step is to understand and agree that everyone, with few exceptions, should have the opportunity to earn the right at some point to have statutory bars to jobs or other services lifted, as well as to have civil rights and public benefits reinstated.

Conclusions

Kurlychek and her colleagues have produced pioneering work to 'determine whether individuals whose last criminal record occurred many years ago exhibit a higher risk of acquiring criminal records than do individuals with no record at all' (2007: 64). It was pioneering on at least three grounds. Firstly, it brought into focus the likelihood of future crime by *non-offenders* which is an area that has been neglected. Secondly, their evidence suggested that, after a significant crime-free period, 'there is little to no distinguishable difference between [the non-offending and offending] groups' in terms of subsequent convictions (ibid.). Thirdly, their evidence links with policy implications that 'after a given period of remaining crime free, it may be prudent to wash away the brand of "offender" and open up more legitimate opportunities to this population' (Kurlychek *et al.* 2006: 483–4).

The statistical gaze produces a clear picture. However, in getting policies adopted following an acceptance of our results and those of Kurlychek *et al.*, it is crucial to consider the potential credibility gap. While statistically, many, if not most, released murderers are low risk, for example, this is probably not the public perception. The relationship between perception and reality needs to be addressed. The media, for example, trade in developing and endorsing stereotypes which may be divorced from reality. In brief, we need to know much more about the public perceptions of risk and how these can be brought closer to the evidence. Certainly in pursuing an educative role, criminologists interested in criminal career research have a long way to go.

Chapter 9

What's wrong with criminal careers? Moving forward

Concluding a book is a challenging task. It is tempting to be cautious and simply regurgitate what has gone before. Others may strike out boldly with new extravagant claims which attract attention. We aim to be cautiously bold! Our title 'What's wrong with criminal careers?' is perhaps suitably arresting. However, it tells only half the story. We need first to recognise what has been achieved in the two decades or so since criminal careers became a distinctive sub-discipline of criminology. The two volumes of Blumstein and his colleagues in 1986 is a good marker of this transition. Before that, of course, there had been some important work, particularly the pioneering efforts of Sheldon and Eleanor Glueck, which still has resonance. However, since the mid-1980s there has been a debate, both implicit and explicit, about how one can most appropriately study criminal careers.

We have explained the 'Great Debate' and believe in the importance of longitudinal studies in positing the 'Great Solution'. We have also emphasised the crucial importance of understanding the separate, but related, issues of onset, persistence and desistance. Similarly, our review of the topics of specialisation and prediction and risk has highlighted a number of issues that criminologists need to confront. Further, we have tried to move the debate forwards by emphasising that making a definitive distinction between offenders and non-offenders is unwise. Indeed, everyone should be included in the study of criminal careers.

Much has been achieved by researchers within the ambit of criminal careers, particularly with the use of data from longitudinal studies. However, we want to use the remainder of this chapter as an opportunity to highlight some further issues. We maintain that there are still traditional issues to address as well as contemporary approaches to challenge and future possibilities to embrace. We cannot consider them all, but two matters stand out. First, the issue of heredity versus environment still has not been fully resolved. Secondly, the reluctance to recognise the importance of social change needs to be highlighted.

Heredity versus environment

This is a familiar chestnut in social science. First, it is perhaps useful to try to clarify the terms. Environment is normally taken to be the host of factors which influence a child's upbringing, including parental rearing, neighbourhood and community effects. Genetic effects, on the other hand, are taken to be inherited factors through the effect of genes on behaviour. In criminology, its founding father, Cesare Lombroso, in effect introduced the issue. The story is a familiar one. Lombroso rejected the established Classical School, an approach which embraced free will and essentially recognised crime as a social construction. Lombroso introduced the positivist revolution which popularly dates from the publication in 1876 of *L'Uomo delinquente*. The new positivist programme focused not on the *crime*, but on the *criminal*; it did not assume rationality, free will and choice (typical concepts within the classical debate); instead, determinism – with biological, psychological or social constraints – challenged the notion of individual choice. This new tradition began to identify the criminal as a special person or a member of a special class (Soothill *et al.* 2002: 2). In brief, Lombroso started a debate which has had reverberations in the discipline ever since. However, it is only recently that the debate has been reopened, for in many respects the issue has been tucked away and not been fully discussed. Most criminologists have been ashamed of their founding father and feel that Lombroso set criminology on the wrong journey. It is often regarded as a past that needs to be buried. However, more recently, Lombroso's contributions have been reappraised. The stereotype that he simply talks of 'big ears and big noses' has been replaced by a greater recognition of his subtleties. Gatti, for instance, in a plenary address at the 2007 European Criminology Conference in Bologna and also in an earlier paper (Gatti and Verde 2004), stressed that there were many more facets to Lombroso's work than most commentators had appreciated. Certainly the resurgence of interest in genetics has encouraged more focus on earlier scholars who, implicitly or explicitly, have something to say about the importance of heredity. In fact, genetics potentially resurrects the notion of biological determinism in its strong form. Further, one cannot deny that genetics has become important in many other fields and criminology – which has largely had a tradition developed since the early Chicago School of an environmental thrust in seeking explanations – needs to meet the challenge.

Most criminologists seem to be in denial, either failing to recognise the general impact that genetics is making or denying its importance for criminology. Denial is understandable for the scientific arguments are complex. However, denial is a mistake. Genetics has the potential to be an explosive issue in the matter of understanding criminal careers. It provides a simple solution that can be readily embraced by the tabloids, even if criminologists are not interested. The solution provides comfortable reading for many in suggesting that criminals are somehow different by having a gene that is different from the rest of us. The explanation becomes part of the Lombrosian tradition that criminals are intrinsically different from conforming members of society. In policy terms, however, the implications are more serious. A 'faulty' gene implies that little or nothing can be done about the problem. It is a fatalistic and pessimistic conclusion.

One needs to establish a position which is less ostrich-like. Genetics needs to have a place in the House of Criminology for, as we have stated here and elsewhere (Soothill *et al.* 2002), the discipline needs to be multi-disciplinary in the fullest sense. However, disciplinary imperialism, particularly with a deterministic slant, is not helpful. Elsewhere, we have argued that these attempts at what Soothill (2005) calls 'capturing criminology' are doomed. Crime and criminal behaviour are too complex to be explained by just one perspective. Nevertheless, one still needs to estimate justly a particular discipline's potential contribution to criminology and to the understanding of criminal careers in particular.

There is much effort being expended on genetic research and perhaps one should be cautious by taking a provisional position, but the evidence is beginning to be persuasive. Crime covers a very broad range of activity and, in trying to assess the worth of a genetic explanation, one perhaps needs to consider its potentially stronger claims by focusing upon a type of crime that seems more likely to have genetic links. Violence seems an appropriate candidate to consider. The reports of a recent discussion meeting of the Royal Society on 'The neurobiology of violence: implications for prevention and treatment' (Hodgins *et al.* 2008) seems a good place to start.

There are methodological issues to consider. As Loeber and Pardini stress:

> The majority of investigations of neurobiological factors have been cross sectional (or retrospective). As a consequence, conceptualisations about the dependent variable of aggression/ violence have been mostly static rather than dynamic and have not reflected individuals' developmental changes in aggression and violence during the life course as evident from longitudinal studies. (2008: 2499).

In short, examining the evidence from longitudinal studies is crucial.

The stakes are high. The WHO report on Violence and Health (World Health Organisation 2002) suggested that each year over 1.6 million are killed through violence and, thus, violence prevention is one of the most important of global concerns. There has been a plethora of studies indicating the political, social, psychological and economic risk factors for violence, but we now need to clarify the possible importance of biological risk factors as a predisposition to violence. Some strong claims are emerging. Indeed, Moffitt (2005) claims that many environmental risk factors that are traditionally thought to be social may actually reflect genetic vulnerability. Viding and her colleagues (2008: 2519) perceptively suggest, 'The question is not really: "Is it in their genes?" or "what environmental factors are to blame?" It is: how do genetic and environmental factors interact to produce specific types of AB [antisocial behaviour]?' In fact, to discover how the gene-environment interplay actually works, a focus on twin and adoptive research into the nature and nurture issue is crucial.

As Viding *et al.* (2008) stress, the twin method is a natural experiment that relies on the different levels of genetic relatedness between MZ or monozygotic (identical twins produced by the splitting of a single egg) and DZ or dizygotic (non-identical twins produced from separate eggs) twin pairs to estimate the contribution of genetic and environmental factors to individual differences in any behaviour of interest. The basic premise of the twin method is that, if identical twins who share 100 per cent of their genetic material appear more similar on a measure than fraternal twins who share on average 50 per cent of their genetic material (like any siblings), then one can infer that there are genetic influences on the behaviour in question. In a similar manner, in adoption studies, the occurrence of behaviour may be compared between adoptive and biological relatives. However, because adoptions have become much less common since the 1970s, most quantitative genetic studies designed in recent years have used the twin method.

The statistical methods to probe the data are complex – Plomin *et al.* (2008) is a useful source. However, Viding *et al.* (2008: 2520) emphasise two important points that are relevant to our later discussion on other issues. Firstly, all the estimates about relative heredity and environmental contributions 'derived from both twin and adoption data pertain to a particular population at a particular time; *should the environmental circumstances change dramatically then so would the proportion of variance accounted for by genetic/environmental factors*' (emphasis added). In short, these authors recognise that social change – the second issue which we wish to highlight – may be important.

Twin and adoption research, of course, has had its critics. As Viding *et al.* (2008: 2520) note, 'twin studies have been criticized on account of equal environments assumption (EEA) and representativeness of twins, while the adoption studies have been criticized on account of representativeness of adoptive families and resultant restricted environmental variance'. Rutter (2005: 41–4) usefully considers these in detail. In fact, definitions of 'environment' are contentious and Viding *et al.* (2008: 2524) suggest that 'the challenge for social scientists is to perfect environmental measurement'. There are certainly problems with the approach but the crucial question is whether the potential flaws fundamentally undermine the conclusions. We suspect not.

Viding and colleagues report on a range of relevant studies, but the conclusions seem to point in a similar direction in relation to behavioural studies which are closest to our criminological interests. It is the gene–environment interaction or, as it is technically known, G × E, which is crucial. To follow Rutter, the G × E refers to genetically influenced individual differences in the sensitivity to specific environmental factors. An example – shown in Box 9.1 – illustrates the complexity of the ideas that have to be grappled with in order to gain a full understanding of the issues. However, we need to move from the world of twins and adopted children to its wider implications.

What emerges is that the crucial ingredient for future trouble seems to be – at least for conduct disorder – the combination of a genetic predisposition and a high-risk environment. However, what also seems to be emerging is that a low-risk environment may

---

Box 9.1   Gene–environment interaction (G × E)

Within twin design, gene-environment interaction (G × E) can be demonstrated when response to environmental risk occurs as a function of genetic vulnerability. Those MZ (identical) twins whose co-twin is affected with a disorder are at the highest risk of developing any disorder that has a genetic component which responds to environmental risk. The DZ (non-identical) twins whose co-twin is affected are at the second highest risk to develop the disorder. The DZ twins with an unaffected co-twin are less vulnerable, but show a higher genetic risk than the MZ twins with an unaffected co-twin.

Comparing twin pairs with different levels of genetic vulnerability, Jaffee *et al.* (2005) studied child conduct problems in physically maltreated and non-maltreated individuals. In line with the G × E hypothesis they found that maltreated MZ twins with an affected (i.e. antisocial) co-twin were at the highest risk of developing conduct problems after physical maltreatment, while the MZ twins with unaffected co-twins showed the lowest risk of developing conduct problems. The DZ twins with affected and unaffected co-twins fell in between the two types of MZ pairs, as predicted.

Adapted from Viding *et al.* (2008: 2524).

---

well moderate an adverse genetic predisposition. This finding is important to conjure with. While – to date – one cannot do much about the genetic component, the environmental component is open to change. In other words, genetic risk can be effectively moderated by environmental intervention and leads to such prescriptions as proposing that 'at-risk families should be monitored and helped regardless of the child's or parent's genotype' (Viding *et al.* 2008: 2524). This quotation leads to two points. Firstly, does the genetic information therefore add anything? The protagonists argue that 'even if environmental interventions are already provided, the scope to make them better lies within better understanding of the mechanisms of gene-environment interplay' (ibid.). Greater understanding is always useful, but the application in this case is not perhaps so clear.

The second point to make is that the 'environmental interventions' conventionally discussed seem rather limited. 'Treatment' usually seems to consist of encouraging positive intervention with parents. Viding *et al.* (2008: 2524) argues that 'early intervention strategies have potentially substantial cost benefits for the tax payer. High quality intervention has been shown to be cost effective in the US (Schweinhart and Weikart 1998)'. However, one also needs to take on board the criticisms of early intervention which have been discussed earlier (see Chapter 7). In fact, there is more to 'environmental interventions' than simply a direct focus on parents. We need to recognise that 'environment' can encompass a range of wider factors such as social structure and culture.

The focus on individuals has, of course, been the logic of the study of criminal careers. Criminal careers seem to be about individuals and the importance of wider social factors can be easily overlooked or downplayed. Genetics certainly needs to find its rightful place within the understanding of criminal careers, but a greater focus on sociological issues is perhaps more pressing. In short, the increasing dominance of psychology and the psychological approach within criminology needs to be viewed with caution.

The psychological tradition tends to seek explanations within the individual rather than from the context of broader society. So it is perhaps not surprising that this tradition re-emerged strongly within criminology at a time when conservativism in its narrow political sense as well as in its wider cultural sense was rampant. The 'treatment' recommended by psychology tends to move towards recalcitrant parents, as we have stressed above, rather than encouraging a focus on wider social concerns. It is, of course, cheaper to monitor 'at-risk families' than to try to do something about the wider structural inequalities within society that produce social tensions at both the societal and individual levels.

Life course or developmental criminology is part of this burgeoning influence within both criminal careers and criminology in general. It has been a very helpful contribution in identifying changes within an individual over time in contradistinction to the Gottfredson and Hirschi insistence that there is little such change over time. However, without dismissing the important contributions of developmental criminology, we also need to embrace other aspects of explanation which will contribute towards a fuller understanding of criminal careers. In brief, we need to consider social change but, in order to do so in relation to criminal careers, there is much to consider. There are both technical and empirical issues to confront. The technical issue concerns attempts to measure individual behaviour in the context of social change.

Age, period and cohort effects

More specifically, the technical issue lies in trying to separate out the different effects of age, year (or period) and cohort. Smith (2002) outlines the distinctions in the following way. Age effects are deemed changes that occur as an individual proceeds through the life cycle regardless of time period and location. Year (or period) effects are described as changes over historic time that affect all individuals regardless of age, and cohort effects are seen as effects affecting all individuals sharing a common experience such as being born at the same time and passing through changing society at the same ages. Cohort effects might be observed when younger generations are committing more crime more frequently than other generations, whereas period effects might be observed when proportionately more crime is being committed by all ages in particular years. The separation of these effects can help to inform political debate – for example, changing offending patterns through period effects may be due to factors such as legislative changes in the criminal justice system and local factors such as unemployment, whereas cohort effects can be used by commentators to explain how some generations of children can increase offending rates by being more criminal than other generations (Hymowitz 1999).

Most academic studies of offending behaviour have been based on the analysis of single longitudinal cohorts of offender histories. However, these datasets, by definition, do not allow investigations of cohort effects. There have been some sophisticated attempts to separate out the effects of age, period and cohort on criminal activity (e.g. Francis *et al.* 2004a), but it is not easy to understand the complexities of modelling official crime rates through an age-period-cohort statistical model. However, there are other more modest attempts which focus on particular offences. Soothill *et al.* (2004), for instance, use the exemplars of burglary, robbery and violence, and drugs offences, all of which have been the source of some concern in recent years.

Using six birth cohorts derived from the Offenders Index (see Chapter 2 for a description – the six birth cohorts are born in 1953, 1958, 1963, 1968, 1973 and 1978 respectively), Soothill *et al.* (2004) focus on the crime profile of offending at the defining moment of the first criminal conviction. They consider changes over time in two ways: changes within a birth cohort and changes between birth cohorts. They begin to indicate how age, period and cohort effects may all come into play in different ways. First, burglary unequivocally shows the effects of age. In other words, the proportions of new recruits convicted of burglary are always high – for each of the six birth cohorts – at the younger ages, with the proportions of burglary new starters declining rapidly after the age of 15 years.

In contrast, the curves for robbery and violence show a rather different pattern. In fact, for each successive cohort, the *proportions* convicted of robbery and violence increase in relation to age, i.e. each successive cohort seems increasingly attracted to robbery and violence as their entry offence to the criminal justice system. However, here interpretation becomes crucial and one must try to distinguish between a possible behavioural change (that is, people's behaviour is changing) or a system change (the criminal justice system itself is changing). In fact, a behavioural change would suggest a cohort effect, with successive cohorts increasingly focusing on this more serious offence. In contrast, a system change relates to period effects – changes in the criminal justice system which mediate such apparent changes in behaviour. While not mutually exclusive, the latter explanation that would reflect the gradually increasing use of discretionary strategies, particularly for offences *other than* robbery and violence, is perhaps more persuasive in this case. The possibilities in this example are considered more fully elsewhere (Soothill *et al.* 2004), but certainly trying to understand whether apparent changes are the result of actual changes in behaviour or the effect of changes in the system is crucial for policy-making.

The final exemplar of drugs offences produces yet another pattern. The analysis seems to demonstrate a mixture of period and cohort effects. Patterns and proportions of drug use are changing from cohort to cohort; in addition, drugs policy and cautioning are changing over time. In other words, since the mid-1970s, the proportions convicted of drug offences at their first conviction have risen, irrespective of gender, or age. In fact, this conforms to what one might have expected from the common knowledge of the increase in drug use and convictions.

The work by Soothill *et al.* (2004) recognises there are potentially important age, period and cohort effects that need to be considered in discussing change. The results in this study have important theoretical implications. If having a criminal conviction is a crucial defining moment in a criminal career and the nature of the offence is involved in the defining process, then one needs to recognise that there are important and significant shifts over time. As they stress (Soothill *et al.* 2004: 417), Garfinkel (1956), Becker (1963) and Matza (1969) have all powerfully argued in their different ways that having a conviction results in a person taking stock. If having a conviction helps to create a criminal identity, it can be argued that contemporary criminal recruits are likely to have been convicted of a more serious criminal offence than earlier criminal recruits in establishing this identity. Whatever else, we have, hopefully, clarified why we think there should be a much greater focus on the changing patterns of offending behaviour (see also Soothill *et al.* 2002, Francis *et al.* 2004b).

Moving forward – the importance of social change

In this chapter, we have tried to confront the question of whether the foundations laid down in criminal careers research to date are sound ones or whether those interested in criminal careers research need to rip up the foundations and make a totally fresh start. In brief, while we believe that there has been much of value that has emerged from the investment in criminal careers research, where we differ is that we do not concur with the notion that we simply need more of the same. It is our view that we need to widen our horizons both literally and figuratively. In contrast, most commentators seem to be happy to continue to plough the same furrows.

However, we argue that one needs to be bolder in trying to understand criminal careers. Certainly, the recognition that the study should be truly inter disciplinary is one way forward. We have pointed to the need to incorporate genetics into the web of explanation. In a similar way, sociologists – who are perhaps among those most likely to dismiss the claims of genetics – are also fighting for their rightful place in the study of criminal careers. In a field which seems to be increasingly dominated by psychologists, the world view of sociologists should be recognised. Certainly some psychologists are importantly dynamic in recognising change within an individual over time but most psychologists are remarkably static in thinking about societal change. There are exceptions, of course. David Farrington has insisted since the late 1980s that to fully understand change, one needs to follow a series of cohorts longitudinally over time. He seems to be thinking about taking a series of cohorts over time within the same society, but we also need to know differences between societies. This, of course, is an area fraught with difficulties. Perhaps a brief focus on some serious crimes can be illustrative.

Heinous crimes and national image

The truly appalling crimes of Josef Fritzl in relation to his daughter Elizabeth and the seven children she bore him has been held up as illustrative of a much darker side of Austria (*The Independent*, 30 April 2008: 'Heinous crimes and national image') with the media reminding the world that Austria was the birthplace of Adolf Hitler, a country where many hailed the Anschluss with enthusiasm, and the first member of the European Union to admit a far-right party to government. However, *The Independent* leader writer argues that 'to conclude from this, however, that Austria and Josef Fritzl were somehow uniquely made for each other takes an exercise in national stereotyping too far'. Nevertheless, the leader writer also admits that 'Austria might seem to have more than its fair share of cruel and devious men with a penchant for a particular type of crime', reminding the readers of the shocking case two years earlier of Natascha Kampusch – a young Austrian girl kidnapped on her way to school and kept in a nearby basement for eight years. Elsewhere, Alison Pearson of the *Daily Mail* maintained that this small country of Austria had seen 'not just one, but *three* girl-in-a-cellar scandals over the past three years' (*Daily Mail*, 30 April 2008). Usefully, *The Independent* leader writer, in contradistinction to suggesting something peculiar happening simply in Austria, asks us to remember Fred West and the torture chamber that he and his wife kept in their terraced house in Gloucester which was all dramatically revealed in the early 1990s, adding that 'it was coincidence, but a telling one, that the Fritzl case burst into the news as a 68-year-old man was arrested in connection with the discovery of concealed chambers and human remains at a former orphanage in Jersey. No nation has a monopoly on cruelty.' The final sentiment is absolutely right but the form of cruelty may vary markedly from country to country. Alison Pearson reminds us that 'Elfriede Jelinek, Austria's Nobel Prize-winning novelist, has been criticised in the past for her "hysterical" portraits of a repressive society which breeds sexual perversity, suppressed violence and human degradation'. As Pearson points out, Jelinek may not have been hysterical after all.

Forms of extreme crime do vary from country to country. Serial killing is an obvious instance. The rate of serial killing in the United States is much higher than elsewhere. Is this a statistical fluke or does the United States have more psychologically flawed persons than most other countries? When one of us was trying to suggest at a criminological conference that the high rates in the United States may be linked to its societal structure and culture, an American criminologist countered by saying that the rates were probably similar elsewhere but the serial killers had just not been caught in these other countries with lower rates. Such responses illustrate both a country and a criminology that is in denial.

In trying to identify serial killers – a task which is obviously crucial for their detection – there is largely an appeal to psychological explanations. However, the question of why more serial killers seem to exist in some historical times than others and in some countries but not others may be difficult to confront using explanations which have purchase only at the individual level. We believe that more recourse to explanations at the societal or structural level is necessary, but these have tended to be neglected (Soothill, forthcoming).

One of the problems is that the so-called 'experts' in the area of serial killing – as in the study of criminal careers in general – are largely psychologists or psychiatrists who tend to individualise social problems. They look for the cause of aggression within the individual and tend to regard the source of the problems as wrapped in some form of psychopathology. However, this cannot explain why there are significant variations in the rates of serial killing over time and between societies.

A Canadian anthropologist, Elliott Leyton (1986), has probably provided the most useful insights beyond an individualistic analysis of this apparently increasing social problem. In his book, *Hunting Humans: The Rise of the Modern Multiple Murderer*, he argues that the multiple murderer is in many senses the embodiment of the central themes in his (and, much more unusually, her) civilisation as well as a reflection of that civilisation's critical tensions. The implications of his analysis, published in the mid-1980s, were quite simply political dynamite. In a world in the 1980s when the 'American dream' was being glorified as the Communist Bloc was so dramatically crumbling, Leyton posed a fundamental challenge to a dream which was becoming a nightmare with respect to serial killing. In brief, Leyton suggested that American society might provide the key to the development and existence of cultural forms which actually fed this nightmare. There has largely been an 'ostrich response' to this provocative thesis, which was less likely to excite the interest of the news media than the hint of a criminal gene.

Elsewhere (Soothill, forthcoming) we have considered why there is more serial killing in some countries than others. The differences between countries in terms of the numbers of serial killers can be quite striking. Certainly the contrast between England and Germany in the 1930s is thought-provoking. As far as can be ascertained, no serial killers were captured or at large in Britain during this time, whereas at least a dozen examples were recorded in Germany.

So what might structural and cultural explanations of the phenomenon look like? Certainly in Germany in the 1930s curious cultural and structural arrangements came together rather dangerously. The structural conditions were problematic for some groups. The aftermath of the First World War produced new stresses and tensions in Germany, particularly for the aspiring lower-middle and working classes. Recruitment into Hitler's Brown Shirts and various Fascist groups was one solution for many of the frustrated and disenchanted. However, the focus here is on serial killing and sexual murder.

Tatar's book, *Lustmord: Sexual Murder in Weimar Germany* (1995), produces some fascinating clues as to what happened in Germany between the Wars which may have had a bearing on the issue. In focusing on the politically turbulent Weimar Republic, she produces evidence of one of the most disturbing images of twentieth-century western culture: that of the mutilated female body. The images abound in painting, literature and films of the time, but Tatar argues that this history has remained a closely guarded secret. She points, for example, to 'the sheer number of canvases from the 1920s with the title *Lustmord (Sexual Murder)*'. In examining these images of sexual murder, she produces a powerful study of how art and murder have intersected in the sexual politics of culture in Weimar Germany. In fact, Tatar shows male artists openly identifying with real-life sexual murderers: George Grosz posed as Jack the Ripper in a photograph with his model and future wife as the target of his knife. Further, there are the corpses of disembowelled prostitutes in Otto Dix's paintings and so on. Tatar has a complex argument, but she essentially suggests that 'violence against women reflects more than gender trouble and can be linked to the war trauma, to urban pathologies, and to the politics of cultural production and biological reproduction' (dust cover). This recognition of the importance of both structure *and* culture is an important contribution towards helping us to understand why some societies provide the conditions under which serial killing flourishes.

Serial killing is, thankfully, an unusual crime but we need to become much more cognisant of the social context and the possibility of social change in relation to all types of crime. We need to remember that many of the people coming before the courts today would not have done so at the turn of the twentieth century before the widespread use of the motor car. Similarly, the current enthusiasm for the use of the Internet has many advantages but it may also change the form and content of crime.

A dynamic view of the social environment

In understanding how the social context may impact on crime, we argue for a dynamic view of the social environment, which is important at a number of levels. For example, technological advances, such as those that have led to widespread use of the Internet, have introduced new opportunities for criminal behaviour and led to new types of crime. Indeed, this is reflected in the content of criminology courses: while modules on 'cybercrime' would have been unheard of a few decades ago, they are increasingly commonplace.

At a different level, changes in the wider society will arguably have an impact on crimes that already exist. At the time of writing, there is much concern about the global 'credit crunch' and the economic crisis facing many western nations. Just days after the Chancellor, Alistair Darling, declared that the UK was facing its worst economic crisis in 60 years, a draft Home Office letter was leaked to the British media in September 2008, predicting that crime levels would rise as a result of the economic downturn (*Daily Telegraph*, 3 September 2008). Specifically, the draft letter to Downing Street (which had not been cleared by the Home Secretary) forecast more smuggling of fuel, alcohol and tobacco. It also predicted increased hostility towards migrants as a result of heightened competition for employment. In addition, the letter suggested that, based on experience of the British recession in the 1990s, both property crime, such as burglary, and violent crime may well go up. Interestingly, the letter further suggested that an economic downturn could prevent the alcohol industry from reducing their prices which could have a knock-on effect in reducing drink-related violence in town centres. It was reported that cocaine use would also be expected to fall as people's finances were stretched (*BBC News*, 1 September 2008). For the purposes of the current discussion, this leaked document clearly highlights how changes in the wider society, and in particular economic difficulties, may be absolutely crucial in understanding changes in crime rates over time.

If we place these two processes in the context of our earlier discussion of age, period and cohort effects, we would identify different effects for each. Increasing criminal use of the Internet would be a cohort effect. New generations are far more comfortable with the technology and its potential for illegality than are older generations. The credit crunch, however, is a period effect which affects all generations equally. Increases in traditional crimes of property are likely across the age range.

Conclusions

In our view, the kinds of social and economic changes referred to above are important not only for understanding changes in societal crime rates, but also for understanding individual criminal careers. This brings us back to the first theme discussed in this chapter and the focus on heredity versus environment. As we argued above, commentators are increasingly recognising the importance of gene and environment (or G × E) interactions in understanding the development of criminal behaviour within individuals (e.g. Viding *et al.* 2008), and criminologists must take on board the contribution of genetics. Indeed, they neglect this area at their peril. That said, current understandings of 'society' and 'environment' in the emerging research agenda on gene–environment interactions seem worryingly static and are often poorly defined. It is at this point that criminologists, particularly those working within the sociological tradition, may have something very useful to offer in arguing for a dynamic view of society and a dynamic view of environment.

If genetic risk can be effectively moderated by a low-risk environment, it seems that our future focus of attention must surely be on improving the social environment and ensuring that the societal conditions do not facilitate criminality. Thus, while taking on board the biological factors associated with offending behaviour, the wider society and the social environment become absolutely key. Herein lies the challenge for criminal careers researchers. To date, much research on criminal careers has successfully highlighted the possibility of change within offending behaviour and has adopted a dynamic understanding of the individual. This dynamic approach must now be extended to society, with questions being raised about whether research on one generation at a particular time period is equally applicable to later generations living in very different eras. This also leads on to the question of whether ongoing longitudinal research, which we have earlier described as the 'gold standard' in methodological terms, may produce out-of-date and obsolete findings by the time the study comes to an end.

In taking account of the social context, we also need to increasingly consider whether findings from one country or continent are applicable across international borders. There are some commendable efforts to do just this, for example, in the area of recidivism among ex-prisoners. O'Donnell *et al.* (2008) note that 'the question of whether and how rates of recidivism may vary across nations is an important one' (p. 141), and they highlight a number of societal features that may impact on this. These features range from the availability of jobs and drug treatment to public perceptions of ex-prisoners and the degree to which people are willing to accept living near or employing ex-prisoners. O'Donnell *et al.* report that there is currently an effort to field large-scale recidivism studies in several European nations simultaneously, using a consistent format for data capture, measurement and analysis. As the authors observe, 'this is precisely the kind of endeavour needed to deepen the reservoir of knowledge about how particular societal conditions help or hinder the ability of released prisoners to turn away from crime' (2008: 142). In our view, this emphasis on the importance of societal conditions across time and space arguably charts a very productive way forward for criminological research in general, and for research on criminal careers in particular.

References

Adams, T. (2006) 'Forgive me, my sons, for I have sinned', *The Observer*, 30 April.

Albrecht, H.J. and Moitra, S. (1988) 'Escalation and specialization – a comparative analysis of patterns in criminal careers', in G. Kiser and I. Geissler (eds), *Crime and Criminal Justice*. Freiburg: Max Planck Institute.

Armstrong, T.A. (2008) 'Exploring the impact of changes in group composition on trends in specialization', *Crime and Delinquency*, 54: 366–89.

Barbaree, H.E., Langton, C.M. and Peacock, E.J. (2006) 'The factor structure of static actuarial items: its relation to prediction', *Sexual Abuse: A Journal of Research and Treatment*, 18: 207–26.

Barry, M. (2006) *Youth Offending in Transition: The Search for Social Recognition*. London: Routledge.

Bateman, T. (2005) 'Reducing child imprisonment: a systemic challenge', *Youth Justice*, 5 (2): 91–105.

Beck, U. (1992) *Risk Society: Towards a New Modernity*. London: Sage.

Becker, H. (1963) *Outsiders: Studies in the Sociology of Deviance*. New York: Free Press.

Blokland, A.J. (2005) *Crime Over the Life Span: Trajectories of Criminal Behavior in Dutch Offenders*. Leiden: Netherlands Institute for the Study of Crime and Law Enforcement.

Blumstein, A. and Cohen, J. (1987) 'Characterizing criminal careers', *Science*, 237 (4818): 985–91.

Blumstein, A., Cohen, J. and Farrington, D.P. (1988a) 'Criminal career research: its value for criminology', *Criminology*, 26: 1–35.

Blumstein, A., Cohen, J. and Farrington, D.P. (1988b) 'Longitudinal and criminal career research: further clarifications', *Criminology*, 26: 57–74.

Blumstein, A., Cohen, J., Roth, J.A. and Visher, C.A. (1986a) *Criminal Careers and 'Career Criminals'*, Vol. I. Washington, DC: National Academy Press.

Blumstein, A., Cohen, J., Roth, J.A. and Visher, C.A. (eds) (1986b) *Criminal Careers and 'Career Criminals'*, Vol. II. Washington, DC: National Academy Press.

Blumstein, A., Cohen, J., Somnath, D. and Moitra, S.D. (1988) 'Specialization and seriousness during adult criminal careers', *Journal of Quantitative Criminology*, 27: 303–45.

Brown, S. (1998) *Understanding Youth and Crime: Listening to Youth?* Buckingham: Open University Press.

Budd, T., Sharp, C. and Mayhew, P. (2005) *Offending in England and Wales: First Results from the 2003 Crime and Justice Survey*, Home Office Research Study No. 275. London: Home Office.

Burnett, R. (1992) *The Dynamics of Recidivism: Summary Report*. Oxford: University of Oxford, Centre for Criminological Research.

Bushway, S. (2008) *Are All Individuals Equally Risky?* Paper presented to the Conference on 'Analysis of Criminal Career Data', London, 24 January. Online at http://www.maths.lancs.ac.uk/ncrm/workshops/januaryconference

Carrington, P.J., Matarazzo, A. and de Souza, P. (2005) *Court Careers of a Canadian Birth Cohort*. Ottawa: Statistics Canada, Canadian Centre for Justice Statistics.

Caspi, A. and Moffitt, I.E. (2006) 'Gene–environment interactions in psychiatry: joining forces with neuroscience', *Nature Reviews Neuroscience*, 7: 583–90.

Christoffersen, M.N., Francis, B. and Soothill, K. (2003) 'An upbringing of violence? Identifying the likelihood of violent crime among the 1966 birth cohort in Denmark', *Journal of Forensic Psychiatry*, 14 (2): 367–81.

Christoffersen, M.N., Soothill, K. and Francis, B. (2005) 'Who is at most risk of becoming a rapist?', *Journal of Scandinavian Studies in Criminology and Crime Prevention*, 6 (1): 39–56.

Christoffersen, M.N., Soothill, K. and Francis, B. (2008) 'Risk factors for a first-time drink-driving conviction among young men: a birth cohort study of all men born in Denmark in 1966', *Journal of Substance Abuse Treatment*, 34 (4): 415–25.

Clarke, R.V. (1999) *Hot Products: Understanding, Anticipating and Reducing Demand for Stolen Goods*, Home Office Police Research Series, Paper 112. London: Home Office.

Clarke, R.V. and Cornish, D.B (1985) 'Modeling offenders' decisions: a framework for research and policy', *Crime and Justice*, 6: 147–85.

Cohen, L.E. and Felson, M. (1979) 'Social change and crime rate trends: a routine activity approach', *American Sociological Review*, 44 (4): 588–608.

Cohen, N. (2002) 'You don't have to be mad ...', *The Observer*, 27 October.

Copas, J. and Marshall, P. (1998) 'The offender group reconviction scale: a statistical reconviction score for use by probation officers', *Journal of the Royal Statistical Society Series C*, 47 (1): 159–71.

Cusson, M. and Pinsonneault, P. (1986) 'The decision to give up crime', in D.B. Cornish and R.V. Clarke (eds), *The Reasoning Criminal: Rational Choice Perspectives of Offending*. New York: Springer-Verlag.

Deane, G., Armstrong, D.P. and Felson, R.B. (2005) 'An examination of offense specialization using marginal logit models', *Criminology*, 43 (4): 955–88.

DeLisi, M. (2005) *Career Criminals in Society*. London: Sage.

Department for Children, Schools and Families (2008a) *Outcome Indicators for Children Looked After: Twelve Months to 30 September 2007, England*. London: Department for Children, Schools and Families.

Department for Children, Schools and Families (2008b) *Children Looked After in England (Including Adoption and Care-Leavers) Year Ending 31 March 2008*, Statistical First Release. London: Department for Children, Schools and Families.

Department of Health (1994) *Guidance on the Discharge of Mentally Disordered People and Their Continuing Care in the Community*, NHS Executive HSG(94)27 and LASSL(94)4. London: Department of Health.

Douglas, J.W.B., Ross, J.M., Hammond, W.A. and Mulligan, D.G. (1966) 'Delinquency and social class', *British Journal of Criminology*, 6: 294–302.

Evans, I.H. (1970) *Brewer's Dictionary of Phrase and Fable*. London: Cassell.

Ezell, M.E. (2007) 'The effect of criminal history variables on the process of desistance in adulthood among serious youthful offenders', *Journal of Contemporary Criminal Justice*, 23 (1): 28–49.

Farrall, S. and Bowling, B. (1999) 'Structuration, human development and desistance from crime', *British Journal of Criminology*, 39 (2): 252–67.

Farrell, G., Phillips, C. and Pease, K. (1995) 'Like taking candy – why does repeat victimization occur?', *British Journal of Criminology*, 35 (3): 284–399.

Farrington, D.P. (1986a) 'Stepping stones to adult criminal careers', in D. Olweus, J. Block and M. Radke-Yarrow (eds), *Development of Antisocial and Prosocial Behavior*. Orlando, FL: Academic Press.

Farrington, D.P. (1986b) 'Age and crime', in M. Tonry and N. Morris (eds), *Crime and Justice: An Annual Review of Research*, Vol. 7. Chicago: University of Chicago Press, 189–250.

Farrington, D.P. (1992) 'Criminal career research in the United Kingdom', *British Journal of Criminology*, 32: 521–36.

Farrington, D.P. (1997) 'Human development and criminal careers', in M. Maguire, R. Morgan and R. Reiner (eds), *The Oxford Handbook of Criminology*, 2nd edn. Oxford: Clarendon Press.

Farrington, D.P. (2003) 'Developmental and life-course criminology: key theoretical and empirical issues – the 2002 Sutherland Award Address', *Criminology*, 41 (2): 221–5.

Farrington, D.P. (2005) 'The integrated cognitive antisocial potential (ICAP) theory', in D.P. Farrington (ed.), *Integrated Developmental and Life-Course Theories of Offending*. New Brunswick, NJ: Transaction Publishers.

Farrington, D.P. (2007) 'Childhood risk factors and risk-focused prevention', in M. Maguire, R. Morgan and R. Reiner (eds), *The Oxford Handbook of Criminology*, 4th edn. Oxford: Oxford University Press.

Farrington, D.P. and Loeber, R. (1999) 'Transatlantic replicability of risk factors in the development of delinquency', in P. Cohen, C. Slomkowski, and L.N. Robins (eds), *Historical and Geographical Influences on Psychopathology*. Mahwah, NJ: Lawrence Erlbaum.

Farrington, D., Coid, J., Harnett, L., Jolliffe, D., Soteriou, N., Turner, R. and West, D. (2006a) *Criminal Careers and Life Successes: New Findings from the Cambridge Study in Delinquent Development*, Home Office Research Findings No. 281) London: Home Office. Online at: http://www.homeoffice.gov.uk/rds/pdfs06/r281.pdf.

Farrington, D., Coid, J., Harnett, L., Jolliffe, D., Soteriou, N., Turner, R. and West, D. (2006b) *Criminal Careers up to Age 50 and Life Success up to Age 48: New Findings from the Cambridge Study in Delinquent Development*, 2nd edn, Home Office Research Study No. 299. London: Home Office. Online at: http://www.homeoffice.gov.uk/rds/pdfs06/hors299.pdf.

Ferri, E. (1897) *Criminal Sociology*. New York: Appleton.

Fitzpatrick, C. (forthcoming) 'Looked after children and the criminal justice system', in K. Broadhurst, C. Grover, J. Jamieson and C. Mason (eds), *Safeguarding Children: Critical Perspectives*. Oxford: Blackwell.

Francis, B. and Crosland, P. (2002) *The Police National Computer and the Offenders Index: Can They Be Combined for Research Purposes?* London: Home Office. Full report available at: http://www.homeoffice.gov.uk/rds/pdfs2/pncandoir170.pdf.

Francis, B. and Soothill, K. (2000) 'Does sex offending lead to homicide?', *Journal of Forensic Psychiatry*, 11 (1): 49–61.

Francis, B. and Soothill, K. (2005) 'Explaining changing patterns of crime: a focus on burglary and age-period-cohort models', in M. Peelo and K. Soothill (eds), *Questioning Crime and Criminology*. Cullompton: Willan.

Francis, B., Liu, J. and Soothill, K. (2008) *Using the Offenders Index to Investigate Patterns of Offending*. Paper given at the 13th Governmental Statistical Service Methodology Conference, 23 June, The Congress Centre, London. Online at http://www.ons.gov.uk/about/newsroom/events/thirteenth-gss-methodology-conference--23-june-2008/programme/index.html

Francis, B., Soothill, K. and Piquero, A. R. (2007) 'Estimation issues and generational changes in modelling criminal career length', *Crime and Delinquency*, 53 (1): 84–105.

Francis, B., Soothill, K. and Ackerley, E. (2004a) 'Multiple cohort data, delinquent generations, and criminal careers', *Journal of Contemporary Criminal Justice*, 20 (2): 103–26.

Francis, B., Soothill, K. and Fligelstone, R. (2004b) 'Identifying patterns of offending behaviour: a new approach to typologies of crime', *European Journal of Criminology*, 1 (1): 47–87.

Furedi, F. (1997) *Culture of Fear*. London: Cassell.

Garfinkel, H. (1956) 'Conditions of successful degradation ceremonies', in E. Rubington and M.S. Weinberg (eds) (1968) *Deviance: An Interactionist Perspective*. London: Macmillan.

Gatti, U. (1998) 'Ethical issues raised when early intervention is used to prevent crime', *European Journal on Criminal Policy and Research*, 6: 113–32.

Gatti, U. and Verde, A. (2004) 'Cesare Lombroso: una revisione critica', *Materiali per una storia della cultura giuridica*, 2: 295–314.

Gibbons, D.C. (1973) *Society, Crime, and Criminal Careers*, 2nd edn. Englewood Cliffs, NJ: Prentice-Hall.

Gibbons, D.C. (1975) 'Offender typologies – two decades later', *British Journal of Criminology*, 15: 140–56.

Gigerenzer, G. (2002) *Reckoning with risk: learning to live with uncertainty*. Harmondsworth: Penguin.

Gigerenzer, G. (2008) *Rationality for Mortals: How People Cope with Uncertainty*. Oxford: Oxford University Press.

Glueck, S. and Glueck, E. (1950) *Unraveling Juvenile Delinquency*. New York: Commonwealth Fund.

Glueck, S. and Glueck, E. (1968) *Delinquents and Nondelinquents in Perspective*. Cambridge, MA: Harvard University Press.

Goffman, E. (1978) 'The moral career of the mental patient', in E. Rubington and M.S. Weinberg (eds), *Deviance: The Interactionist Perspective*, 3rd edn. New York: Macmillan.

Goldson, B. (2007) 'Child criminalisation and the mistake of early intervention', *Criminal Justice Matters*, 69: 8–9.

Gottfredson, M. and Hirschi, T. (1986) 'The true value of lambda would appear to be zero: an essay on career criminals, criminal careers, selective incapacitation, cohort studies and related topics', *Criminology*, 24: 213–34.

Gottfredson, M. and Hirschi, T. (1987) 'The methodological adequacy of longitudinal research on crime', *Criminology*, 25: 581–614.

Gottfredson, M. and Hirschi, T. (1988) 'Science, public policy, and the career paradigm', *Criminology*, 26: 37–55.

Gottfredson, M. and Hirschi, T. (1990) *A General Theory of Crime*. Stanford, CA: Stanford University Press.

Greenberg, D. (1991) 'Modeling criminal careers', *Criminology*, 29: 17–46.

Greenberg, D. (2006) 'Criminal careers', in E. McLaughlin and J. Muncie (eds), *The Sage Dictionary of Criminology*, 2nd edn. London: Sage.

Grove, W.M. and Meehl, P.E. (1996) 'Comparative efficiency of informal (subjective, impressionistic) and formal (mechanical, algorithmic) prediction procedures: the clinical-statistical controversy', *Psychology, Public Policy, and Law*, 2: 293–323.

Haapanen, R., Britton, L. and Croisdale, T. (2007) 'Persistent criminality and career length', *Crime and Delinquency, 53: 133–55.*

Hagell, A. and Newburn, T. (1994) *Persistent Young Offenders*. London: Policy Studies Institute.

Haldane, J.B.S. (1946) 'The interaction of nature and nurture', *Annals of Eugenics*, 13: 197–205.

Hall, O. (1948) 'The stages of the medical career', *American Journal of Sociology*, LIII (March): 243–53.

Hanson, R.K. and Thornton, D. (1999) *Static 99: Improving Actuarial Risk Assessment for Sex Offenders*, User Report 1998-01. Ottawa: Department of the Solicitor General of Canada.

Hanson, R.K., Scott, H., and Steffy, R.A. (1995) 'A comparison of child molesters and nonsexual criminals – risk predictors and long-term recidivism', *Journal of Research in Crime and Delinquency*, 32 (3): 325–37.

Hanson, R.K., Gordon, A., Harris, A.J.R., Marques, J.K., Murphy, W., Quinsey, V.L. and Seto, M. C. (2002) 'First report of the collaborative outcome data project on the effectiveness of psychological treatment for sex offenders', *Sexual Abuse: A Journal of Research and Treatment*, 14: 169–94.

Hawkins, J.D. and Catalano, R.F. (1992) *Communities That Care*. San Francisco: Jossey-Bass.

Hayslett-McCall, K. and Bernard, T.J. (2002) 'Attachment, masculinity and self-control: a theory of male crime rates', *Theoretical Criminology*, 6 (1): 5–33.

Haywood, T.W., Kravitz, H.M., Grossman, L.S., Cavanagh, J.L., Davis, J.M. and Lewis, D.A. (1995) 'Predicting the "revolving door" phenomenon among patients with schizophrenia, schizoaffective, and affective disorders', *American Journal of Psychiatry*, 152: 856–61.

Hazel, N., Hagell, A., Liddle, M., Archer, D., Grimshaw, R. and King, J. (2002) *Detention and Training: Assessment of the Detention and Training Order and Its Impact on the Secure Estate Across England and Wales*. London: Youth Justice Board.

Heidensohn, F. and Gelsthorpe, L. (2007) 'Gender and crime', in M. Maguire, R. Morgan and R. Reiner (eds), *The Oxford Handbook of Criminology*, 4th edn. Oxford: Oxford University Press.

Henderson, G.C. (1924) *Keys to Crookdom*. New York: Appleton.

Hindelang, M.J. (1971) 'Age, sex and the versatility of delinquency involvements', *Social Problems*, 18: 522–35.

Hirschi, T. and Gottfredson, M. (1983) 'Age and the explanation of crime', *American Journal of Sociology*, 89: 552–84.

Hobbs, D. (1988) *Doing the Business: Entrepreneurship, the Working Class, and Detectives in the East End of London*. Oxford: Clarendon Press.

Hobbs, D. (1995) *Bad Business: Professional Crime in Modern Britain*. Oxford: Oxford University Press.

Hobbs, D., Hadfield, P., Lister, S. and Winlow, S. (2003) *Bouncers: Violence and Governance in the Night-Time Economy*. Oxford: Oxford University Press.

Hodgins, S., Viding, E. and Plodowski, A. (eds) (2008) 'The neurobiology of violence: implications for prevention and treatment', *Philosophical Transactions of the Royal Society*, 363 (1503): 2483–622.

Home Office (2004) *Preventative Approaches Targeting Young People in Local Authority Residential Care*, Home Office Development and Practice Report 14. London: Home Office.

Home Office (2008) *Youth Crime Action Plan*. London: Home Office. Online at: http://www.homeoffice.gov.uk/documents/youth-crime-action-plan/.

Home Office Communications Directorate (2004) *Joint Inspection Report into Persistent and Prolific Offenders*. London: Home Office.

Hornung, E.W. (1899) *The Amateur Cracksman*. New York: Schribner's.

Hughes, E.C. (1945) 'Dilemmas and contradictions of status', *American Journal of Sociology*, L (March): 353–9.

Hughes, E.G. (1958) *Men and Their Work*. New York: Free Press.

Hymowitz, K. (1999) *Ready or Not: Why Treating Children as Small Adults Endangers Their Future – and Ours*. New York: Free Press.

Information Commissioner's Office (2007) 'Police told to delete old criminal conviction records', press release, 1 November, 2007. http://www.ico. gov.uk/upload/documents/pressreleases/2007/press_release_criminal_ conviction_records.pdf. http://www.ico.gov.uk/upload/documents/press releases/2007/%20press_release_criminal_conviction_records.pdf

Jaffee, S.R., Caspi, A., Moffitt, T.E., Dodge, K.A., Rutter, M., Taylor, A. and Tully, L.A. (2005) 'Nature X nurture: genetic vulnerabilities interact with physical maltreatment to promote conduct problems', *Development and Psychopathology*, 17 (1): 67–84.

Jamieson, J. (2005) 'New Labour, youth justice and the question of "respect"', *Youth Justice*, 5 (3): 180–93.

Kempf, K.L. (1987) 'Specialization and the criminal career', *Criminology*, 25: 399–420.

Kemshall, H. (2003) *Understanding Risk in Criminal Justice*. Maidenhead: Open University Press.

Klein, M.W. (1971) *Street Gangs and Street Workers*. Englewood Cliffs, NJ: Prentice-Hall.

Klein, M.W. (1984) 'Offence specialization and versatility among juveniles', *British Journal of Criminology*, 24: 185–94.

Kurlychek, M.C., Brame, R. and Bushway, S.D. (2006) 'Scarlet letters and recidivism: does an old criminal record predict future offending?, *Criminology and Public Policy*, 5: 483–504.

Kurlychek, M.C., Brame, R. and Bushway, S.D. (2007) 'Enduring risk: old criminal records and predictions of future criminal involvement', *Crime and Delinquency*, 53 (1): 64–83.

Laub, J.H. and Sampson, R.J. (2001) 'Understanding desistance from crime', in M. Tonry (ed.), *Crime and Justice: A Review of Research*, Vol. 28. Chicago: University of Chicago Press.

Laub, J.H. and Sampson, R.J. (2003) *Shared Beginnings, Divergent Lives: Delinquent Boys to Age 70*. Cambridge, MA: Harvard University Press.

Laub, J.H., Nagin, D.S. and Sampson, R.J. (1998) 'Trajectories of change in criminal offending: good marriages and the desistance process', *American Sociological Review*, 63: 225–38.

Leibrich, J. (1993) *Straight to the Point: Angles on Giving up Crime*. Otago, New Zealand: University of Otago Press.

Lettice, J. (2007) 'Spotting tomorrow's criminals in today's pushchairs', *The Register*, 29 March. Online at: http://www.theregister.co.uk/2007/03/29/blair_crime_review_children/print.html.

Leyton, E. (1986) *Hunting Humans: The Rise of the Modern Multiple Murderer*. Toronto: McClelland & Stewart.

Litwack, T.R. (2001) 'Actuarial versus clinical assessments of dangerousness', *Psychology, Public Policy and Law*, 7 (2): 409–43.

Loeber, R. and Le Blanc, M. (1990) 'Toward a developmental criminology', in M. Tonry and N. Morris (eds), *Crime and Justice: A Review of Research*, Vol. 12. Chicago: Chicago University Press.

Loeber, R. and Pardini, D. (2008) 'Neurobiology and the development of violence: common assumptions and controversies', *Philosophical Transactions of the Royal Society*, 363 (1503): 2491–503.

Loeber, R., Farrington, D.P., Stouthamer-Loeber, M., Moffitt, T.E., Caspi, A., White, H.R., Wei, E.H. and Beyers, J.M. (2003) 'The development of male offending: key findings from fourteen years of the Pittsburgh Youth Study', in T.P. Thornberry and M.D. Krohn (eds), *Taking Stock of Delinquency: An Overview of Findings from Contemporary Longitudinal Studies*. New York: Kluwer/Plenum.

Lombroso, C. (1876) *L'Uomo Delinquente*. Turin: Fratelli Bocca.

Lovald, K. and Stub, H.R. (1968) 'The revolving door: reactions to chronic drunkenness offenders to court sanctions', *Journal of Criminal Law, Criminology and Police Science*, 59 (4): 525–30.

Lundman, R.J. (1993) *Prevention and Control of Juvenile Delinquency*. New York: Oxford University Press.

Lussier, P. (2005) 'The criminal activity of sexual offenders in adulthood: revisiting the specialization debate', *Sexual Abuse: A Journal of Research and Treatment*, 17 (3): 269–92.

McAra, L. and McVie, S. (2007) 'Youth justice? The impact of system contact on patterns of desistance from offending', *European Journal of Criminology*, 4 (3): 315–45.

McCord, J. (1978) 'A thirty-year follow-up of treatment effects', *American Psychologist*, 2: 284–9.

McCord, J. (1992) 'The Cambridge-Somerville Study: a pioneering longitudinal experimental study of delinquency prevention', in J. McCord and R.E. Tremblay (eds), *Preventing Antisocial Behavior-Interventions from Birth through Adolescence*. New York: Guilford Press, pp. 196–206.

McCormack, H. (2006) 'High thresholds for referral to criminal justice system are key to cutting offending', *Community Care*, 25–31 May, 18–19.

McGloin, J.M., Sullivan, C.J., Piquero, A.R. and Pratt, T.C. (2007) 'Local life circumstances and offending specialization/versatility – comparing opportunity and propensity models', *Journal of Research in Crime and Delinquency*, 44 (3): 321–46.

Mannheim, H. (1965) *Comparative Criminology*, Vol. 1. London: Routledge & Kegan Paul.

Marshall, P. (1997) *The Prevalence of Convictions for Sexual Offending*, Home Office Research Findings No. 55. London: Home Office Research and Statistics Directorate.

Martinson, R. (1974) 'What works? Questions and answers about prison reform', *Public Interest*, 35: 22–54.

Maruna, S. (2001) *Making Good: How Ex-convicts Reform and Rebuild Their Lives*. Washington, DC: American Psychological Association.

Maruna, S. and Matravers, A. (2007) 'N = 1: criminology and the person', *Theoretical Criminology*, 11 (4): 427–42.

Matza, D. (1969) *Becoming Deviant*. Englewood Cliffs, NJ: Prentice-Hall.

Mayhew, H. (1851) *London Labour and the London Poor: A Cyclopedia of the Conditions and Earnings of Those That Will Work, Those That Cannot Work, and Those That Will Not Work*. London: George Woodfall & Son.

Milner, J. and Campbell, J. (1995) 'Prediction issues for practitioners', in J.C. Campbell (ed.), *Assessing Dangerousness: Violence by Sexual Offenders, Batterers, and Child Abusers*. Thousand Oaks, CA: Sage.

Moffitt, T.E. (1993) '"Life-course persistent" and "adolescence-limited" antisocial behavior: a developmental taxonomy', *Psychological Review*, 100: 674–701.

Moffitt, T.E. (2006) 'Life-course persistent versus adolescence-limited antisocial behaviour', in D. Cicchetti and D. Cohen (eds), *Developmental Psychopathology*, 2nd edn. New York: Wiley.

Moffitt, T.E., Caspi, A. and Rutter, M. (2006) 'Measured gene–environment interactions in psychopathology', *Perspectives on Psychological Science*, 1 (1): 5–27.

Moffitt, T.E., Caspi, A., Harrington, H. and Milne, B.J. (2002) 'Males on the life-course persistent and adolescence-limited antisocial pathways: follow-up at age 26 years', *Development and Psychopathology*, 14: 179–207.

Moffitt, T.E., Caspi, A., Rutter, M. and Silva, P.A. (2001) *Sex Differences in Anti-social Behaviour: Conduct Disorder, Delinquency and Violence in the Dunedin Longitudinal Study*. Cambridge: Cambridge University Press.

Nacro (2005) *A Handbook on Reducing Offending by Looked after Children*. London: Nacro.

Nacro (2008) *Some Facts about Children and Young People who Offend – 2006*, Youth Crime Briefing March 2008. London: Nacro and the Howard League for Penal Reform.

Nagin, D.S. and Farrington, D.P. (1992) 'The onset and persistence of offending', *Criminology*, 30 (4): 501–23.

Nagin, D.S., Farrington, D.P. and Moffitt, T.E. (1995) 'Life-course trajectories of different types of offenders', *Criminology*, 33: 111–39.

New York Times (1908) 'Criminals are no longer general practitioners – the specialist has become even more of a necessity among crooks today', 24 May, p. 7.

O'Donnell, I., Baumer, E. and Hughes, N. (2008) 'Recidivism in the Republic of Ireland', *Criminology and Criminal Justice*, 8 (2): 123–46.

Olds, D., Henderson, C.R. Jr, Cole, R., Eckenrode, J., Kitzman, H., Luckey, D., Pettitt, L, Sidora, K., Morris, P. and Powers, J. (1998) 'Long-term effects of nurse home visitation on children's criminal and antisocial behavior: 15-year follow-up of a randomized controlled trial', *Journal of the American Medical Association*, 280 (14): 1238–44.

Osgood, D.W. and Rowe, D.C. (1994) 'Bridging criminal careers, theory, and policy through latent variable models of individual offending', *Criminology*, 32 (4): 517–54.

Osgood, D.W. and Schreck, C.J. (2007) 'A new method for studying the extent, stability, and predictors of individual specialisation in violence', *Criminology*, 45 (2): 273–311.

Pearce, F. (1976) *Crimes of the Powerful: Marxism, Crime and Deviance*. London: Pluto Press.

Peeters, H. (2002) *Gerrit de Stotteraar: Biografie van een Boef*. Amsterdam: Uitgerverij Podium.

Perry, C.L., Williams, C.L., Veblen-Mortenson, S., Toomey, T., Komro, K.A., Anstine, P.S., McGovern, P.G., Finnegan, J.R., Forster, J.L., Wagenaar, A.C. and Wolfson, M. (1996) 'Project Northland: outcomes of a community-wide alcohol use prevention program during early adolescence', *American Journal of Public Health*, 86: 956–65.

Piquero, A.R. (2000) 'Frequency, specialization, and violence in offending careers', *Journal of Research in Crime and Delinquency*, 37 (4): 392–418.

Piquero, A.R., Farrington, D.P. and Blumstein, A. (2003) 'The criminal career paradigm', in M. Tonry (ed.), *Crime and Justice: A Review of Research*, Vol. 30. Chicago: University of Chicago Press.

Piquero, A.R., Farrington, D.P. and Blumstein, A. (2007) *Key Issues in Criminal Career Research: New Analyses of the Cambridge Study in Delinquent Development*. Cambridge: Cambridge University Press.

Piquero, A.R., Mazerolle, P., Brame, R. and Dean, C.W. (1999) 'Onset age and offense specialization', *Journal of Research in Crime and Delinquency*, 36: 275–99.

Piquero, N.L. and Benson, M. (2004) 'White-collar crime and criminal careers', *Journal of Contemporary Criminal Justice*, 20 (2): 148–65.

Pittman, D.J. and Gordon, C.W. (1958) *The Revolving Door: A Study of the Chronic Police Inebriate*. New York: Free Press.

Plomin, R., DeFries, J., McClearn, G. and McGuffin, P. (2008) *Behavioral Genetics*, 5th edn. New York: Worth.

Powers, E. and Witmer, H. (1951) *An Experiment in the Prevention of Delinquency: The Cambridge-Somerville Youth Study*. New York: Columbia University Press.

Prime, J., White, S., Liriano, S. and Patel, K. (2001) *Criminal Careers of Those Born between 1953 and 1978*, Home Office Statistical Bulletin 4/01. London: Home Office.

Quinsey, V.L., Harris, G.T., Rice, M.E. and Cormier, C.A. (1998) *Violent Offenders: Appraising and Managing Risk*. Washington, DC: American Psychological Association.

Reed, G.E. and Yeager, P.C. (1996) 'Organizational offending and neoclassical criminology: challenging the reach of a general theory of crime', *Criminology*, 34 (3): 357–82.

Roth, P. (2006) *Everyman*. London: Cape.

Rutter, M. (1988) 'Longitudinal data in the study of causal processes: some uses and some pitfalls', in M. Rutter (ed.), *Studies of Psycho-social Risk: The Power of Longitudinal Data*. Cambridge: Cambridge University Press.

Rutter, M. (2005) *Genes and Behaviour: Nature-Nurture Interplay Explained*. Oxford: Blackwell.

Sampson, R.J. and Laub, J.H. (1993) *Crime in the Making: Pathways and Turning Points Through Life*. Cambridge, MA: Harvard University Press.

Sampson, R.J. and Laub, J.H. (1995) 'Understanding variability in lives through time: contributions of life-course criminology', *Studies on Crime and Crime Prevention*, 4: 143–58.

Sampson, R.J. and Laub, J.H. (2003) 'Life-course desisters? Trajectories of crime among delinquent boys followed to age 70', *Criminology*, 41 (3): 555–91.

Sampson, R.J. and Lauritsen, J.L. (1990) 'Deviant life-styles, proximity to crime, and the offender-victim link in personal violence', *Journal of Research in Crime and Delinquency*, 27 (2): 110–39.

Sampson, R.J. and Wooldredge, J.D. (1987) 'Evidence that high crime rates encourage migration away from central cities', *Sociology and Social Research*, 70 (4): 310–14.

Sare, J. (2008) 'The danger of Sarah's Law', *New Statesman*, 22 September.

Schweinhart, L.J. and Weikart, D.P. (1998) 'High/Scope Perry Preschool Program effects at age twenty-seven', in J. Crane (ed.), *Social Programs That Work*. New York: Russell Sage Foundation.

Scott, P. (1996) *Gentleman Thief – Recollections of a Cat Burglar*. London: HarperCollins.

Shannon, L.W. (1982) *Assessing the Relationship of Adult Criminal Careers to Juvenile Careers*. Washington, DC: US Department of Justice.

Shaw, C.R. and McKay, H.D. (1942) *Juvenile Delinquency and Urban Areas*. Chicago: University of Chicago Press.

Sherman, L.W, Smith, D.A., Schmidt, J.D. and Rogan, D.P. (1992) 'Crime, punishment and stake in conformity: legal and informal control of domestic violence', *American Sociological Review*, 57: 680–90.

Shore, H. (2000) 'The idea of juvenile crime in 19th-century England', *History Today*, 50 (6): 21–7.

Shover, N. (1996) *Great Pretenders: Pursuits and Careers of Persistent Thieves*. Boulder, CO: Westview.

Simon, L.M.J. (1997) 'Do criminal offenders specialize in crime types?', *Applied and Preventive Psychology*, 6: 35–53.

Simpson, E.H. (1949) 'Measurement of diversity', *Nature*, 163: 688.

Simpson, S.S. and Piquero, N. (2002) 'Low self-control, organizational theory, and corporate crime', *Law and Society Review*, 36 (3): 509–47.

Smith, D. (2003) 'New Labour and youth justice', *Children and Society*, 17: 226–35.

Smith, D.J. (2002) 'Crime and the life course', in M. Maguire, R. Morgan and R. Reiner (eds), *The Oxford Handbook of Criminology*, 3rd edn. Oxford: Oxford University Press.

Smith, D.J. (2007) 'Crime and the life-course', in M. Maguire, R. Morgan and R. Reiner (eds), *The Oxford Handbook of Criminology*, 4th edn. Oxford: Oxford University Press.

Smith, D.J. and McVie, S. (2003) 'Theory and method in the Edinburgh Study of Youth Transitions and Crime', *British Journal of Criminology*, 43: 169–95.

Social Exclusion Unit (2002) *Reducing Re-offending by Ex-Prisoners*. London: Social Exclusion Unit.

Soothill, K. (1974) *The Prisoner's Release*. London: Allen & Unwin.

Soothill, K. (ed.) (1999) *Criminal Conversations: An Anthology of the Work of Tony Parker*. London: Routledge.

Soothill, K. (2001) 'Opening doors and windows for Tony Parker', *The British Criminology Conferences: Selected Proceedings*, Vol. 2. Online at: http://www.britsoccrim.org/bccsp/vol04/soothill.html.

Soothill, K. (2003) 'A new report on violence: a welcome and a warning' (editorial), *British Journal of Psychiatry*, 182: 3–4.

Soothill, K. (2005) 'Capturing criminology', in M. Peelo and K. Soothill (eds), *Questioning Crime and Criminology*. Cullompton: Willan.

Soothill, K. (2008) *A Window on the Law: A Historical Study of the Local Media Reporting of Judges' and Barristers' Comments in Rape Cases*. Workshop on Law and Popular Culture held at the Onati International Institute for the Sociology of Law, May 2008.

Soothill, K. (forthcoming) 'Serial killing', in Loucks, N. (ed.), *Why Kill?* London: Middlesex University Press.

Soothill, K. and Francis, B. (1997) 'Sexual reconvictions and the Sex Offenders Act 1997', *New Law Journal*, 147: 1285–6 and 1324–5.

Soothill, K. and Peelo, M. (2007) 'Constructing British criminology', *Howard Journal of Criminal Justice*, 46 (5): 476–92.

Soothill, K., Ackerley, E. and Francis, B. (1997) 'The value of finding employment for white-collar ex-offenders: a twenty-year criminological follow-up', *British Journal of Criminology*, 37 (4): 582–92.

Soothill, K., Ackerley, E. and Francis, B. (2003) 'The persistent offenders debate: a focus on temporal changes', *Criminal Justice*, 3 (4): 389–412.

Soothill, K., Ackerley, E. and Francis, B. (2004) 'Profiles of crime recruitment: changing patterns over time', *British Journal of Criminology*, 44 (3): 401–18.

Soothill, K., Francis, B., Ackerley, E. and Humphreys, L. (2008a) 'Changing patterns of offending behaviour among young adults', *British Journal of Criminology*, 48 (1): 75–94.

Soothill, K., Ackerley, E. and Francis, B. (2008b) 'Criminal convictions among children and young adults: changes over time', *Criminology and Criminal Justice*, 8 (3): 297–315.

Soothill, K. and Francis, B. (forthcoming) 'When do ex-offenders become like non-offenders?', *Howard Journal of Criminal Justice*.

Soothill, K., Francis, B., Ackerley, E and Sanderson, B. (2000) 'Sex offenders: specialists, generalists … or both? A 32-year criminological study', *British Journal of Criminology*, 40: 56–67.

Soothill, K., Francis, B., Ackerley, E. and Fligelstone, R. (2002) *Murder and Serious Sexual Assault: What Criminal Histories Can Reveal About Future Serious Offending: Full Report*, Police Research Series No. 144. London: Home Office. Online at: http://www.homeoffice.gov.uk/rds/prgpdfs/prs144.pdf.

Soothill, K., Peelo, M., and Taylor, C. (2002) *Making Sense of Criminology*. Cambridge: Polity Press.

Stander, J., Farrington, D.P., Hill, G. and Altham, P.M.E. (1989) 'Markov chain analysis and specialization in criminal careers', *British Journal of Criminology*, 29 (4): 317–35.

Stanley, C. (2006) cited in McCormack, H. (2006) 'High thresholds for referral to criminal justice system are key to cutting offending', *Community Care*, 25–31 May 2006.

Sullivan, C.J., McGloin, J.M., Pratt, T.C. and Piquero, A.R. (2006) 'Rethinking the norm of offender generality: investigating specialization in the short term', *Criminology*, 44 (1): 199–233.

Sutherland, E.H. (1949) *Principles of Criminology*, 4th edn. Philadelphia: J. B. Lippincott.

Sutton, C., Utting, D. and Farrington, D. (2004) *Support from the Start: Working with Young Children and Their Families to Reduce the Risk of Crime and Anti-social Behaviour*, Research Brief No. 524, March. London: Department for Education and Skills.

Sykes, G. (1958) *The Society of Captives*. Princeton, NJ: Princeton University Press.

Tatar, M. (1995) *Lustmord: Sexual Murder in Weimar Germany*. Princeton, NJ: Princeton University Press.

Taxman, F.S. and Piquero, A. (1998) 'On preventing drunk driving recidivism: an examination of rehabilitation and punishment approaches', *Journal of Criminal Justice*, 26 (2): 129–43.

Taylor, C. (2001) 'The relationship between social and self-control: tracing Hirschi's criminological career', *Theoretical Criminology*, 5 (3): 369–88.

Taylor, C. (2006) *Young People in Care and Criminal Behaviour*. London: Jessica Kingsley.

Taylor, R. (1999) *Predicting Reconvictions for Sexual and Violent Offences: Using the Revised Offender Group Reconviction Scale*, Research Findings No. 104. London: Home Office.

Thistlethwaite, A., Wooldredge, J. and Gibbs, D. (1998) 'Severity of dispositions and domestic violence recidivism', *Crime and Delinquency*, 44 (3): 388–97.

Thornton, D. (2000) 'Scoring Guide for Risk Matrix: 2000'. Unpublished manuscript.

Tidmarsh, D. (1997) 'Risk assessment among prisoners – a view from a parole board member', *International Review of Psychiatry*, 9: 273–81.

Ventura, L.A. and Davis, G. (2005) 'Domestic violence – court case conviction and recidivism', *Violence Against Women*, 11 (2): 255–77.

Viding, E., Larsson, H. and Jones, A.P. (2008) 'Review. Quantitative genetic studies of antisocial behaviour', *Philosophical Transactions of the Royal Society*, 363 (1503): 2519–27.

Wallerstein, J.S. and Wyle, C.J. (1947) 'Our law-abiding law breakers', *Probation*, April, 107–12.

Webster, C., Douglas, K., Eaves, D. and Hart, S. (1997) *HCR-20 Assessing Risk for Violence: Version II*. Burnaby, British Columbia: Mental Health, Law & Policy Institute, Simon Frazier University.

Weisburd, D. and Waring, E. (2001) *White-Collar Crime and Criminal Careers*. New York: Cambridge University Press.

Weisburd, D., Wheeler, S., Waring, E. and Bode, N. (1991) *Crimes of the Middle Classes: White-Collar Offenders in the Federal Courts*. New Haven, CT: Yale University Press.

West, D.J. (1969) *Present Conduct and Future Delinquency*. London: Heinemann.

West, D.J. (1982) *Delinquency, Its Roots, Careers, and Prospects*. London: Heinemann.

West, D.J. and Farrington, D.P. (1973) *Who Becomes Delinquent?* London: Heinemann.

West, D.J. and Farrington, D.P. (1977) *The Delinquent Way of Life*. London Heinemann.

Wikstrom, P.-O.H. and Butterworth, D.A. (2007) *Adolescent Crime: Individual Differences and Lifestyles*. Cullompton: Willan.

Wolfgang, M.E., Figlio, R.F. and Sellin, T. (1972) *Delinquency in a Birth Cohort*. Chicago: University of Chicago Press.

Woods, P. and Lasiuk, G.C. (2008) 'Risk prediction – a review of the literature', *Journal of Forensic Nursing*, 4 (1): 1–11.

World Health Organisation (2002) *World Report on Violence and Health*. Geneva: WHO.

Young, J. (1999a) 'Cannibalism and bulimia: patterns of social control in late modernity', *Theoretical Criminology*, 3 (4): 387–407.

Young, J. (1999b) *The Exclusive Society: Social Exclusion, Crime and Difference in Late Modernity*. London: Sage.

Index